Transnational
Adoption

NATION OF NEWCOMERS
Immigrant History as American History

Matthew Frye Jacobson and Werner Sollors
GENERAL EDITORS

Beyond the Shadow of Camptown:
Korean Military Brides in America
Ji-Yeon Yuh

Feeling Italian:
The Art of Ethnicity in America
Thomas J. Ferraro

Constructing Black Selves:
Caribbean American Narratives and the Second Generation
Lisa D. McGill

Transnational Adoption:
A Cultural Economy of Race, Gender and Kinship
Sara K. Dorow

SARA K. DOROW

Transnational Adoption

A Cultural Economy of Race, Gender, and Kinship

NEW YORK UNIVERSITY PRESS
New York and London

NEW YORK UNIVERSITY PRESS
New York and London
www.nyupress.org

Library of Congress Cataloging-in-Publication Data
Dorow, Sara K.
Transnational adoption : a cultural economy of race, gender, and kinship /
Sara K. Dorow.
p.   cm. — (Nation of newcomers)
Includes bibliographical references and index.
ISBN-13: 978-0-8147-1971-8 (cloth : alk. paper)
ISBN-10: 0-8147-1971-6 (cloth : alk. paper)
ISBN-13: 978-0-8147-1972-5 (pbk. : alk. paper)
ISBN-10: 0-8147-1972-4 (pbk. : alk. paper)
1. Intercountry adoption—China. 2. Intercountry adoption—United States.
3. Ethnicity—China. 4. China—Social life and customs.   I. Title. II. Series.
HV875.58.C6D67 2006
362.7340951—dc22   2005034182

New York University Press books are printed on acid-free paper,
and their binding materials are chosen for strength and durability.

Manufactured in the United States of America

c 10 9 8 7 6 5 4 3 2 1
p 10 9 8 7 6 5 4 3 2 1

CONTENTS

ACKNOWLEDGMENTS

I do not know exactly how to begin to thank and acknowledge the many people and organizations that have supported this project, spiriting me through what has been a remarkably enjoyable journey. I have been graced by their friendship, advice, and responsiveness. They have made this book possible, even as any flaws or offenses contained herein fall squarely with me.

Most of the people who made the book possible cannot be directly thanked on paper, but I want to start with them. I am humbled by the many people in China and the United States who were open to my participation in their stories, and to their participation in mine: adoptive families, adoption agency administrators and social workers, adoption support groups, adoption facilitators, orphanage administrators, caregivers and foster families, local and state officials, and children both adopted and not. As with any project, some individuals played a key role in steering me down useful and otherwise obstructed paths, and I am forever grateful.

I am also thankful that there are many whom I can directly acknowledge. This project took shape in concert with many individuals and groups. I owe thanks to Jennifer Pierce for instilling in me respect for the power of ethnographic work, and for exceptional mentoring; to Ron Aminzade for good-humored advocacy and an intellectual atmosphere supportive of all brands and breeds of sociological research and teaching; to Doug Hartmann for nurturing a vision of critical theory, the racialization of culture, and scholarly collaboration; to Dan Kelliher for provocative conversations on childhood, adoption, and everyday Chinese politics; and to Erika Lee for insights on migration histories, especially those of Asian Americans. I also thank Barbara Laslett for a vision of sociology that preemptively tips the balances in favor of real rigor and real people.

The list of colleagues to whom I am grateful is long and continues to grow. My thanks to participants in the Workshop on International Adoption (Amherst, Massachusetts, May 2001) for inspiration that extends far beyond our weekend together—especially Kay Ann Johnson,

Barbara Yngvesson, Ann Anagnost, Amy Klatzkin, Françoise-Romaine Ouellette, Eleana Kim, Deann Borshay Liem, and Toby Volkman. Other much appreciated fellow travelers in the realm of adoption research include Sandra Patton-Imani, Jiannbin Lee Shiao, Mia Tuan, Cathy Ceniza Choy, Andrea Louie, and Rebecca Hurdis. Mirim Kim has kept me on my toes with her honesty and grace. Amy Blackstone, Alyssa Goolsby, and Amy Ronnkvist regaled me with welcome feedback and friendship, as did members of Piercing Insights, Ron's Salon, and Bees Nest. Amy Kaler and Huang Jinzhou have been the best kind of scholar-friends.

Most chapters in the book have benefited from input from panelists and audience members at various conferences, including the Association for Asian American Studies (May 2003), the American Sociological Association (August 2000, 2001, and 2002), the American Studies Association (November 2004), the Canadian Intercountry Adoption Policy Research Roundtable (March 2004), and the Ethnic Studies Graduate Student Conference at Harvard University (February 2004) to which I was generously invited by Werner Sollors.

The flow of funding into this project is important not only for its material value but because it came with people support. The MacArthur Interdisciplinary Program on Global Change, Sustainability, and Justice at the University of Minnesota provided funding throughout my graduate career and, more important, an exceptional and dedicated group of colleagues. I am especially indebted to participants in the MacArthur Gender Consortium.

I am very grateful to the Social Science Research Council (SSRC) for funding in the form of the Advanced Disciplinary Training Fellowship in 1998–99 and the International Migration Fellowship in 2000–1. The former allowed me to spend a pivotal year with faculty and students at University of California-Berkeley, among whom I especially acknowledge Raka Ray, Barrie Thorne, Arlie Hochschild, Tom Gold, Aihwa Ong, Donald Moore, Theo Goldberg, Damani Partridge, Nan Kim, and Jacqueline Adams. The latter fellowship allowed me to travel to China to continue my fieldwork. Both fellowships included conferences with lively colleagues; my thanks to SSRC conference participants in Phoenix (October 1998) and Dallas (March 2002).

I also sincerely thank Professor Hou Junsheng and Mr. Han Keqing of Nankai University, Professor Huang Banghan of the Anhui Agricultural

University, Professor Wang Liyao of the Anhui Academy of Social Sciences, Professor Bian Yanjie of the Hong Kong University of Science and Technology, and Professor Hong Yang of the China Center at the University of Minnesota for so kindly assisting me with research in China.

Expert understanding of what makes a book "work" came from a number of sources. In addition to several anonymous reviewers, I am grateful to Eric Zinner and Emily Park of New York University Press for their professional handling of my questions and quests, and ultimately of the text itself. Marty Dorow lent her expertise to indexing.

It is difficult to separate personal and professional acknowledgments, but I end by focusing on the former. Thanks to Jim and his housemates, as well as Li Qing, for providing a home away from home in Beijing; to Margaret for doing the same in Berkeley; and to Brian Boyd and everyone else at Yeong and Yeong for good books and unfailing generosity. And to my family and friends, thank you for believing that I must have been doing something worthwhile all these years, and for keeping my feet on the ground. This book is for you.

Finally, a word to adoptive families and adoption practitioners. As with my earlier books (*When You Were Born in China* and *I Wish for You a Beautiful Life*), you and other readers with an interest in transnational, transracial adoption are the intended audience of this book. But unlike these other texts, it is also a book for academic audiences; and so it is written in a voice that combines everyday stories with theoretical discourses. I hope that it is accessible and compelling for most readers, and that above all it illuminates what China/U.S. adoption practices might teach us about ways of being and belonging.

Introduction

Adoption Moves

> We could argue that these adoptions are all about individuals, on both sides of the Pacific: individual Chinese women are choosing to give up their daughters and individual Americans are choosing to adopt those children. But clearly, this individual behavior—as successful as it might be for a particular individual in achieving her goals—is possible, is even regular, because of the social contexts, politics, and norms in both societies. To see this we must understand the larger social institutional involvement in these practices.
>
> —Nancy Riley (1997: 94)

On the first day of February 1997, I walked across a snow-covered school parking lot in Minnesota to join the Chinese New Year celebration of the organization Families with Children from China (FCC). The sidewalk was lined with signs pointing the way, each adorned with a large colorful dragon; "FCC Chinese New Year Celebration" was printed in English on each sign in the jagged-edged font that jauntily signals things Asian. Inside, long cafeteria tables were set with the red paper placemats and chopsticks found at Chinese restaurants across North America. White adults and preschool-age Chinese children milled about, some of the latter wearing little silk jackets and dresses. I found myself moved by this scene of family ties: "How warm and hopeful," I thought.

Three years later, I once again entered a room full of adoptive families, this time at one of the "baby hotels" in China where foreign families concentrate when they travel to meet the children with whom they have been matched. I came down to a breakfast buffet that could have been at almost any three-star hotel in the world, offering the fluted orange slices, croissants, and omelettes of Western fare. Across the room, about twenty white American adults sat around a group of tables, feeding and holding the Chinese babies and toddlers they had adopted just days before—some of the children wore fresh Baby Gap–like outfits. A twinge of neo-colonial discomfort surfaced: "They're taking the children," said a voice in my head.

Together, these ethnographic vignettes represent moments and spaces in a process that brings thousands of Chinese children into American families every year. China/U.S. adoption currently constitutes the largest transnational movement of adopted children,[1] and the least studied among significant new forms of East Asian migration. It is a process inflected by the movement of children through and across uneven racial, national, class, and gender spaces. These relationships of power are seen, heard, felt, narrated, and even smelled in the practices through which children—the vast majority of them girls—are abandoned[2] and then moved from intermediary care in Chinese welfare institutions to adoptive families in the United States—the vast majority of them white, well educated, and relatively well-off. In this book I interrogate the ways in which meaning, identity, and value are constructed around adoptees by the actors and institutions that participate in adoption migration on both sides of the Pacific; I take China/U.S. adoption to be the kind of process, as described by Gupta and Ferguson (1992), "on which cultural difference, historical memory, and societal organization are inscribed" (7).

While it is a distinct form of transnational migration, China/U.S. adoption nonetheless speaks insistently to the raced and gendered relations by which individual, family, and national identities are produced and negotiated. Along these lines, my opening description of two distant but interconnected rooms of adoptive families is meant to beg a series of questions: By what sets of imaginaries and practices—both individual and institutional, inclusive and exclusive—have these parents and children come together? How do the histories of one space carry over into the history of the other, and how do they together shape a horizon of possible identity formations for Chinese adopted children? How do we account for the divergent but simultaneous meanings of transracial adoption migration—for instance, the joyful intimacy of making family next to the unjust history that it might recall?

By asking who and what the Chinese adopted child can be, and through what practices and stories she is made to belong, I mean to investigate conditions of social citizenship in the late capitalist, globally powerful, liberal multicultural United States. In the field of adoption research, this means resisting a tendency to put the behaviors and attitudes of individual adoptees, and their dyadic relationships to their parents, under a psychosocial microscope (Ouellette and Belleau 2001; Tuan and Shiao 2001; Hollingsworth 1997); there is in some of the sociological canon on adoption a parallel to early studies of "immigrant America" that concerned themselves more with the so-called adjustment of immigrants than with the historical conditions of migration and citizenship. We could do right by adopted persons, and learn from them in the process, by turning our sights on the anxieties, disciplining practices, and transformative possibilities that shape their belonging. This takes us outside the United States to China and back again, affording a multisited vision of which *kinds* of difference *make* a difference to claims on political and cultural subjectivity. The racial formations, gendered relations, class practices, and national imaginaries through which people labor to embrace the adopted Chinese child, to make her kin and citizen, have also conditioned her departure and arrival—her transfer from birth home to orphanage to adoptive family, and her movement from the margins of China to the normalized spaces of largely white middle- and upper-class neighborhoods in the United States. How the histories she carries with her reproduce and contest these spaces is not just a matter of her adjustment but of our collective response-ability to those histories (see also Anagnost 2000).

There are a number of exciting ways in which the case of China/U.S. adoption reaches beyond adoption itself to demonstrate poignantly what Cruz (1996) calls the "social hieroglyphics" of identity formation.

> Identity formations . . . are not fixed and frozen, but subject to shifting configurations of power and multiple modes of appropriation that refract underlying social relations. This is so, not because social

identities are distinct and unique, or based on pristine and preformed essences, but because they are constructed in the shifting field of historically constituted social relations. . . . Theoretical reflection might enable us to generate great inventories of existing and possible combinations of identity formations, but situated subjects are not necessarily free to pick and choose among the cornucopia of options to make themselves anew. (The desire to make the world anew, to scrap bad histories and begin over again, with the belief that this involves not much more than self-willed redefinitions of identity, is fundamentally American. . . .) This underscores the importance of assessing *identity formations as social hieroglyphics.* (25–26; emphasis in original)

Transnational adoption research can contribute to theorizing the social hieroglyphics of identity formation by examining the strands of difference that characterize the child's history. As recent work by and about transnationally/transracially adopted people demonstrates, the experience of difference in adoption is multiple and disjointed (Yngvesson and Mahoney 2000; Register 1991; Hoffman-Riem 1990; Bishoff and Rankin 1997; Ito and Cervin 1999). I remember explaining to Karen, a single white mother of a school-age Chinese daughter, my research interest in the overlapping issues of race, abandonment, gender, culture, markets, migration, and kinwork. Karen started to smile and shake her head at the overwhelming complexity of her daughter's identity narrative, and soon she and I were chuckling together at the image conjured: both parent and sociologist poised in nervous anticipation, trying to keep up with multiple social categories as they popped up in overlapping and random succession.

But then, this image of "watching" for complex identity might miss Cruz's point: identity is always already relational, never "out there" to be observed in discrete individuals. In other words, categories of "race," "class," "gender," and so forth are convenient analytical tools that tend to oversimplify and too neatly explain the rich reality of multiply determined identity processes. The image Karen and I conjured must also treat the spectacle of difference as a construct of similarity, a projection of the fantasies of personhood that dominate American culture in this historical moment. (Why do particular markers of identity appear to pop up, and not others?) Adoption poignantly exemplifies how identity is constructed *"in situ,* in relation to symbolically and physically constructed 'home,' 'place,' voluntary and involuntary dis/locations and dis/placements of physically distinguishable and marked human bodies and subjectivities" (Luke and Luke 1998: 732).

It is also important, and instructive, that adoption places these questions of subjectivity into the heart of family. Adoption is a "no" to naturalized forms of kinship that invites us "to a new way of seeing, a way of looking relationally at the betwixt and between and beforehand of received social categories" (Weston 2001: 151). How much more is this the case in transnational, transracial adoption, where the disparate sites and subjects of a global political economy are brought into the intimate sphere of everyday kinship, in both China and the United States. At the same time, however, adoption's particular set of institutionalized practices and exchanges leans toward reproducing the latter—middle-class American kinship and its hegemonic whiteness and heterosexuality (Anagnost 2000; Eng 2003; Melosh 2002; Ortiz and Briggs 2003). The child is plunked into this intimate proximity to difference through a series of cultural-racial imaginaries and marketized exchanges, and through dislocation from biological kin. As a result, as I try to show throughout this book, the labor of producing the parent-child relationship and of narrating the adoptee's belonging is especially intense and overt.

On the one hand, the private, nuclear family is an important mediator in this racialized process of creating individual and national identities, not just because families are sites of national reproduction and signs of social respectability (Anagnost 2000; Eng 2003) but also because the nation is imagined as family (Balibar 1988b; McClintock 1995; Manzo 1996; Yngvesson 2000). On the other hand, family is a site of contestation (Stoler 1995); families formed interracially, as well as across uneven borders of nation and wealth, might prove to be "key sites where new forms of cultural, social class, and gender identity are reconstructed" (Luke and Luke 1998: 728). As Rapp (1999) suggests, we stand to learn new things "when we approach nonnormative or problematic family making—the production, circulation, and integration of anomalous progeny and the embattled, diffuse solidarity that attends them—in contemporary U.S. culture" (xii–xiii).

The impossible (but promising) contradictions of nonnormative family making unfold across the chapters of this book, from American parents' decisions to adopt from China, to the state and market processes that produce abandoned and adoptable children, to the birth mothers and racialized national histories that haunt the construction of children's identities. To put the commands of *political economy* (circuits of exchange and value) in conversation with the desires of *kinship* is a potent mixture. Writer and adoptive mother Janice Williamson poignantly captures this powerful alchemy of history and intimacy in the slide "My adopted daughter's wish is my command," part of her visual and textual narrative of adopting from China (see Figure 1).[3]

Finally, the case of China/U.S. adoption demands attention to how the domestic family/nation is constructed through racialized imaginaries of transnational migration. In this way it is wedged in the false dichotomy of forced and voluntary migration (Mahler 1998; Ong 2004)—the child is emigrated "for her own good," but not through her own choice—and illuminates the coexistence of processes that both absorb and exclude national subjects. My approach thus focuses not on the adopted person's self-constructed identity but on the constellation of sites and actors who read and make and tell who she is. Accounting for adoptive parents' perspectives, for example, has especially important implications for what Kang (2003), drawing on Appadurai and Chuh, calls "two different transnations in the United States . . . 1) a diasporic transnation where immigrants might desire and sustain a belonging to a distant homeland; and 2) a xenophobic and racist transnation where a state can imprint its own citizen-subjects with foreign membership as the proof of their inexorable un-belonging in 'America'" (39). To read these transnations from the perspective of the immigrant or racialized minority is one thing, but given the relative silence of Chinese adoptees (for now, but not for long), our attention shifts to how parents and adoption practitioners, on behalf of and in response to adopted children, deal with the tensions arising from the coexistence of these two transnations. White American parents are in the position of desiring (or not) a connection to the homeland for their children and of confronting (or not) the stamp of foreignness on their children. Whiteness and the nation thus become immediately and intimately relational concepts (Frankenberg 1993), problematizing any neat analytical and categorical distinctions among "Asian American," "white American," "white," or "American" (Kang 2003).

Figure 1
My adopted daughter's wish is my command

月 宮 小 客 人

The difference between our lives is this gap between desire and command that floats between us. Between my longing and desire for a child and my ability—economic, social, political—to fetch you from there so far away.

Poster is part of the IISH Stefan R. Landsberger Collection (http://www.iisg.nl/~landsberger).

Baobao En Route

I am moved by my daughter's inability to do anything but be literally carried away by the adoptive process, a command performance. Bao did not choose to take herself in hand and make her way to the Guangdong Foreign Adoption Office. She did not study and select my photo and documentation from a file of waiting parents. She did not interview me to discern whether I would fulfill my promises. She did not write out her wish list for an adoptive mother. She did not have an opportunity to think about whether she wanted to remain in her home province after all. She did not choose to be abandoned. But that's another story.

The South Asian critic Gayatri Spivak (1990) writes: "[T]he so-called non-West's turn toward the West is a command. That turn was not in order to fulfill some longing to consolidate a pure space for ourselves, that turn was a command" (from *The Post-Colonial Critic: Interviews, Strategies, Dialogues,* edited by Sarah Harasym. London: Routledge, p. 8).

We must consider in particular the production of kinship and citizen-ship around children *from China* (the FCC support group uses this phrase in its name). In some ways, they exemplify Lowe's (1996) argument about the role Asians have played in the construction of American history, as the "foreigners" at the edge of national membership:

> Throughout the twentieth century, the figure of the Asian immigrant has served as a "screen," a phantasmatic site, on which the nation pro-jects a series of condensed, complicated anxieties regarding external and internal threats to the mutable coherence of the national body: the invading multitude, the lascivious seductress, the servile yet treacher-ous domestic, the automaton whose inhuman efficiency will supersede American ingenuity. Indeed, it is precisely the unfixed liminality of the Asian immigrant—geographically, linguistically, and racially at odds with the context of the "national"—that has given rise to the necessity of endlessly fixing and repeating such stereotypes. (Lowe 1996: 18–19)

At the same time, however, children adopted from China complicate the differentiation of national body and foreign other; for example, they are granted automatic citizenship in the bosom of white middle-class Amer-ica. Either way, I argue that practices around them pose impossible con-tradictions of belonging. Their presence in domestic America demands a reckoning with liminality, especially at the busy intersections where in-ternal relations of race and capital meet trans-Pacific practices of ex-change. A number of writers and artists who were adopted from Korea as children, for example, have eloquently written of their adoptive origins as a product of the respective local social histories of Korea and the United States and the global political and economic relations that link them (Ahn 1994; Bishoff and Rankin 1997; Trenka 2003). This places their Asian/American identities—their autobiographical inquiries—on the fault lines of historical contingencies, often heightened by a lack of information on the specifics of their individual histories. "I never asked to be born to those who wouldn't have me . . . I never asked to become the son of a white couple . . . I never asked to be stared at/called a gook and a chink," writes Korean adoptee Ellwyn Kauffman (1997). "I miss my own past" (158–59).

The narrative of this book thus moves toward "restoring history to the process of constructing the [adopted] child's subjectivity" (Anagnost 2000: 414); it is spurred by asking, as Eng (2003) has, "what kind of histories and historical contradictions might be returned to the practice of transnational adoption in order to analyze more fully its global and domestic genealogies" (9). This is not a matter of filling in the sequence of events in individual life stories but of unpacking the histories that shape why and how adoptees might miss their past. But which histories, and how do we "restore" historical contradictions to a process of identification? One way to cheat the silences of time, the occlusion of particular histories, is to travel theoretically and methodologically across spaces (Marcus 1995). Adopted children at a Minnesota Chinese New Year celebration are brought together through a set of institutionalized practices and complex desires that once brought their future parents to hotels in China to meet them. Aihwa Ong (1998) has said that the analysis of the cultural logic of a global process like this one

> cries out for a sense of political economy and situated ethnography. What are the mechanisms of power that enable the mobility, as well as the localization and disciplining, of diverse populations within these transnationalized systems? How are cultural flows and human imagination conditioned and shaped within these new relations of global inequalities? (11)

Global Ethnography and the Cultural Economy of China/U.S. Adoption

LAX, the short-lived television series about executives at the Los Angeles International Airport, premiered in September 2004. At the end of the show's first hour, the characters played by actors Heather Locklear and Blair Underwood have spent a long and exhausting day fighting the dangers of global border crossing: drug smuggling, illegal immigrants, bomb threats, hijackers. And then, as sweet music plays, the screen switches to the scene of an airplane, which we learn is a flight from Shanghai, pulling up to the gate; the subtitle for the segment reads, "The Orphan Plane." In slow motion, families of every stripe come off the

plane with young Chinese children in their arms: a gay couple with a
baby, a straight white couple leading a little girl in a silk dress, black parents with a toddler, a white dad with twin boys. The two stars of the
show watch this scene with a look that says, "*This* is what makes everything we do worthwhile." In this moment, Chinese adoption is mobilized
as the shining exemplar of all that is good about transnationalism, the
reason that borders must be protected and kept (conditionally) open.
America is made safe for these adoptees, its multicultural achievements
reproduced in the bosom of kinship.

The numbers of children adopted from China into the United States
are not huge; in 2004, there were seven thousand such placements (out
of nearly twenty-three thousand intercountry adoptions, and only 10 to
15 percent of American adoptions in any one year are intercountry).[4] But
the practices of China/U.S. adoption—and the children themselves—
have taken on forms of public and symbolic significance that exceed
what the numbers suggest; not only *LAX* but a number of other television shows of the early twenty-first century, from *Sex and the City* to *The
Simpsons,* have featured story lines about Chinese adoption. In the case
of *LAX,* it is probably not worth protesting that planes carrying new
adoptive families almost always come not from Shanghai but from
Guangzhou (where U.S.-bound children receive immigrant visas). But
other features of China/U.S. adoption lost in the show's feel-good depic-
tion should certainly matter, starting with the fact that adoptions of
Chinese children by gay couples and black families have been in practice
rationed or rare. It should also matter that children placed for intercountry adoption every year are fewer in number than those adopted domestically in China and do not come close to the several hundred thousand in Chinese orphanages.[5] And it should also matter that a special set
of institutionalized practices facilitates the smooth migration and settlement of adopted Chinese children across borders, in direct contrast, for
example, to those rules that Locklear and Underwood enact to bar "dangerous" immigrants from entry.

By leaving the space of the Los Angeles airport, by looking at the
specific spaces that come before and after this moment of arrival, we can
put multisited global ethnography to the task of connecting local experiences and practices to transborder processes, taking into account the
unevenness of globalization as it is both experienced and produced

across different localities.[6] The global ethnography of adoption that shapes this book thus moves between sites in China and the United States, with the specific intent of understanding how actors across these sites—orphanages, government offices, tourist hotels and destinations, adoption agencies, adoptive family organizations, adoptive homes—assign meaning to the raced, gendered, and classed identities of adoptees and to their migration. My goal is not to compare and contrast variant perspectives in this global process but "instead to build a montage that lends greater insights into the whole, into the connections, disconnections, and reconnections" (Burawoy 2001: 15–16).

Moving back and forth across these local meanings and practices begs for methods that can discover the mechanisms that link and separate them. One methodological key to doing so is to follow the path taken by a person or object. For "even though from a *theoretical* point of view human actors encode things with significance," as Appadurai (1986) argues, "from a *methodological* point of view it is the things-in-motion that illuminate their human and social context" (5). So while adopted Chinese children are not the direct subjects of this ethnographic inquiry, they are its organizing principle, its raison d'être, the subjects whose particular journey illuminates frontiers. An ethnography that travels across the hotels where they meet their parents, to the orphanages where they have stayed, to the official agencies that have matched them, and to the homes where they settle gestures toward the restoration of history.

From the perspective of prospective adopters in the United States, the adoption process in China looks something like this. Parents select an agency in the United States, where they proceed with the necessary paperwork for the agency, the Chinese government, and the U.S. government, and sometimes receive preadoption training. Meanwhile, welfare institutions in China that care for children eligible for adoption send paperwork on individual children (called "referrals") to the CCAA (China Center of Adoption Affairs) in Beijing;[7] those children might reside in small orphanage facilities, large orphanage facilities, or foster homes. Once parents' preadoption work is complete (including application through U.S. immigration services for the child's visa), their paperwork is sent to the CCAA, approved, and matched with a child referral. They are then approved for travel to China, where they spend about two weeks. Families usually stay in local hotels, where they receive their children in the first couple of days, and then are guided through local adoption and U.S. consulate procedures by Chinese or American facilitators before flying home. The entire process, from application to travel (most of it made up of waiting), usually takes at least one year and costs more than U.S. $20,000.

There are other ways to tell the story of China/U.S. adoption, of course. The one told in this book is a cultural economy of transborder identity practices; it is important to explain how it came to be. What began as a small, local ethnographic project was eventually built on some eighty informal interviews and three hundred hours of participant observation gathered from adoptive parents and adoption agencies in two metropolitan areas in the United States, as well as orphanages and state adoption organizations in eight urban locations in China. (See Figure 2 for a diagram illustrating the sites through which adopted Chinese children travel, and hence through which I traveled.) My interest, as in many academic pursuits, came from my own experiences; I had spent a number of years in China, had supervised East Asian programs at an adoption agency in the United States, and had written a book for adopted children called *When You Were Born in China*.[8] In 1997, I initiated a pilot project in the Twin Cities of Minneapolis and St. Paul,[9] examining how white adoptive parents, as well as adoption agencies and the local chapter of the parent-run organization Families with Children from China, constructed the cultural and racial identities of their children adopted from China. As my theoretical interest grew, so did the methodological scope of my ethnography. Starting in 1998, I expanded the project to include adoptive families and agencies in a second geographic location in the United States, the San Francisco Bay Area. These two sites have offered some compelling comparisons, especially given their different histories of Chinese migration, which are highlighted at several different points in the book.

As I gathered the forty-some interviews with adoptive parents that constitute the heart of this project—solicited through online requests, snowball-sampled referrals, and sometimes the help of agencies or my own personal contacts—I strove not for a random sample but for a sample representative of the range of people that have entered China/U.S. adoption: white and Asian American, straight and queer, single and partnered, with and without birth children. That perhaps one-quarter of families in San Francisco adopting from China include at least one Asian American parent, in most cases Chinese American, adds a crucial dimension to the theorizing of difference in identity. (The stream of parents coming off the "orphan plane" on *LAX* did not include Asian adult parents with Chinese children; otherwise, how would we recognize the race-transcendent meaning of the moment?) Whenever possible, I interviewed couples together, and in their homes. Launched with some version of the invitation "So, tell me your adoption story," interviews lasted from one to seven hours, but usually for about two. Interviewees' adopted Chinese children were girls in all cases but one; most were healthy and had been adopted when between five and twenty-four months of age, although a few had been preschool or school-age.[10] Interviews with parents were supplemented with observations at FCC events (such as the one with which I opened) and of some online newsletters and Listserv groups, and with fieldwork at adoption agencies in both cities whose China programs were a substantial part of the services they offered.

But it was not enough to know only the American "end" of what I increasingly saw as a transnational political economy organized around the child's adoptive relocation; to capture the specificity of circuits in which the United States is "the host pole of the transnational migrant field" (Lauria-Pericelli 1992: 251) requires looking to locations external to it. The project thus expanded to include adoption-related actors and organizations across China, where I spent four months in the autumn and winter of 2000–1. I visited eight different orphanages, and in three of them (Beigang, Dayang, and Hongqi) I spent from one to three weeks volunteering alongside regular staff to care for infants and school-age children. Both formal and informal interviews with caregivers, orphanage administrators, social workers, and government officials provided insight into their relationships to transnational adoption and to the children for whom they were responsible. These ranged from scheduled conversations at the offices of adoption tour guides to friendly debates over lunch with orphanage staff. Providing crucial links "between" the locations of adoption are the Chinese and Chinese American facilitators who broker and translate the exchanges that bring parent and child together. While most of my interactions in China were in Mandarin, my ten interviews with facilitators were usually in English. Also, as I traveled around China

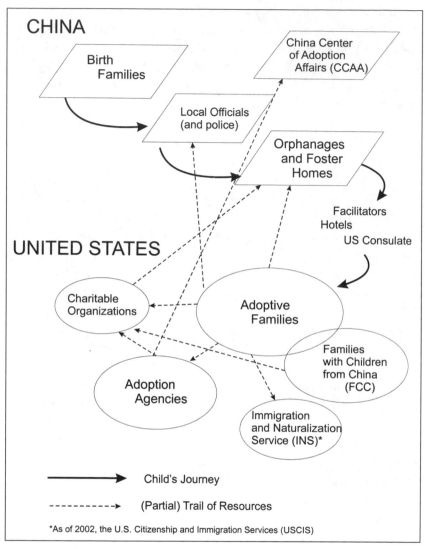

Figure 2. China Adoption Field.

I tried to gather a sense of people's knowledge of and response to transnational adoption by talking informally with fellow train passengers, taxi drivers, and other chance acquaintances.

The shadowy presence of birth families among my ethnographic subjects reflects the social reality that they are difficult to find (the work of Kay Ann Johnson and others notwithstanding; see Johnson et al. 1998 and Johnson 2004). Whatever the circumstances under which they leave their children, there is no legal avenue in China by which birth parents can place their children for adoption; and so they leave their children in public places, usually with vague or no clues about who the birth families are. The looming absence of birth families is reflected in the trajectory of adopted children's lives; it is one of the points of disconnection that, shaped by unequal class and gender relations, makes the child's relocation possible. Along with children in both China and the United States who are not adopted or not considered adoptable, immigrants whose entry is circumscribed or denied, the kinds of children desired and not received by parents on both sides of the Pacific, people not able to adopt, and the lives in China adoptees might have had, birth families are the "ghostly doubles" (Gordon 1997; Eng 2003; Yngvesson 2002; Anagnost 2000) of the transnational processes that reproduce adoptive families. Their absence or exclusion urges analysis of how

> [t]he propagation of money, technology, goods, services, and people are indeed rooted in inequalities of power between transmitter and receiver. There is a hierarchical chain, which can be disrupted and diverted. The ruptures and local violences produced beyond the chain are as important as the links within the chain. The marginalization of people denied access to the chain is as important as the appropriation of resources along the chain. (Burawoy 2000: 5–6)

As Gordon (1997) so eloquently writes, those people "not present" are signs of unsettled histories of exclusion, and they demand attention.

My global ethnography, then, labors to defetishize the transnational processes that produce abandoned and adopted children. This does not mean recreating a linear chain of production and consumption but rather analyzing together a panoply of meanings and materials that circulate through and across the institutions and practices of China/U.S. adoption: for example, the images of beautiful Chinese girls that grace glossy adoption ads, the gifts facilitators give to officials, the names given to adopted children first by caregivers and then by parents, the U.S. citizenship now automatically granted to children adopted abroad by Americans, and the public welfare support being withdrawn in postsocialist China. These various pieces of the process are linked by "the interplay of economic interests with markets, economic organizations, political power, and cultural distinctions" (J. Hall 1992: 31), including quasi-markets that, like adoption, circulate sentiment and emotion.[11] They push us to consider how class projects are embedded "in the efforts of families or kin groups to reproduce themselves" (Lauria-Perricelli 1992: 252–53). It is this plethora of meanings and values around the child—the cultural logics of exchange—that my global ethnography seeks to discover.

The Impossible Contradictions of Belonging

Where and what is the Chinese adopted child in these two intertwined forms of reproduction: of kinship and of the adoption system itself? She is many things and, perhaps most important, never exactly what people might desire or command her to be. It is the contestations over and tensions around her belonging that help us see some of the configurations of power that shape national and familial membership, especially in contemporary America. Practices around and representations of children point toward the intricate relationships of biological and social reproduction that link everyday kinship bonds to seemingly far-flung global circulations (Ginsburg and Rapp 1995; Stephens 1995; Thorne et al. 2001); as Lal (2002) puts it, "battles over children have always involved forces far larger than the seemingly private family" (175). What the child is and is not—what she can be narrated to be—is multiply determined within the proliferation of sites across which she travels and, more specifically, in the acts of exchange that move her across those sites (Appadurai 1986; Yngvesson 2002). The histories that condition her dislocation and relocation *are* her history; and what's more, they converge on her from both China and the United States, from both her past and her future, and they animate each other. For example, the racialized politics of being an Asian child adopted into a white American family of privilege recalls the gendered politics of being an abandoned girl-child of an unknown and likely poor Chinese family.

Three contradictions in particular emerge around the identification of adopted Chinese children; these are "impossible" contradictions because they refuse to be either ignored or resolved.[12] While these are woven throughout the book and help form the framework of chapter 1, I briefly introduce them here, drawing on narrations of adoption I encountered in both the United States and China.

I point first to the uneasy relationship between *commodification and care,* or market and rescue, a relationship that asks the troublesome question, who is adoption *for*? (Lal 2002). Transnationally adopted children are not bought and sold, but neither are they given and received freely and altruistically; the people and institutions around them enter into social relationships of exchange, meaning, and value that are both caring and consumptive. On the one hand, children become sacralized as "a crucial modern symbol of nature and the object of protection and enculturation" (Stephens 1995: 10), a " 'gift of love' that makes a family (complete)" (Yngvesson 2002: 235). On the other hand, children become objects of desire and consumption, each of them distinguished as "a 'resource' that has been contractually alienated from one owner so that it can be attached to another" (235). In a hearing before the House Committee on International Relations in May 2002, Susan Soon-keum Cox, vice president of Public Policy and External Affairs at Holt International Children's Services, warned of the commodification of desire that (inevitably?) attends the transfer of a child across terribly uneven global territories:

> *An unfaltering commitment of adoption should be that it is intended as a means to provide families for children, rather than children for families.* This is especially critical in international adoption where it is the children of one country being taken to another. The simplistic assumption that a poor child in a developing country will have a preferred life with a family in a "rich" country is misguided, imperialistic and overlooks the sacrifice and loss, not only to the sending country, but to the child. [Emphasis in original.][13]

Cox's warnings are evidence of the anxiety in intercountry adoption over catering to parents as clients, even if in the name of "saving" a child, and possibly in the name of sustaining the business of adoption.

At the same time, however, some adoptive parents worry that the adoption industry maintains itself at the expense of children who need homes and parents who want them. One group has formed the association ACAP (Adoption Consumer Assistance and Protection Service); in September 2004 a letter sent to various Internet Listservs asserted that "in the last 15 years, 43% of the most popular countries that U.S. Citizens adopt from have closed—most often in the wake [sic] accusations about child trafficking and other illegal activity. Yet, adoption is one of the least regulated industries in America. If we don't fix it soon, we will lose it!" It is impossible to extricate the consumer-parent from the caring-parent in this statement, and the child who is object of the market from the child who is object of love. Difficult contradictions form around the child; to count fully as family, she and the bonds with her adoptive parents must be protected and distinguished from the very market forces of adoption in which parents and agencies are increasingly implicated. This is why the question "How much did she cost?" which parents report hearing, might doubly sting.

While commodification may be a fascinating but nonetheless unsurprising facet of intercountry adoption, the contradictions it builds around the sacralized child become all the more salient when considered from the "sending" country of China. One young scholar in China said to me that adopting a Chinese child seemed to be a kind of trend for American parents, like buying the latest color television. He was being deliberately provocative, but the broader context of his statement—China's relative place in the global order—resonated with other readings of children being adopted out of China. Abandonment and adoption were together interpreted by Chinese observers as signs of their nation's status between backwardness and modernity, its place in the world still somewhat subject to Western and more specifically American economic power, its uneven resources and policies inadequate to the job of preventing or caring for abandoned children, and its national pride resentful of external humanitarian intervention (Madsen 1995; Guo 2004). Chinese passersby may give an approving, admiring "thumbs up" to groups of foreign adoptive families they encounter on the streets, even as they are skeptical of motives of consumerism and convenience; when I asked one taxi driver in southern China what he thought about international adoption, he replied, "American women don't like to give birth, do they?"

When they are yoked together, we see in practices of care and market—especially the conversion of economic and social capital into the symbolic capital of having (the right kind of) a child (Zelizer 1985)—the unmistakable imprint of distinctions among sending and receiving nations, and of children adopted and left behind. Of course, almost all children in Chinese orphanages, whether adopted or not, have been "left behind" by way of abandonment in places ranging from back alleys to orphanage gates. But that such dislocation from birth origins should itself be a condition of adoptive kinship poses a second impossible contradiction between the demands of *dislocation and relocation,* which are also the demands of biological origins and culturally "chosen" kinship. On the one hand, abandonment signals the potential loss of some kind of rooted essence or primal connection (Lifton 1994, referenced in Yngvesson 2003)—to blood kin but also to the culture and nation with which those blood ties are associated; on the other hand, it makes possible the kind of "clean break" from those ties (Duncan 1993; Ouellette and Belleau 2001; Gailey 2000) that signals a freestanding child, ready to be made anew:

> The clean break separates the child from everything that constitutes her grounds for belonging as a child to *this* family and *this* nation, while establishing her transferability to *that* family and *that* nation. With a past that has been cut away—an old identity that no longer exists—the child can be re-embedded in a new place, almost as though he or she never moved at all (Yngvesson 2003: 7)

It is not surprising, then, that professional adoption discourse often calls for a "balance" of old and new selves; adoption expert Freundlich (2000), for example, writes, "The challenge for policymakers, service providers, and most particularly the parents who adopt cross-nationally will be to find that special balance that permits a child to acknowledge his or her roots while experiencing a sense of belonging and acceptance within their new family and culture" (114). Such a call for both roots and transformation must be understood as an artifact of American national culture. The desire "to scrap bad histories and begin over again," as Cruz (1996) points out, is fundamentally American; but then, so is the idea that motherhood and birth origins "naturally" tell us who we are (Ginsburg 1989). In China/U.S. adoption we will see that "roots and wings" (as one adoption magazine has been called)—the inescapability of a naturalized birth identity and the promise of self-made beginnings—do not always so seamlessly coexist. Indeed, Chinese children are desirable to many prospective parents in part because, through abandonment, their attachments to birth families seem not so rooted after all.

Despite the relief of "clean breaks," the conditions that dislocate Chinese children from birth families are not easily silenced. Chinese adoptees quite literally embody the history of China's bid to develop and succeed as a nation on the global stage by reducing the size and increasing the quality of its population.[14] Abandonment in China is a result of the stringency with which the family-planning policy has been implemented, combined with material and cultural structures of family and gender relations, especially in rural areas (Johnson 2004; Greenhalgh and Li 1995). It is usually girls (often second daughters),[15] promising less in the way of economic security or social status, who are abandoned; they make up what Anagnost (1995) calls the "surfeit of bodies" that resulted from China's national population policies. But gender does not necessarily trump health or other social stigma, as many special-needs children and an increasing number of children (of both sexes) of single mothers are also brought to orphanages each year. In all cases, social policies that limit family size and undermine social support services (including medical coverage) interact with individual circumstances so that certain families feel they must give up their children, even after trying to keep them; others might have the social networks, financial means, or tenacity to hang onto their children.[16] International adoption finds permanent homes for children while bringing in U.S. $3,000 per child and freeing the Chinese state of bodies made excess, at least in part, by its own policies. These symbolic and material considerations, marked on the gendered, raced bodies of adoptees, defy the creation of an identificatory "clean break."

On both sides of the Pacific, naturalized understandings of familial and national membership are embedded in a third salient impossible contradiction, namely, *fixed and flexible racialized imaginaries;* mutable characterizations of Asianness coexist with histories that have continually invented ways to fix and contain it. In some ways, the adopted Chinese child's migration suggests racial flexibility, by virtue of the proximity to whiteness and class privilege that in turn ease her global mobility. In other ways, that very proximity recalls the periphery from which she came, the body from which she came, and the histories of migration and racist cultural formation that have shaped the Asian America to which she has moved (Lowe 1996; Omi and Winant 1994; Palumbo-Liu 1999). As I try to demonstrate at different points throughout the book, the meanings attached to Asian adopted children also highlight the reproduction of whiteness that, in the racial politics of the United States, so often occurs in nervous relation to blackness.

People may "recognize" or "assign" race on the basis of everything from hair color to speech pattern to family name, but that recognition is utterly intertwined with historical, cultural, geographic, and socioeconomic meanings and effects. As Omi and Winant (1994) define it, race is that set of practices and discourses that "signifies and symbolizes social conflict and interests by referring to different types of human bodies" (55). While this phraseology is quite consciously counterposed to the definition of race as inherent biological difference (as it was entrenched in the colonial era of scientific racism; see McClintock 1995; Goldberg 1993), there is in adoption an oblique return of biologism to the racialization of "different types of human bodies." This is because in transracial adoption, race doubles as an expression of biological difference between parent and child. So even as kinship might shrink the distance between differently racialized bodies, the adoptive family is also compelled to translate and explain its own peculiar hybridity. When observers ask white American parents of Chinese children, "Are those your *real* kids?" they read and thus demand a simultaneous narration of race and kinship. In China as well, people to whom I talked differed in what they thought adoption meant for the cultural and national identities of children adopted abroad but usually averred that these children continued to have a "blood" connection to China.[17]

The racialized bodies of Chinese adoptees signal not only biological difference but also the particular forms of difference history has assigned to Asian immigrants as those "in between" immigrant and citizen,

insider and outsider. In a section of his book subtitled "Impossible Ar-
rivals," David Eng (2001) argues, "Suspended between departure and arrival, Asian Americans remain permanently disenfranchised from home,
relegated to a nostalgic sense of its loss or to an optative sense of its unattainability" (204). This history of impossible arrival is complicated in
China/U.S. adoption by the circuits of desire that mark Asian children of
white parents as nonbiological kin, and by the compulsive move toward
the new American home.

I want to make clear that the "impossible contradictions" I use to
frame my story are not dead ends or spinning wheels but rather an invitation to think in new ways about the stuff of which identification is
made, narrated, and imagined—that is, if we can live with the contradictions. Smelser (1998) argues that Americans are not very good at living with ambiguity. But adoptive parents—who do not get the racially
flexible, unequivocally detached, or needy child they might have imagined—are pushed to live with it. Transnational, transracial adoption
reproduces itself through dichotomies of sending/receiving nations,
white/nonwhite parents and children, birth/adoptive families, and
poverty/privilege, and yet it constantly defies and unfixes these very dichotomies. It pushes us to address the "in between" of race as neither
essence nor illusion (Cheng 2001) but rather as historically relational and
fluid (Stoler 1997); it pushes us to consider all forms of familial and national kinship as unstable concoctions of blood and culture (Weston
2001; Ginsburg and Rapp 1995); and it pushes us to recognize that social
relatedness is made in exchanges both marketized and humanitarian.

I suggest, then, that these contradictions pose possibilities for turning
the gaze of identity back on the historical and social struggles that make
it possible to think an identity in the first place. Put another way, they
might help us avoid the pitfalls of two problematic responses to difference: the first embraces difference in the name of relativism, and the second eschews difference in the name of universalism (Calhoun 1995: 135).
As Appadurai (1996) does in his study of mobile "postnational" orders,
we might too quickly revel in the endless possibilities of difference (Ong
2004)—as if hybridity and the proliferation of difference are automatic
antidotes to the essentializing of race or gender or kinship (Cheng 2001).
Or, as with liberal universalism and color blindness, we might too
quickly revel in the irrelevance of difference (Newfield and Gordon 1996;

Omi and Winant 1994), as if race or gender or kinship ties didn't matter. Each of these positions in its own way might circumvent the injuries of the past that constitute the identificatory system of dominant white America (Goldberg 1993). A multisited cultural economy of adoption allows us to study gender, class, and race neither as always already of no consequence nor as only "out of place" and dislodged, but rather as relocated in particular ways. Perhaps adoption is thus an especially effective vehicle for examining how unsettled transnational histories of dislocation and oppression have made their way into the psyches of both dominant and minority subjects, where they continue to haunt (Gordon 1997; Anagnost 2000; Cheng 2001); it further invites us to attend to those subjects who, "confined to the edges of globalization have attenuated, and often no legal claims to 'family,' 'home,' or 'nation'" (Eng 2003: 8).

Transnational Adoption Scholarship and the "Post" of Adoption

In the summer of 2000, I sat in the home of Jennifer Bartz,[18] a white American mother, listening to the story of her adoption from China. In the middle of the interview, in the space of about five minutes, I found out three significant things. First, Jennifer had commissioned a sculpture in memory of the child she was originally supposed to adopt, but who seemed so ill when Jennifer met her in China that she felt she could not agree to adopt her. Second, Jennifer later found out that the girl the Chinese orphanage director had instead placed with her—who was now in the other room doing her homework—had been a favorite of one of her orphanage caregivers in China. The caregiver had wished she could adopt this girl herself but could not afford to. Third, and not surprising, Jennifer wrestled with if, how, and when to tell her daughter these things, given that explaining abandonment and transracial, transnational adoption was fraught enough as it was.

This kind of history, linked to the quotidian details of individual lives both present (here and now) and not, puts the "posts" of adoption in question. Jennifer's story counters a particular strain of scholarly research that has treated the U.S.-based aftermath of adoption—what is referred to in the adoption profession as the *post*adoption phase—as a linear and developmental process. Much of this literature has focused on outcomes for children's self-esteem and identity coherence.[19] Within this body of work, large-scale surveys have tended to demonstrate that transracially adopted children are doing "just as well" as the general population of children or same-race adopted children, while small-scale clinical or qualitative studies tend to highlight problems children are having or issues that create tensions in identity formation (Tuan and Shiao 2001; Ouellette and Belleau 2001). (In both cases, the adoptive relationship is usually "evaluated in terms of how closely it approximates the cultural ideal of a family, composed of a heterosexual couple and the children born to them" [Ouellette and Belleau 2001: 11].) This "post" of adoption is thus often constructed as a time of individual psychosocial healing of the potential or actual traumas of losing birth family and birth stories, or of adjustment to being a minority among a white majority. As a result, the dislocations of the adoption process are analyzed and debated in terms of the "broken" (or not) child (Volkman 2003; Yngvesson 2003). A myopic developmentalist script emerges around the pathologized child and his family wherein traumas of birth loss and injuries of racist exclusion are pinned to the individual identity of the postadopted child, rather than being located in collective sets of relationships found equally in preadoption practices.

What if we turn the research gaze away from the (potential) brokenness of the adopted child out to that which shapes or denies such brokenness—to the broader histories and structures that make us wonder and worry for her to begin with (Derrida 1994; Anagnost 2000; Watkins 2004)? My goal is to frame the adoption story in this way, by refiguring the "post" of adoption itself. Such a deconstructive move recognizes the powerful heterogeneity of the "pre" of adoption (Derrida 1994)—the globalized cultural and capitalist production of disrupted kinship, racialized desire and exclusion, and gendered cultural scripts.

Fortunately, and fruitfully, these questions compel some of the scholarship on transnational, transracial adoption that has emerged since the late 1990s. These works embed struggles over domestic transracial adoption in the broader political projects that hierarchically racialize women and citizens (see, for example, Patton 2000; Solinger 2001; and Kirton 2000). Lovelock (2000) has argued that intercountry adoption is a neglected form of migration to the United States whose history can be traced to global political economies of military action, social strife, and economic expansion. Briggs (2003) expands on this history of adoption by showing how it has helped shore up the notion of a humanitarian America, especially through discourses of victimized Third World women. Riley (1997) links this framework of unequally located sending and receiving nations and families to American parents' decisions to adopt from China. Recognizing transnational adoption as increasingly marketized, Anagnost (2000) and Eng (2003) have used the case of China/U.S. adoption to pry open questions of whiteness and commodification in globalized kinship construction. While they look largely at representations by and of adoptive parents (particulary motherhood, both straight and queer), Yngvesson (2002, 2003) draws on the experiences and narratives of transnational adult adoptees to reconstruct the routes of exchange and value that haunt the dislocations of adoption. Choy and Choy (2003) and Kim (2000) interrogate the autoethnographic cultural productions of adult Korean adoptees as particular cases of Asian American identity formation in transnational context.

In these texts, as in my own, transnational adoption is treated not as a linear process of individual or familial identity formation, moving from "pre" to "post," but as a cultural economy of circulating relationships of power and exchange. This is a move from asking who we are to asking how we came to be located in the particular social spaces where we reside (Mirza 1997). The individual adopted child's history recalls the multiple histories around her, from the gendered disciplinary circumstances of her abandonment, to the transnational movement of resources that help prepare her for adoption, to the racial and national discourses that both invite and potentially compromise her citizenship. In other words, the "identity issues" of postadoption are not just the result of leftover feelings of loss and rejection or individual experiences with racial prejudice; rather, they surface because the historical raced, gendered, and classed conditions of abandonment and adoption are *still present*. This is why a number of these scholars, including myself, have employed the language of "haunting," which refers to the ghosts of unsettled pasts, foreclosed relationships, and excluded others that haunt the present and push for recognition and for the restoration of history to the present (Yngvesson 2002; Anagnost 2000; Eng 2003; Dorow and Hartman 2000).

Haunting is double-edged in that it not only exposes adoptive families to structures of inequity but also pushes for something to be done
about them (Gordon 1997). It is a reminder that transracial, transnational
adoptive kinship might just as readily transform as reproduce forms of
injustice, might just as easily forge new cultural politics as ignore the
constraints of existing ones. When it comes to racial formations in the
United States, for example, China/U.S. adoption might be just another
case of whiteness fortifying itself by "taking in the other-made-ghostly"
(Cheng 2001: 8), and/or it might enact "what it means, for social, political, and subjective beings *to grieve*" the racial injuries that live at the
core of the nation (7; emphasis in original). Eng (2003) reminds us:

> Parents of transnational adoptees should not be held any more ac-
> countable than the rest of us to the political, economic, social vicissi-
> tudes of globalization. Nevertheless, the practice of transnational
> adoption presents an exemplary—perhaps radical opportunity for
> white, middle-class subjects to confront and to negotiate difference
> ethically within the social configurations of the new global family. (33)

Recent examinations of transnational, transracial Asian adoption have
posed the question of how, and to what extent, such kinship can be considered "poststructural" (Anagnost 2000; Eng 2001; Watkins 2004; Yngvesson 2003; Dorow 2006)—how does it reproduce the power relations
of difference, and how does it challenge and transform them?

Narrating Adoption: The Trouble with Stories

How are any of us invited to tell the stories of who we are and how we
got to where we are? The style and content of such an invitation might
reveal the horizon of possible ways of being, the limits and promises of
everyday experiences of difference. In adoption, the stories and activities that happen between adopted children and the people around them
constitute what Hall (1996a) calls *identification*—a process that "entails
discursive work, the binding and marking of symbolic boundaries, the
production of 'frontier-effects.' It requires what is left outside, its consti-

tutive outside, to consolidate the process" (3). In other words, identification is a process that happens *between* individual psyches and the subject positions invented by culture, politics, and markets (Fuss 1995). My book is especially concerned with the discursive work found in the narratives people tell to and about children adopted from China, because these narratives animate the migration of adopted children and invent them in particular ways. Resituating the child in a host of stories is all the more salient a process when adoption itself spells a narrative rupture in her life: a separation from the stories normally/naturally associated with the family of origin. Identity narratives—including not just stories but the photos, objects, and practices through which stories are socially transmitted—are meant to bring coherence and unity to identity, telling us who we are (Widdershoven 1993; Denzin 1990). We might think of the "broken" narratives of adoptees and, more important, the various narratives used by parents, social workers, facilitators, and officials to "fix" them as the identificatory work between individual and collective, local and transnational, past and present.

Jennifer Bartz, the mother who had commissioned the memorial sculpture, told me that perhaps more compelling than knowing the facts of her daughter's story was "how you invite her to tell the story back to herself, or how you invite her to explore it." What is suggested here is that getting a story "right" is as much a matter of expecting something unanticipated as it is a matter of the facts of its contents. It recognizes the partiality of knowledge as a mingling of inseparable fact and fiction and grapples with that which is not understandable (Gordon 1997). "The truth about stories," Thomas King (2003) reminds his readers, "is that that's all we are" (2). This goes for adoptees, and it goes for researchers. The story told in this book is meant to be read in light of these things. It is one iteration of the China/U.S. adoption story, made possible by bringing stories and practices together that are multiply positioned and intertwined. Yet it does so with an argument that is consciously mine; the particular way in which it represents China/U.S. adoption comes from the stuff *between* me and the people and places and practices I studied. It does not pretend to be the whole story but instead suggests that there is more to the story than we might think. It is also an invitation to explore how we might give subjectivity to the ghostly object (the excluded, the marginalized, the unrecognized); as Cheng (2001) argues, to pose a different, perhaps more emancipatory relationship between the self and the conditions of dislocation is an appropriate way to grieve.

One couple I interviewed, when reading a shorter piece I had written, told me they did not quite recognize themselves—and not just because I had changed their names or other identifying details about them, as I have done with most people who appear in this book. They knew they had said those things I quoted but also knew that they had changed, or were unsure, or had fuller lives than had been conveyed. Indeed, the people in this book are not the people I interviewed and observed, in part because they cannot be and in part because conveying the fullness of individuals' lives in relation to themselves or to their immediate context is not the only intent here. When I take a quote from an interview or a piece from my field notes or a chunk of text from a publication, I do so in relation to other pieces less immediately obvious—to the broader set of social institutions, discourses, and practices that make up the political economy of adoption from China. This rewoven narrative is meant to speak to the breadth and complexity of social discourses and practices that inform and are informed by the process of transnational, transracial adoption. People directly experiencing adoption on a daily basis—adoptive parents, adoptees, orphanage caregivers, agency social workers, immigration officers—may not usually think about it in this way. But I have borrowed from them to contend and demonstrate how adoption as a social process speaks to a range of broader questions: the racial topographies of American culture, the border crossers who illuminate the class and gender contours of the nation, the transnational political economy of exchanges that produce and challenge those relationships, and the locus of kinship through which various forms of belonging both wither and bloom.

Finally, however, it is important to note the impossible contradiction of narrating adoption to the satisfaction of all whom it affects. As not only a transnational political economy but also a very personal experience, it invites intense debate. This is why I probably should not have been surprised when an earlier manuscript was reviewed with the following result. "Too critical," said one reviewer, protesting that it was too hard to review because too hard on adoption. "Not critical enough!" said a second reviewer, suggesting that I was too intent on accommodating adoptive parents. "Just right," said the third reviewer, declaring that I had found the right balance of respect and critique. All three reviews struck a chord (and were invitations to reread my story in particular ways), because although it has become almost a cliché to speak of what haunts ethnographic researchers, those ghost stories are there—the obligation to people who have entrusted their time and stories and even secrets to me, the multiple and sometimes conflicting hats I wear of researcher and friend and former adoption administrator, the impossibility of knowing exactly what my project is until it is produced, the challenge to find the right balanced relationships between the big stuff (the social, political, economic, structural-historical) and the little stuff (the personal, everyday, immediate). But such sensitivities are also themselves sociological evidence of the continuous and elusive attempt to tell the stories of who we are.

The Chapters to Come

As indicated above, the Chinese adopted child's path serves as the "spine" for the narrative flow of this project, which moves from practices in both China and the United States that prepare children and parents for each other, to the exchange practices through which children migrate, to the stories and practices parents use to narrate abandonment and cultural-racial identity. It also moves from the transnational histories of adoption's political economy to everyday constructions of kinship, especially as expressed by adoptive parents. Each chapter of the book builds in a new "layer" of contradictions, exploring how actors variously experience and respond to those contradictions. The multiple determinations of identification are perhaps most densely encountered when parents travel to China to meet their children (chapters 3 and 4), although they certainly continue to unfold upon return to the United States in the form of stories told to and about adopted children. But I have also tried to convey that this is not a linear story. The China and birth family of a child's preadoption story make themselves felt in postadoption narratives of motherhood and racialized class positions, just as the histories of American national and racial imaginaries shape parents' decisions to adopt from China. In some ways, then, the book lends itself to being read as a whole, even as individual chapters focus on particular facets of the China/U.S. adoption process.

The first chapter, "Why China? Identifying Histories," is foundational to ensuing chapters. It lays out the histories of Chinese immigration, international adoption, and China/U.S. adoption itself, arguing that these histories animate American parents' decisions to adopt from China. Each of these histories highlights one of the contradictory impetuses for adoption discussed here in the introduction: flexible racialization, marketized rescue, and exclusive kinship. In doing so, the chapter provides what I see as important historical and theoretical contexts for understanding China/U.S. adoption as a political and cultural economy of exchange and migration, while also introducing readers to some of the racialized desires and gendered contingencies that shape the popularity of the China program.

The dislocations of abandonment bring children into a system of circulating ideas and resources that remake them for adoption. Chapter 2, "Matches Made on Earth: Making Parents and Children for Each Other," examines the practices and narratives of the preplacement stages of the story. I write across the sites in both China and the United States where marginalized children are selected and prepared as adoptable, but also where prospective parents are produced as able to adopt. The practices of Chinese state and welfare institutions charged with caring for relinquished children are thus articulated with the practices of adoption agencies and "waiting" parents in the United States; I pay particular attention to the resources and ideologies that circulate between them. Analyzing Chinese and American preadoption narratives in tandem brings to light the power relations that reproduce hierarchies of migrating subjects, even before they physically migrate, and that at the same time make possible the reclamation of marginalized subjects. Constructions of the material and symbolic value of differentiated subjects—children who are adoptable, parents who are able to adopt—are shown to be simultaneously consumptive and caring. The labor to "match" parents and children is embedded in this contradictory linkage, which tends toward favoring parents as agents of choice.

Many adoptive parents trace the originary moments of kinship with their adopted children to the receipt of a referral photo, when a child halfway around the world becomes "real." I briefly discuss this process in a short chapter called "Picturing Kinship." As in the process of adoption itself, chapter 3 serves as the link between processes in China and the United States that set the stage for matching parent and child and for their actual meeting. Chapter 4, "Client, Ambassador, and Gift: Managing Adoption Exchange," examines how the labor of transferring children from Chinese institutions to American adoptive families is accomplished through the three tropes of client, ambassador, and gift. The labors of exchange are especially intense during the two weeks when parents travel to China to meet their children; this encounter briefly brings together a myriad of people with connections to the child, creating a kind of multivocal space between the past and future, the here and there of the adopted child's life. I draw in particular on observations and interviews conducted when I accompanied two groups of American adoptive families as they arrived at hotels in China, met their children and their children's caregivers, filled out paperwork, and performed as tourists. Not just the child's identity but also the identities of those who narrate her as ambassador, client, and gift are articulated through the differences that attend her exchange. Of particular importance are the Chinese facilitators and officials who manage this process, as well as the caregivers and birth mothers who hover at its edges.

Even before American adoptive parents leave China, they travel through transnational spaces that privilege adoption as a special form of migration. This is most poignantly illustrated in adoptive parents' last stop in China before they return to the United States: the U.S. consulate on Shamian Island in Guangzhou. Chapter 5, "Shamian Island: Borders of Belonging," is the most ethnographically dense of the book's chapters. I describe the series of hotels, shops, and state offices that serve as a pivotal transnational point in the remaking of the adopted Chinese child across borders. Photos of Shamian Island solicited from adoptive parents several years after my visit are included alongside my written observations.

When Chinese children cross the Pacific with their American parents, they carry with them these histories of transnational exchange, as well as imprints of the racialized histories of Asian migration that are inextricably part of American national culture. Chapter 6, "Storied Origins: Abandonment, Adoption, and Motherhood," picks up on the gendered relationships that have brought children into the transnational adoption system and argues that these relationships haunt constructions of white, middle-class motherhood. It is especially concerned with the impossible contradictions of dislocating and relocating children between "two mothers" marked by differentiated race and class positions. The problems of good and bad mothers, of reading children's belonging through biology and culture, and of imagining fated kinship are evident in the stories adoptive mothers tell about their children's origins.

Transnational, transracial adoption compels narration not only because of disrupted biological kinship but also because of the way race underwrites the making of nations and identities. The final substantive chapter, "American Ghosts: Cultural Identities, Racial Constructions," examines how both white and Chinese American adoptive parents try to give coherence to their children's identities as they cross into the domestic spaces of nation and family. Parents' approaches to their children's "Chineseness" are more varied than is popularly thought, but whether they emphasize assimilation, ethnic immersion, or some version of multiculturalism, they must all deal with the ghosts of difference and unsettled relationships of power—racial formations, national claims, kinship ties, gendered expectations, class inequalities—stirred by the dislocation and relocation of their children. Parents' organizational activities, social practices, and family stories renarrate their children's identities in the midst of these differences, both reproducing and struggling to transform them. I argue that constructions of the racially flexible Chinese child run into the impossible contradictions of particularized forms of social citizenship.

In the conclusion, "Akin to Difference," I address the question of transformation that is latent throughout the preceding chapters. Drawing on Gordon (1997) and Derrida (1994), I assert that the case of China/U.S. adoption shows us that possibilities for justice begin precisely where inequalities are reproduced, namely, at proximities of multiple difference. The haunting of material and symbolic exclusions and inequalities in the child's migration story pushes for, as Gordon (1997) puts it, "something to be done." I suggest ways in which something is already being done and explore to what extent we might consider China/U.S. adoptive families to constitute "poststructural" kinship.

The trajectory of these chapters relies on the narratives of adults in the China/U.S. adoption process, and most often adoptive parents, but is ultimately guided by the animated histories of children themselves. Indeed, children adopted from China who have become old enough to tell their own stories often do so in surprising and evocative ways. One of my favorite stories appeared in the newsletter of FCC–Minnesota, *Blessings from China;* it was a series of captioned drawings submitted by the four-year-old of a single mother. It begins with a little girl in an orphanage, where a "little present came in a box. The baby opened the present and a mommy popped out" (*Blessings from China,* June 2001: 6). Turning the reproductive and migratory story on its head coaxes us to consider the adoption process from differing locations, and thus to link the subjectivities of adopted children to transnationally circulated resources and meanings.

CHAPTER 1

Why China?

Identifying Histories

> We should not conflate a haunted
> history with nonspecificity; on the
> contrary, haunted history alerts us
> to context.
> —Anne Anlin Cheng (2001: 28)

Contemporary poststructural and psychoanalytic theorists define *identification* as a process that occurs where individual lives meet the haunting of social relationships—a process that "names the entry of history and culture into the subject" (Fuss 1995: 3; see also Cheng 2001).[1] In this sense, there are several overlapping histories that "identify" Chinese adopted children: trans-Pacific migration, the social and legal contexts of domestic and international adoption, and the unfolding dynamics of China/U.S. adoption itself. I see the traces of these histories in the stories American parents tell about how they decided to adopt a child or children from China. As prospective adoptive parents sift through their options, the ways in which they imagine the child that might become "our own" conjure elements of these histories. The title of this chapter, "Why China?" thus refers to two things at once: (1) parents' reasons for choosing to adopt from China and (2) the historical forces that might explain the popularity and growth of the China adoption program.[2]

The histories that are invoked when parents choose *transnational* adoption tell us about racialized and gendered citizenship in the *domestic* nation and family. Yet my focus on parents is not meant to put them on the spot. Rather, parents' expressions of transnational family building should lead us to interrogate the historical weight of dominant social discourses and practices that reach beyond—and inform—individual beliefs and everyday interactions in contemporary American social life more generally (Anagnost 2000; Eng 2003). For the adoption process itself, this means we should try to understand how parents' choices are shaped within institutionalized practices in state and social service agencies. So while parent motivations for adopting are portrayed in the literature as notoriously difficult to pin down (Kirton 2000: 43–44), this becomes a problem for "knowledge about adoption" only when motivations are assumed to spring from inside the bounded individual decision maker, rather than from the juncture of individual and collective practices. I take the messiness of parents' decisions as evidence of the circulating forces of history that shape the possible horizons of identification for them and their children.

Throughout the following pages, I focus in particular on moments in my ethnographic data when adoptive choices meet racialized exclusions—those places where histories of color blindness, salvation, and universal humanism meet their dialectical partners of white privilege, marginalization, and particularity. My intention is not to attempt any kind of exhaustive history, nor to permanently hitch contemporary China/U.S. adoption to specific historical sign posts, but rather to suggest resonances of a discursive and practical nature. When it comes to racial formations, for example, I am more interested in how adoption decisions might play off of the shifting topography of imagined black-white-Asian relationships than I am in reinforcing the imprint of a racial hierarchy on American culture.

I begin with the story of just one adoptive parent to suggest what historical traces I mean, and what I intend to argue in this chapter on "why China." When we spoke in 1998, Jackie Kovich was a single white woman who had only recently adopted a daughter from China. Like most adoptive mothers and fathers I interviewed, Jackie began her adoption story with an explanation of her decision to adopt at all. She drew on humanitarianism and nonbiological parenting as naturally linked in a tacitly white embrace of a "different" child:

> I've always had the feeling that adoption was what people ought to do, from a political perspective, and from a, from a social justice perspec-

tive also. And I've never had the need to reproduce, to see a child that looks like me. . . . And I've always worked with underserved people and in the Third World.

This expressed commitment to and familiarity with global political and social inequities recalls a long-standing but selectively invoked thread of adoption discourse in the United States, fulfilling national and familial discourses of generous humanitarian outreach (Briggs 2003; Modell 2002). But it also laid the narrative groundwork for Jackie's choice to adopt from China in particular:

> [A]bout three months after I came back from a business trip to China, I went to see my sister. And she said, "Oh, did you see the thing on TV about the Chinese orphanages?" And I said, "Yeah, and you know, those children are so beautiful. There are no ugly Asian children." And my sister said, "Why don't you adopt one?" Okay? And I'd never mentioned anything to her [about wanting to adopt]!

In Jackie's account, a prescient remark by her sister seals her destiny with China, but only because overdetermined by the dual desirability of Chinese children as both needy and beautiful. "The thing on TV" refers to a 1995 media exposé of poor conditions in Chinese orphanages, beginning with a documentary titled *The Dying Rooms,* that ended up influencing a number of parents in their decision to adopt from China. At the same time, "there are no ugly Asian children" resonates with a history of American and European fascination with aestheticized, feminized Oriental others (Said 1994 [1978]; R. G. Lee 1999; Register 1991).

Taken together, these transnational expressions of need and desire figure through yet a third lens of domestic racialized history. A bit later in our discussion, Jackie had just finished telling me how important she thought it was to teach her daughter about Chinese culture, when she continued, "I mean, look at the black community. If they truly had pride in who they were, the community wouldn't be disintegrating. . . . I think the reason why the Asian communities have excelled in our society is that they *do* have pride in who they are." Simultaneously referencing discourses of the culture of poverty (associated with blacks), the model minority (associated with Asians), and globalized humanism (associated with whites), Jackie imagines what her daughter is and can be against what she is not and will not be. A racially and culturally proud, desirable, redeemable Asian child is distinguished from the racially and culturally abject, marginalized, and possibly irredeemable black (collective) body. As Cheng (2001) asserts, the "strain of Asian euphoria" that marks the model minority discourse "serves to contain the history of Asian abjection, as well as to discipline other racialized groups in America" (23). Explanations for transnational family building sometimes expose not only the historical blinders of American multiculturalism invoked by Cheng and others (Okihiro 2001; Omi 1996; Prashad 2003) but also its unspoken whiteness (which has little need to be culturally proud). Jackie's story of choosing or being fatefully chosen for China—while more overt in its racial constructions than was the case in most of my interviews—brings to the surface several histories that reproduce/transform white middle-class subjectivity at the juncture of domestic and transnational practices and through the migrating adoptee.

Flexible Difference: Adoption as a Chapter in Trans-Pacific Migration History

China/U.S. adoption came along at the right time, or perhaps more accurately, because the times were right—that is, a confluence of historical processes made it both possible and attractive. It is toward this claim that my argument in this chapter is aimed, organized around three kinds of history that weave through Jackie's story. In subsequent sections I deal with adoption histories themselves, but I begin with the migration of people, cultural imaginaries, and material objects between China and the United States, a history that is in some ways the least recognized of contextual histories of adoption, yet which leaves a certain imprint on the reasons people give for adopting from China. Parents imagine their and their children's relationships to China through the traces of a long history of "trans-Pacific flights" of people, ideas, and sentiments. In other words, the reasons parents give for adopting from China are inseparable from the images and sociopolitical relationships that characterize the history of China/U.S. migration (Shiu 2001).

I do not want to suggest a direct and continuous link from century-old images and constructions of China to the present, but as Gungwu Wang (2001) has argued,

[A]ny study of Chinese today must take account of the historical experiences of those who left China in the 19th and early 20th centuries, whose descendants form the majority of those abroad who are still identified as Chinese in some ways. Those experiences provide an important background to what it has meant for Chinese to live among different kinds of non-Chinese during the last hundred years or so. (119–20)

China/U.S. adoption fits Wang's general description of migration yet reworks the relationship between contemporary and past experiences of Chinese migration. Because Chinese adoptees enter at a young age into the legal and social embrace of (usually) white American homes, adoption migration abruptly raises the question of what it means to "live among" non-Chinese and at the same time suggests a path free of some of the usual obstacles to doing so. Chinese adopted children leapfrog into the national interior across boundaries of kinship, class, nation, and race. And it is for that very reason that their presence compels explanation.

Adoption migration thus turns our gaze to non-Chinese and, more specifically, white American imaginaries of the immigrant past. It forces us to consider the Chinese experience of migration as it both shapes and is shaped by Western images of China—those familiar and contradictory historical traces that "have designated China in a range of ways, as worthy of admiration, sympathy, curiosity, fear, ridicule, hostility, conversion to Christianity, or as a means of profit" (Mackerras 1989: 11). One kind of American discourse of China has placed it at the center of an increasingly transnational and "borderless" world, for instance, as invoked in the notion of the open economy of the Pacific Rim (Palumbo-Liu 1999). At the same time, however, representations of the Pacific Rim tend to recover East/West binaries; its Orientalized others, as Said's (1994 [1978]) pivotal work demonstrated, "recuperate a specific western individual at the core of reality" (Palumbo-Liu 1999: 339). These different but simultaneous imaginaries of China have developed through migration in both directions across the Pacific, for example, missionaries to China and railway workers to California. The cultural economy of adoption similarly occurs through the movement of people, ideas, and resources both from and to China.

The question of trans-Pacific migration must address the different historical contexts of the two areas in which I conducted research in the United States: the San Francisco Bay Area and the Minneapolis–St. Paul metropolitan area. The former has a 150-year history of Asian and especially Chinese immigration. Starting in the mid–nineteenth century, American westward expansion included the idea of developing East Asia (Dirlik 1993, referenced in Palumbo-Liu 1999), with San Francisco as its gateway to trade with China (Takaki 1989) and as the gatekeeper of Chinese immigrants who would provide labor for American nation building (E. Lee 2003; Takaki 1989). This means that in the contemporary Bay Area, where 30 percent of the population reports being Asian, Chinese American people and cultural representations are more pervasive as well as more variable than in the Twin Cities, where significant Chinese immigration is one or two generations old and only about 8 percent of the population is Asian.[3] Thus, the Asian America of the Twin Cities is an instance of the more recent expansion of Chinese and other East Asian student, business, and family immigration to North America. Also significant is that in San Francisco, an estimated one-fourth to one-third of families adopting from China include at least one Asian or Asian American parent (mostly Chinese American but also some who identify as Japanese American and Filipina American, for example)[4]—a proportion substantially higher than Minneapolis–St. Paul and probably most any other location in the United States. For these reasons, the question of "why China" begs consideration of geographic location. Of course, location must always be considered alongside other social factors. Jackie Kovich, for example, contrasted her child's identity to that of adoptive families living just over the hill from her in the Bay Area; she drew on the "free" cultural resources of her multiethnic working-class neighborhood, while wealthier white adoptive parents a few miles away could afford to send their children to private schools offering formal programs in Mandarin language and Chinese cultural arts.

Whether in San Francisco or the Twin Cities, parents' narratives of "choosing China" both echo and challenge a central theme of the history of China/U.S. migration: the American construction of the Asian Other as both strange and familiar, as insider and outsider, and as variably suited to incorporation into national projects of citizenship (Lee 2003; Palumbo-Liu 1999; Lowe 1996). Since the nineteenth century, immigration policies and practices have sometimes invited, sometimes forced, and sometimes barred the migration of Chinese workers and students and the relatives (including "paper sons")[5] who have joined them. From the Chinese Exclusion Act of 1882, to the 1965 reforms abolishing official race-based immigration, to the grounding of the *Golden Venture* that stranded hundreds of illegal Chinese immigrants in New York Harbor in 1993, China/U.S. migration has been shaped by universal discourses of transnational capital as well as particularizing notions of the uncivilized or exotic Asian, or more recently, the virtuous model minority (Palumbo-Liu 1999; Lowe 1996). The *flexibility* of Asian difference—strange but adaptable—has thus enabled contradictory positions of expansionary transnationalism, nativist exclusion, and assimilationist embrace.

The liminal space occupied by Asian America is and has been accomplished on cultural and racial territory, and in response to material realities. The reaction to increasing labor pressures in California that catalyzed the late-nineteenth-and early-twentieth-century exclusion period, for example, was as much a manifestation of Orientalist discourses of the untrustworthy and uncivilized Chinaman (E. Lee 2003) as it was a class issue. Brought back by American missionaries and traders, these racialized discourses were reproduced "at home" in various ways; one exemplary case is provided in Nayan Shah's (2001) study of political and social responses to Chinatown's "contagion" in turn-of-the-century San Francisco. But then, even as the 1906 establishment of the Angel Island immigration station ensured increasingly standardized practices of keeping out unwanted Asian people (E. Lee 2003), the importation of "Oriental-style" decorative arts and consumer products reached heights previously unprecedented in middle-class white American culture (R. G. Lee 1999).

This dialectic of danger and exoticism has echoed again since the 1960s in the seemingly more benign "model minority" discourse, which Lowe (1996) argues is yet another instance of the projection of American national anxieties onto the site of Asian American immigration. While purporting admiration of "traditional values," the model minority discourse tends also to depoliticize the material realities of racism and to deny histories of labor exploitation by promising "deliverance of minority subjects from collective history to a reified individualism" (Palumbo-Liu 1999: 415). But even so, there is regular confirmation that such transformation is not fully possible, as the case of Wen Ho Lee demonstrated.[6] R. G. Lee (1999) points out that in the late capitalist national American imaginary, Asian Americans have become both model minority and potential enemy within. In discourse echoing some of the nativist tone of the late nineteenth century, Asians are in and to America "economically productive but culturally inauthentic" (191). A more recent surge of "Asian cool"—hip but respectable popular Asian American culture—is perhaps the latest reinvention of America's flirtation with the exotic potential of such inauthenticity (see Galang 2003).

Reasons parents give for adopting from China at times reflect this contradictory history of Asian America, sitting uneasily on the impossible binary of rejecting/embracing images and ideologies of flexible Asian difference. Some of the multicultural promise of adopting children from China hinges on cultural-racial desirability and accessibility. But Asianness may still threaten to exceed the bounds of consumable difference. I argue below that such excess is at least partly kept in check through the construction of black difference as less assimilable difference. As suggested in Jackie's narrative, motifs of model Asian America play off the construction of abject black America and failed black-white relations (Gotanda 2000; Palumbo-Liu 1999), allegedly manifest in welfare dependence, criminality, and ingratitude.

For a select group of parents, feelings of connection to China and Chinese culture come from histories of trans-Pacific migration in their own families. Some Chinese American adoptive parents I interviewed cited a "natural" connection based on cultural heritage, even as they were sometimes quick to distinguish their second-, third-, or fourth-generation Chinese American experience from the Chinese heritage their children seemed more directly to embody. A number of white adoptive parents also cited a direct connection to China because they had relatives who had been missionary, diplomatic, or academic sojourners there or had themselves lived in or frequently visited China as businesspeople or teachers. But most white parents expressed an affinity with Chinese culture that bore more indirect traces of the cultural and political histories of migration discussed above. It was not uncommon, for example, for white adoptive parents to indicate a preexisting or growing interest in "ancient Chinese culture." Some named such an interest as a circumstantial bonus, while others indicated they thought it was a mistake for people to adopt from China if they did not have such an interest. Cultural knowledge and interest on the part of adoptive parents is encouraged by Beijing as well. The China Center of Adoption Affairs has long asked prospective foreign adopters to indicate in writing that they will teach their children about Chinese culture.

White parents usually construed Chinese culture as admirably different but accessible, lending itself to some form of celebration or incorporation into their family lives. Adoptive father John Padding said, "We obviously wanted to adopt for *us,* but maybe another reason it makes it okay is that it's also a good thing, for our daughter, for the world, for multiculturalism"; he later added, "We like Chinese people and food and things and culture, so it was an easy thing to connect to." In the middle of my interview with the Cook family, adoptive mother Nancy stopped mid-sentence to muse, "You know, I was just thinking as we're sitting here, looking at our house . . . we have a lot of Asian influence, and most of this was before we adopted her. This was just our *taste,* I guess." In the San Francisco Bay Area in particular, the accessibility of "things Chinese" contributed to justifications for adopting from China. As Jason Bradley discussed his and his wife's decision to adopt from China, for example, he noted that having lived on the West Coast for so long, "we had had Asian American friends, and had had exposure to that culture." On a number of occasions parents in the Bay Area contrasted its multicultural and especially Asian population to some town in the Midwest that represented a problematic lack of the same.[7] While white parents in Minnesota did not as often or as confidently claim to have been primed for adoption from China through "exposure" to Asian cultures and peoples, their reasons for being attracted to the China program also sometimes referenced the accessible difference of Chinese culture itself, and thus the imagined adaptability of their children.

Accessibility—naming the appeal of Chinese food and art objects or naming Asian American friends—was in turn made possible by the *definability* and *longevity* of Chinese culture. As Mackerras (1989) argues, late-twentieth-century images of China remained focused "on the past, and the strength of its role in present-day China" (217). Parents fairly consistently used words such as *strong, rich,* and *ancient* to describe Chinese culture, suggesting a reliable and contained kind of difference with which children (and parents) could proudly identify and be identified. Lila Noonan said it was important in her and her husband's decision to adopt that "Chinese history is so advanced, so developed. . . . I'm Hungarian American, and growing up with the traditions, the history, the values—it's made me who I am."

The point is not that parents thought they could fully adopt Chinese culture along with the children they brought home; for some, in fact, part of the attraction was that an authentic China remained just out of reach, even as it could be celebrated, admired, and accessed. China itself—"actual" China—was sometimes even narrated as intimidating. Cindy Coombs noted, "At the beginning, it was still a mystery. The idea that China might actually be a place that we could feel comfortable didn't even occur to us." Jennifer Bartz made clear that she knew her daughter's understanding of China through *Mulan* and picture books was an "abstraction from the real thing." This was true as well for a couple of Chinese American parents in the Bay Area who had chosen to adopt from China so they could have a child "like us," yet who laughed ironically at feeling "inauthentic" in relation to the China from which their grandparents or great-grandparents, and now their children, had directly come.

The flexible racialization of Asian subjects in the American imaginary is crucial to understanding the dialectic of strangeness and familiarity that contributed to "why China." This is especially so for white adoptive parents, who sometimes saw their own amorphous racial identities—what Frankenberg (1993: 205) calls the "unadorned, basic, essential" feeling of whiteness—potentially enlivened through transracial adoption. Deena Houston sheepishly admitted she had been somewhat disappointed that her daughter "was so white"; she had imagined one of those darker, rosy-cheeked country girls you saw in *National Geographic,* an outcome that might have made their whole family more interesting. Jennifer Bartz described her experience of the "difference" of China, which was also the experience of her own difference, as a kind of rush:

I was overwhelmed by being in China. I had never been any place like China. There were times when I would just have to stop on the street and let it wash over me. And I would be standing on the street watching the tidal wave of bicycles go by, at sundown, and the sunlight would be filtered through the dust in the air, and you'd hear the sound of bicycle bells, and I would just stand and take it in, and people would be staring at me. You know, people from the country would be staring at me. Or their heads would swivel. And I had never had an experience like that. I liked it. I liked being—I liked having the experience of being Other. Because so rarely in my life have I been Other, except maybe as a lesbian. And even then, it's not like you could pick me out of a lineup . . . I grew up the majority in a Midwestern suburb. So whatever hardwiring and life experience came to be that allowed me to enjoy feeling, most of the time, like Other, that felt good to me.

In Jennifer's description, the experience of being Other exposes the "hardwiring" of whiteness but then just as quickly welcomes relief from its bland normalcy. The transracial, transnational adoptive journey can be a dangerous pleasure, promising mutually beneficial Asian-white relations both through and for the child.

The potential to make whiteness more colorful depends in turn on the racial and cultural flexibility of Chinese children themselves. With particular attention to the commoditization of this process, Eng (2003) explores how the transnationally adopted child is both object and subject, performing the ideological labor of reproducing the white heterosexual nuclear family. He asks, "What does it mean that, in our present age, full and robust citizenship is *socially* effected from child to parent and, in many cases, through the position of the adoptee, its visible possession and spectacular display?" (8, emphasis in original). In this formulation, the American family and nation reproduce whiteness and weak multiculturalism[8] through the embrace of the transnational, transracial adoptee's cultural and racial difference (see also Shiu 2001; Ortiz and Briggs 2003). We are reminded that the history of struggles over the citizenship of Asian immigrants in America was also always about national citizenship in its dominant white patriarchal form (Palumbo-Liu 1999; Lowe 1996). But in the age of multiculturalism, and under the condition of unquestioned legal citizenship for the immigrant adoptee, social citizenship is not so much about making clear distinctions between "us" and "them" as it is about the extent to which "us" and "them" are reconstructed through the uneven exchange of difference.

Model minority discourses are part of the flexible racialization that facilitates the double act of making child and family for each other. While the assimilability of Chinese immigrants was largely questioned and denied up until the mid–twentieth century, the invention of the model minority and changes to immigration law have since allowed for a limited transformation from alien to citizen (Lowe 1996). While many parents saw model minority stereotypes as both a blessing and a curse, reasons for adopting from China found some justification in them. As an adoptive father I met in China put it, his Midwestern hometown was pretty homogeneously white, but he didn't think it would be a problem for his daughter because Asians had a "different kind of stereotype."

Of further importance is that, in some parents' narratives, this "different kind of stereotype" relied on the more weighty abjection of blackness. Discourses of enfranchisement and national identity in the nineteenth century may have relied on black/white binaries to repudiate the uncivilized "Oriental," but by the 1960s the model minority discourse had redeemed Asians as "not black" (R. G. Lee 1999)—a social topography of abjection that echoed in adoptive parent narratives of choosing China. "Real" race and racism were sometimes reserved for blacks, not Asians, whose appreciable cultural characteristics can be read off their bodies. Social worker Rita Jasper described one kind of encounter she has with prospective parents:

> People come in here and they say, "Okay, I'm open to adopting a child from anywhere." I'll say, "Okay, great. So how about doing a domestic adoption, African American child?" "Ooooohhh, no." "Okay, well why?" "Well really, it would be so hard for the child." "Okay, so why would it not be so hard for the child coming from China?" [Here Rita lowers her voice to mimic a parent talking to her in a knowing whisper.] "Well, you know, Rita . . ." [She laughs.] And they're afraid to say it. And what I end up saying is yeah, in this country there is definitely a hierarchy, and the darker color your skin, the more prejudice there is. . . . [She becomes the voice of the rationalizing parent again.] "Oh well, I'm not thinking about us, I'm thinking about the child."

Teresa, a white woman married to a Chinese American, told me, "It seems in the overall scheme of things that as far as stereotypes go, the Asian stereotype tends to be a little more 'favorable' than say the black or Hispanic stereotype." Patty expressed a similar sentiment: "It's really not that harsh for Asians. There's a little bit of, you know, 'they're smarter,' but there's not really the same kind of racism there is against blacks, unfortunate as that is." Aaron Kretz, a Jewish father living in California, owned that racism toward African Americans was embedded in and around him in part because race itself was conflated with black:

> To be honest, with me it was a racial thing. I didn't want a black child, and it was pretty much China or South America, and in South America you could get kids of color, and I didn't want to do that. You can't ask. And I just don't have any biases about Asians, so for me it was an easier fit. . . . I mean, black is still, uh, not only a minority to me in this country, but a minority that doesn't, you know, fit in, as well as some other minorities. And like Jews, the minority of Jews, have chosen to fit in, or do fit in, or whatever, pretty much. There's other minorities that kind of get blended in. . . . I mean, it goes back to why I wanted to do Chinese. For me, [race] doesn't come up. I've gotta admit that if I had a black child, I'd probably think of us as more biracial.

Chinese children were in some instances desirable because they could be imagined as neither white nor black—interesting without being so different that they would not "fit in." We have here the suggestion of a racial "passing" in which the recognition of difference is key to the reproduction of whiteness and kinship. Indeed, the model minority discourse promises to scale down the Asian threat precisely by writing particularized cultural admiration onto racial difference—a far cry from the anxieties of the mid–nineteenth to mid–twentieth centuries that prompted Chinese immigrants to try to "pass" as respectable middle-class non-Chinese, or that produced a series of laws about marriages between Chinese and whites (E. Lee 2003). This does not mean that adoptive parents did not express anxieties about the interracial intimacy of their families, including explaining it to relatives and friends. But where and how parents found ways to explain it points to an aesthetics of racial passing that not only references a broad racial topography but also intersects with gendered and class productions of identity.

In a context in which 95 percent of adoptees are girls, it is important to address questions of how racialized desire might intersect with the construction of Asian *female* bodies. Cheung (2000), for example, argues that in American cultural history Asian women have been endowed with an "excess" of womanhood (alongside the full manhood denied Asian men). And in China/U.S. adoption, mothers Deena Houston and Jackie Kovich were not alone in conjuring the image of beautiful, enthralling Chinese girls. Adoption agencies consistently use photos of cute, dolled-up Asian girls in their advertising; some use phrases such as "From China with Love" to attract would-be parents. Some of those prospective parents said they had become enchanted with their friends' or neighbors' Chinese girls. Margaret Jennings said she saw a photo of a Chinese adopted girl in the paper and "knew I wanted to adopt from China right then." Some expressed embarrassment at what they suspected hinted at "racist love"—embrace of the "acceptable model" of the racial minority (Chan 1972, quoted in Cheung 2000: 309). Just days after she had met her daughter, Barbara and I were discussing what seemed among some new adoptive mothers an obsession with dolling up their daughters, when Barbara stopped to say in a low tone, "I hate to ask this, but are all the children beautiful? It seems like they're all beautiful."

Such raced and gendered aesthetics have bearing on social and legal citizenship, especially when considered along with the class conditions of belonging. Historically, Chinese women and children in particular gained legitimacy through formal kinship ties with respectable citizens (e.g., the War Brides Act that allowed Chinese Americans in the armed forces to bring spouses to the United States) and through other associations with whiteness (e.g., having white witnesses who could attest to nativity at citizenship hearings) (E. Lee 2003: 106–7). Class and capital further differentiated racialized and gendered citizens, and continue to do so. In her work on late-twentieth-century Asian immigrant experiences in the United States, Aihwa Ong (1996) argues that class interacts with race and gender such that "money whitens"; transnational practices and exchanges of capital afford some transnational immigrant subjects more flexibility than others (Ong 1998). And while the model minority discourse in particular has underwritten a successful Asian class position over and above that of African Americans (Gotanda 2000), at the same time there lurks in the recent American imaginary the threat of both cheap Chinese labor and Chinese economic power (E. Lee 2000; Palumbo-Liu 1999).

Yet, as discussed above, China/U.S. adoption simultaneously creates kinship for both citizen parent and immigrant child. And here we must consider issues of class and capital from an angle somewhat different from what the history of immigration might usually suggest: it is the material and social capital of white middle-class citizen families that catalyzes the flexible belonging of Chinese adoptee migrants, who in turn reproduce and transform the family. The class (and race) position of adoptive parents is signified in a series of "choices"—the choice to adopt, the choice to adopt internationally, the choice to adopt from China—which then enable both parents and children to gain fuller social recognition. The point is underscored by cases in which parents' choice to adopt from China is marked by an excess of difference. Even as adoption might help fulfill middle-class family values for gay and lesbian parents (Eng 2003), for example, many choose China because it is one of few options available to them.[9] For Lisa and Gerry, a lesbian couple who are respectively white and Asian American, this choice was overdetermined by historical intersections of race, gender, and class. While they initially considered adopting a white child domestically, one crucial factor that led them to China was the painful awareness that with a white child in her arms, Gerry would be more likely to be read as the child's nanny than her mother. Their story demonstrates that the adoptive family is one of those sites of social formation that reflect, govern, and potentially challenge racialized and gendered social relationships, at the intersection of the national and transnational (Lowe 1996: 172).

Redeeming Acts: China/U.S. Adoption as a Chapter in Domestic and International Adoption Histories

While parents' narrations of "why China" both reiterate and contest the racialized, gendered, and classed relations of power that have marked China/U.S. immigration history, they must equally be understood within

the history of adoption in the United States. This history, when domestic and international adoptions are considered together, especially foregrounds the dialectical relationship between acts of rescue and acts of
market exchange. In my interviews, "saving" Chinese children was usually not first among reasons parents gave for adopting from China, but it
often served as a complementary justification. Humanitarian rescue discourses helped distinguish international adoption from domestic adoption options. But as a number of researchers have pointed out, the idea of
"rescuing a child" does not always sit comfortably with cultures of
choice, value, and upward mobility (Melosh 2002; Modell 2002; Anagnost 2000; Zelizer 1985). Domestic family and nation can be imagined
only by distinguishing themselves from but also imagining influence on
"the global," through a prism of differentiating who can be saved and
how. As I argue in this section, racialized projections of the nation shape
China/U.S. adoption as fulfilling the needs of both humanitarian outreach as well as increasingly commodified formations of kinship and citizenship.

The story of adoption in the United States over the last century reflects a cultural struggle over the commodification and sacralization of
children (Berebitsky 2000; Melosh 2002). In *Pricing the Priceless Child,*
Viviana Zelizer (1985) traces in the period 1870–1930 a transition in the
kind of value assigned to children, from economic usefulness to senti-
mental fulfillment. At the confluence of several broad social trends—differentiation between economic production and home life, the specializa-
tion of women into expert full-time motherhood, and the growing sacralization of the child—domestic adoption began to emphasize the "best
interest of the child" and the emotional fulfillment the child would bring
to adoptive parents. By the 1930s, legal adoption of "strangers" was
much more common, and more focused on middle- and upper-class families looking for an infant to love. But this growing sentimentalization
also meant a growing adoption business, both unofficial and official. "An
apparently profound contradiction was thereby created, between a cultural system that declared children priceless emotional assets, and a social arrangement that treated them as 'cash commodities'" (Zelizer 1985:
201). As Berebitsky (2000) makes clear in her study of the "Child-Rescue
Campaign" run by the magazine *The Delineator* from 1907 to 1911, commodification of children went hand in hand with their rescue, fulfilling

the destiny of the nation. Urban orphans could be rescued from poor and backward Eastern European immigrants and transformed into valuable citizens in the hands of white middle-class mothers. Market exchanges thus facilitated the rescue of children but also the redemption of those upright citizens in whose care they would thrive.

This seeming contradiction between rescue and desire, care and market, continued to haunt adoption practices and narratives in various ways, and adoption professionals and adoptive families in turn sought ways to resolve it. The Child-Rescue Campaign promulgated the notion that "the rescued always paid back the rescuer" (59), anticipating subsequent official and unofficial discourses of adoption that emphasized "parity of need" and "matching" between parents and children. Families (meaning, for the most part, infertile white couples) and children who needed each other could be matched up for the mutual fulfillment of individual, familial, and national identities. Indeed, as adoption was professionalized under the management of state and social service agencies in the first half of the twentieth century, it constructed itself over and against markets, substituting the language of proper placement and matching for that of direct rescue and crass exchange. Parents thus learned to narrate adoption as raising children "like our very own," mirroring biological kinship. At the same time, however, the growth of consumer society meant that professional matching could ensure a child "had the ability to achieve the class position and status aspirations of its parents" (3). The matching criteria seen as most important to doing so have changed over time, but they have continually been crosscut by supply and demand as well as cultural and racial politics.[10]

The post–World War II era ushered in several decades of increasing acceptance of adoption, accompanied by charged discourses of race and rescue and complicated by the growth of international adoption and its relationship to the American imaginary of itself. It began with the placement of war orphans from Europe and Japan; then, in 1949, Pearl S. Buck established her Welcome House program of placing Amerasian orphans. This was followed by adoptions from Korea and Vietnam in the 1950s–70s, the former in numbers that now total more than 150,000.[11] As Lovelock (2000) and others have noted, intercountry adoption programs have often come in the wake of war and strife; "its history maps the global suffering wrought by war, hatred, hunger, and political oppression" (Melosh 2002: 195). The history of intercountry adoption is thus one immediately steeped in notions of rescue and humanitarian outreach. But that is not the whole story, as transnational adoption also sheds light on the valuation of children in relation to race and national origin (Modell 2002: 145). Adoption of war orphans, as Briggs (2003) so well argues, enacted Cold War emphases on the necessity of American intervention, the conflation of family and national security, and the color-blind universalisms that underwrote whiteness. Race and ethnic difference were subsumed under (and perhaps enabled) an ideology of rescuing poor Third World children for a "better life" in the bosom of American households (Lovelock 2000: 922). Gailey (1999) argues that "the adoption of Korean infants seemed at least in some way a laboratory for assimilationist beliefs in the redemptive qualities of capitalist culture. These children were going to become 'real' American Asians, because they would be reared by 'real,' that is, middle class, conservative and patriotic (i.e. military), white Americans" (60).

While rescue and color blindness (or, alternatively, multiculturalism) became impetuses for intercountry adoptions into the United States, especially from an underdeveloped Third World understood to *need* adoption, this history cannot be divorced from the politics of race at home. As many historical accounts of adoption suggest, the expansion of international adoption starting in the 1970s was entangled with at least two important developments in domestic adoption: an increasing demand for infants[12] and protests by the National Association of Black Social Workers (NABSW) against transracial placements, especially of black children with white parents (Lovelock 2000; Modell 2002; Melosh 2002; Patton 2000). Lovelock (2000) has suggested that a double standard emerged that made race an issue in domestic placements but not in international placements. But she goes on to suggest that this double standard was in fact a complementary set of racializations that served the needs of the proper national family and its prospective adoptive parents (922); in other words, the NABSW's cries of cultural genocide may have simultaneously resonated with white segregationist sentiments and fueled white humanitarianism outreach abroad.

Race has thus served as fulcrum for playing international and domestic adoptions off each other, shaping them as respectively "good" and "bad" adoptions (Modell 2002).[13] How so, and to what end? International adoption became increasingly desirable over the last two decades (from eight thousand children in 1989 to more than twenty thousand children in 2004)[14] to prospective adopters who experienced infertility, did not think they met the requirements (age, health, sexual orientation, marital status) for domestic adoption, and sometimes harbored fears of domestic birth parents with questionable backgrounds and the power to reclaim children (Modell 2002) all motivations that shape parents' decisions to adopt from China. As adoptive mother Lila Noonan put it, she was "afraid of contact" with birth families, and besides, she just knew "how traumatic children's life is in the States before they finally get in the system." In addition, domestic adoption of "nonsystem" children, i.e., healthy white infants, also looked increasingly marketized to some parents, as they competed for and even solicited birth mothers; adoptive father Jason Bradley cited the "sort of buy-a-baby tone" to domestic adoption as one motivation for going to China. Ironically, international adoption can be just as and often more expensive than domestic adoption,[15] and there are increasing concerns of trafficking in some international adoption programs, but it is here that multiple racializations help construct international adoption as meeting the needs of both children and parents—the former rescuable from poverty and abandonment, the latter able to fulfill their desire for family. Such discourses bring to the surface the racialized relationship between commodified and sacralized childhoods—between consumption and rescue—that makes some children more adoptable than others. This kind of humanism tends to bind people into sameness through various kinds of conscious or unconscious exclusion (Shiu 2001; Goldberg 1993; Balibar 1988a).

By the mid-1990s, vocal opposition to transracial placements in the United States—meaning, by default, African American and, to some extent, Native American children in white homes—had waned considerably and had even been replaced by a new official color blindness in adoption.[16] But in practice, as Patton (2000) has convincingly argued, this shift killed at least two birds with one stone, favoring the consumptive choices of white heterosexual families while vilifying single black (read "welfare") mothers. The former could be kept safe from the latter through a popular pathologizing of unreliable welfare mothers who gave birth to "crack babies." Despite official race parity, such children could be understandably labeled as unadoptable, while orphans abroad

remained rescuable—what Ortiz and Briggs (2003) call "resilient (overseas) and toxic (U.S.) childhoods" (40). Ortiz and Briggs argue that even
though domestic transracial adoption is promoted, it is promoted in ways
that reproduce proper white families and barely redeemable black children, fixed on the interior as biologically and culturally tainted. Transnational adoption, in contrast, conjures children whose difference makes
them both rescuable and valuable.[17] Instead of being fixed to abject
mothers and cultures, they are innocent victims of "unpromising infra-
structural soil" (Ortiz and Briggs 2003: 43). A complex interplay of interior and exterior racial categories joins family and nation in what Briggs
(2003) calls "a coherent cultural logic that invest[s] the foreign in the
domestic and the domestic in the foreign" (181).

We have already seen how the racial and cultural flexibility of Asianness may contribute to the desire for Chinese children, but it also contributes to notions of rescuability. One adoptive mother suggested that
helping needy children provided some balance for the loss of physical
sameness that would have been produced had infertility treatments been
successful:

> I mean, there was that, there was the fantasy. We would have had, you
> know, a red-haired baby or something. You know, because we both
> had red hair. But for me it was a lot more important to be a parent, and
> to have a baby . . . for there to be a baby that *needed* to have a family.
> And there were real ones there, in that orphanage [in China], waiting!

Jackie Kovich told me she had briefly been tempted to adopt from
Lithuania so she would not have to deal with issues of racial difference.
"But then," she said, "I quickly went back to why I was attracted—why
I wanted to do this in the first place," that is, to help a child in need.
While Jackie had indicated she found Chinese children desirable for
their looks, her reference to Lithuania—where there are children who
might just as easily be seen as needing homes—indicates that Chinese
children are also desirable for being "more" needy. Ortiz and Briggs
(2003) suggest that being Third World and nonwhite makes for more rescuable subjects.

So then, we might also consider how the backwardness that produces
marginalized Chinese children compares through racialized discourses to

the backwardness that produces marginalized American children. For some parents, for example, a 1995 exposé of poor conditions in Chinese orphanages affirmed that China and its orphan children were in need; a few felt, out of religious conviction, that China was a society short on morals; and many referred to a China struggling to develop and modernize, burdened by a large population, low education, and a communist legacy. The American imaginary of such comparisons is, at times, arguably racialized. One white father who had originally looked into domestic adoption told me that when the possibility of adopting a biracial (meaning "black and white") child arose, some family members balked. "Yeah," he said, "we brought back a communist baby from a communist country and that was okay, but not a biracial child in our own country!" The rescuability of Chinese children—from the backwardness of communism and poverty—is contrasted to the abjectness of domestic black children. An adoption social worker was blunt about how this worked in some parents' adoption decisions: "I think there's a romanticism about saving a starving child on the other side of the planet. I'm often amazed that people would take an older child from the other side of the world but won't consider an older child here. I think it's racism." It must be noted, too, that the professional adoption world of which she is a part gives mixed messages about the rescuability of domestic and international children, and of what kinds of parents are right for what kinds of children.

The rescuability of Chinese children is intertwined with several dimensions of imagined racial flexibility. As indicated above, some parents felt they had to give up on the competition and long wait for healthy white infants. Parents also expressed nagging fears regarding the more accessible but less palatable route of domestic public adoption, which usually meant special-needs and/or nonwhite children. Lila Noonan said of the forces that pulled her away from domestic transracial adoption and toward international adoption, "I just knew too much; if I didn't, I would have been more open." Chinese children become flexibly rescuable, then, *in contrast to* a continuity of abject (black, older, special-needs) and unattainable (white, young, healthy) children at home. And just as important, they are seemingly less burdened by a volatile history of intractable black-white relations, read as a cautionary tale by some adoptive parents. African Americans could even be seen as recalcitrant for not making their children available for adoption. June, a white adoptive mother, told me that the newspapers in her hometown of Detroit were full of horror stories about children in foster care who were abused or even returned to abusive homes. She became indignant, then, that "the black community is so against placing black children in white families." Both Chinese and black children needed to be rescued, but it was easier to imagine the former being absorbed into white kinship.

Race and gender thus contribute to making orphans from abroad desirable as citizen-subjects; as some parents see it, children can be not only rescued *from* their unfortunate conditions abroad but also absorbed *into* a new life at home. They are at once strange and familiar, different yet knowable (Yngvesson 2000; Shiu 2001). On the one hand, people may be attracted to Chinese children for the differences of origin that make them both culturally/racially interesting and economically in need of rescue. On the other hand, they may be attracted to the change the children will undergo and enact in their parents. One reason parents gave for choosing China was that while not receiving the best possible orphanage or foster care, the available children seemed to "catch up" quickly. (A number of social workers and parents have lamented that Chinese children in particular are surrounded by a mythology of resilience that sometimes precludes attention to attachment or developmental problems.) As I argue in the next section, the history of the China/U.S. adoption program in particular neatly turns rescue into transformation of both children and parents, through a mutual "matching" of needs.

Light Baggage: History of the China/U.S. Adoption Program

International adoptions have moved from a dominant discourse of rescue and humanitarian outreach for children who need families to one that just as emphatically endorses the needs and desires of prospective adoptive parents (Lovelock 2000; Solinger 2001). Adoption professionals prefer this as a more "honest" acknowledgment that prospective adoptive parents adopt for themselves as much as for children. Parents' expressed reasons for adopting from China are, in fact, dominated by how the characteristics of the program and of available children meet those of their own situation. Chinese children need rescue, and China is underdeveloped, but not so much as to threaten the desire for healthy, young infants whom parents can claim as their own. This symbiotic relationship between choice and rescue, consumption and care, is a necessary backdrop to the history of the China adoption program. "Why China"—why the formal inception and growing popularity of the program in the 1990s—must be understood as a mixture of material conditions of choice in China and the United States through which circulate imagined ways of belonging. We have seen how cultural intrigue, racial mapping, gendered images, and humanitarian national outreach have historically shaped the desirability of Chinese adoptions, but they are so important precisely because they animate the mundane matter of the policies and demographics that institutionalize the "fit" between Chinese parents and their prospective American parents. Fitting and belonging, as I argue in this section, are in large part a matter of smooth dislocations and desirable transformations.

Why the international adoption of Chinese children was implemented when it was and why it developed so quickly are separate but interrelated questions that must take into account perceived needs in both China and the United States. Research to date has not fully traced the developments that led Beijing to draft China's first adoption law in 1991 and increasingly to formalize international adoption in the succeeding few years; the details of this history are murky enough that Melosh (2002) simply assigns it to "unknown reasons" (193). But Kay Johnson's (2004) invaluable work foregrounds a social welfare system underfunded and overwhelmed by abandoned babies, many of them girls.[18] The crisis came to a head in the late 1980s and early 1990s, in part because of crackdowns in the enforcement of the family-planning policy. The resulting upsurge of abandoned children increased the burden on the cash-strapped social welfare system in China, where facilities were quite basic; per-child allowances for food, clothing, and medical care were minimal; and caregivers' salaries even in the year 2000 were rarely more than 400 RMB (U.S. $50) per month.[19] Even though a broadened acceptance of domestic adoption had grown in China, for the state to promote domestic adoption would mean the risk of pointing a finger right back at the sensitive family-planning policy and its drastic gendered effects; besides, argues Johnson, the adoption law was itself meant to combat those who "cheated" on the family-planning policy by adopting children over quota (145–46). In fact, early versions of China's international adoption policy mirrored its domestic regulations, restricting overseas adopters to childless people.

It is here that the question of why China opened to international adoption and the question of why China was so popular for American adopters become closely linked. By the early 1990s, the demand for international adoption in the United States was on the rise, especially as the Korea program decreased in size and domestic adoption became in some ways less attractive, for reasons discussed above (competition for "high-demand" children; age, health, and race of children available; fears of open adoption). Romania and Russia opened up, but by the late 1990s, the rapid increase in placements of Chinese children was matching that of Russia. There is little doubt that the rise in Russian adoptions in the 1990s was due in some measure to the availability of white children, meeting the "as-if-begotten" criterion Modell (2002) argues is still a strong strain in adoption. At the same time, however, "the claim of diversity in being a parent is equally powerful" (Modell 2002: 146), and the flexible racialization of Chinese children as "different, but not too different" made it an attractive adoption option for some.

But there are equally significant explanations that have to do with the matching of supply and demand. The Chinese adoption program offered relatively healthy young infants, free of ties to birth families. As one parent put it to me, she had been attracted to China in part because the children "wouldn't come with a lot of baggage." Things that bind children to a preadoptive identity—such as older age and birth-family contact —can appear especially burdensome to prospective parents who have come to adoption by way of a road strewn with the obstacles of infertility, their own older age, or their partnership status. From the perspective of the "demand" side, then, the less-restrictive requirements and fairly straightforward process of the China adoption program matched the experiences and demographics of an array of people eager to become parents.

In narrating their reasons for adopting at all, most parents, whether married or single, straight or queer, indicated that they had "reached a point" of some kind. Most of the forty families I interviewed had been through brief or extended infertility treatment, had explored various other reproductive alternatives, or had "given up" on looking for the right partner with whom to have a child. As one woman put it, "You reach an age in your life where you know you want to have at least one child. You know, you do not appear to be on the road to producing one of your own, so . . ." For those who had opted for adoption after exhausting medical reproductive alternatives, their narratives often reflected the mantra of professionals that counsel this transition: "we decided it was more important to be a parent than to have a child that shared our DNA." Others—some in their late forties and early fifties—had decided they wanted to be parents at a point in their life course when biological parenting was a risky or missing option. There are both personal and systemic fragilities in "reaching this point." Many domestic and international adoption programs carry restrictions that preclude certain prospective parents[20] or seem risky from the perspective of parents searching for an adoption option. Jason Bradley told me, "It would have been more difficult and a lot more time-consuming for people our age to adopt an infant in the U.S." The China Center of Adoption Affairs in Beijing had and continues to have a fairly generous upper age limit, has been open to single and married applicants, and until the late 1990s seemed to turn a blind eye to placing children with gay and lesbian parents. And apart from quite early in the program, its bureaucratic but uniform process and reasonable timetable seemed to offer reliability and transparency to parents tired of obstacles. As Lila Noonan put it, "I wanted a guarantee. I wanted my baby."

That "guarantee" and "baby" are parallel constructions is significant; it is also significant that Lila went on to say that she badly wanted a daughter. Not only did China seem to want these parents, these parents wanted—and adoption agencies promoted—the healthy young infant girls that seemed to fill Chinese orphanages. Infants are desirable for a number of reasons, but often because their kinship and cultural attachments are seen as not fully formed; this translates into a child ready for a fresh start in her new family and nation.

Being able to make Chinese children "one's own" is a function of the child's age but also of (lack of) kinship ties. This was apparent in the comfort many parents expressed at not having to deal with birth parents who might reclaim children or want to be part of their children's lives. Peggy

Peterson put it this way: "We felt more comfortable with China or Vietnam because they pretty much are not going to want to have the child
back in a year." While media stories of domestic child reclamations
loomed large, so did fears of having to share a child beyond the confines
of the nuclear, adoptive family. One new adoptive mother told me she did
not want a twenty-year-old dropping in six times a year with presents.
"What kind of mother is that?" she asked, adding that one reason she
liked Chinese adoption was that it was "clean, pure." Indeed, Chinese
adoptions fit well with the "clean break" policies and practices of transnational adoption, whereby a child's adoptability is predicated on being
legally and socially "free" of ties to family and place of birth (Yngvesson
2000; Ouellette and Belleau 2001; Gailey 2000).[21] Agencies variously join
in promoting clean breaks. In an unusually stark example of this, one
adoption agency stated on their Web site: "Adopting a Chinese child is
very simple. There will be no birth mother knocking on your door. In
China, it is a crime to abandon a child. If a birth mother changes her
mind and comes back to a welfare home for the child, she will be put in
prison."[22]

It is in statements like these that Chinese birth mothers, safely entangled in social and legal proscriptions, become a racialized medium for the
baggage-free child. They are not only the right kind of mother because,
as marginalized "Third World" women, they cannot touch their children
but also because, in contrast to some other countries and to the United
States, women in China can be constructed as giving up babies for reasons other than being young, unfit, and unhealthy social deviants. When
Ian, a white father, said that he and his wife, Amy, adopted from China
because they knew the children "were very, very healthy," Amy added,
"You know, we knew that some of them were small and maybe not as
well-nourished . . . but we knew that Chinese women didn't typically
drink and smoke, culturally? Isn't that right?" Rather than being made
villains in the story, Chinese birth mothers can be made into unfortunate
but healthy victims. One adoptive mother pointed out that children in
China were abandoned "just because they are girls"; to her and her husband, this meant they would not have to worry about the poor prenatal
care, drugs, and alcohol that characterized the birth mothers—implicitly
black and/or poor—whose children were in the American public welfare
system. Why prospective American adopters prefer girls is complicated,

but that Chinese children were abandoned ostensibly *because* they were girls made them unattached to birth family, and for reasons other than (in many cases) poor health.

The choices that make adoption an act of clean breaks and fresh starts, of detaching and reattaching, are enabled by class distinctions. Of increasing concern to critical observers is that "light baggage"—racial flexibility, good health, young age, distanced birth mothers—comes with a price tag through a stratified system that literally values some children more than others (Solinger 2001; Mansnerus 1998).[23] Most parents who adopt from China make this choice in part because they can—because they have or can find the means to pay the U.S. $20,000-plus that it costs. The material means that drive this choice must be linked not only to the delimited choices of Chinese birth parents but also to the delimited desirability of other children. As I have argued, factors of race, gender, age, and health play into the narratives of choice that imagine the possible relocation of some children, and not others, into adoptive homes; but the imagined transformation of the child in her new adoptive family rests in part on the ability of such a family to enact it through material means.

It should not be surprising, however, that the material means that enable adoption choices remain mostly an arena of silence and indirect reference. The consumptive overtones that haunt adoption exchanges and exclusions (Yngvesson 2000; Modell 2002; Anagnost 2000) are coded in the meeting of needs and the giving of gifts, or narrated in terms of "how much we have to offer" a child. As adoptive mother Wanda Jones put it, "You know, if you were born here, or even being able to come here young, you have so many opportunities. And to be able to give those opportunities to somebody else is really important." Material choices were also tacitly expressed in the photos of nice homes sent in parents' applications to Beijing (and expected by Beijing) and mitigated by allusions to rescue. Barbara, for example, told me that she and her husband had initially considered adopting a white child from Russia. Given "all the problems" the children seemed to have, she and her husband had decided instead to go to China for a healthy infant girl. But for acquaintances who did not otherwise understand why the couple would adopt a child from another country, and especially one that did not look like them, Barbara found "saving a child" a quick and acceptable explanation. When orphaned Chinese children were "saved" by American church groups in the late nineteenth and early twentieth centuries,[24] civilizing benevolence was the guiding principle; in contemporary China/U.S. adoption, rescue discourses are corollary to professionally managed choices, and immigration laws and adoption policies smooth rather than block the way for well-off American citizens adopting Chinese children.

Consumptive choices haunt adoption in a dialectical pair of anxieties: that adoption will be seen as a market and that as a market it will take a downturn. One particular event in the history of China/U.S. adoption exemplifies this tension and highlights the nexus of benevolent desires and material resources in which it is embedded. In 1995, less than two years after international adoptions from China had started to take off, reports of poor conditions, high mortality rates, and intentional neglect in Chinese welfare homes reached a high level of exposure in the Western media, in the form of a Human Rights Watch report and a BBC documentary titled *The Dying Rooms*.[25] The reports had several significant effects: major U.S. media outlets covered the story as a sensational scoop but also covered the counterresponses of agencies and adoptive families; the Chinese government, issuing defensive and propagandistic retorts, shut down Chinese orphanages to foreign and many Chinese visitors;[26] and adoption agencies and adoptive families organized to tone down or discredit the reports through media releases, appeals to Washington, D.C., and letters and faxes to Beijing that claimed conditions were improving, many orphanages were doing their best, and there was no evidence of a national policy of relieving an overburdened orphanage system through deliberate starvation (Johnson 2004).[27] I am most interested in the last response, since it was in part born of a fear that China would shut down adoptions, or at least make the process more difficult, and that it would appear that only very malnourished, poorly cared-for children waited in Chinese orphanages. The human rights exposés had the effect of inspiring some prospective parents to save Chinese orphans through adoption. But adoption organizations cannot let rescue be the dominant motivation for international adoption. It not only portends an unequal parent-child relationship but also suggests children with more "baggage" than the current political economy of adoption choices can sustain. In the ensuing years, a strange equilibrium has resulted from the

1995 reports: China kept open its adoption doors and has increased numbers ever since; Beijing could be seen as struggling but sincere in its efforts for abandoned Chinese children; and those children could be seen as needy, but not too needy.

Conclusion: The Return of the "Whys" of Chinese Adoption

Jeff D. Opdyke, adoptive parent of a Chinese child and personal finance reporter for the *Wall Street Journal,* titled his "Love and Money" column on September 21, 2003 (p. D6): "Why We Decided to Adopt from China." In many ways, it summed up the impetuses for adopting from China I have covered in this chapter: providing hope to a child in the Third World, the ease of a fairly efficient process, availability of healthy infants, and reliable birth mothers. Opdyke set this in the framework of a kind of cost-benefit analysis that made China "worth it," putting in writing the considerations many parents weigh in their decisions but would probably express in less economic terms: "So in the end, an international adoption may not save us much money. But at least we would be assured of getting what we want—an infant." And given all the other factors that entered the equation, China came out on top: "At the end of the day, of course, it all comes down to personal choice for each family . . . and in dealing with those choices, Amy and I came to a unified conclusion: The road to our daughter runs through China."

Of course, individual choices do not occur in a vacuum—they drip with the residue of social relationships and of imaginaries of the identities of self and other. The sketch art that accompanied Opdyke's article showed a simple, stark scene of exchange: a woman handing a swaddled baby across the Great Wall, into the outstretched arms of a man whose female partner stands waiting beside him. Actually, given the particular poses of the characters, the piece could conceivably work the other way: the man *could* be handing the child to the lone woman. But this goes against the grain of what we imagine makes Chinese children and American parents a good match, why China "works": birth *mothers* (enclosed behind the Great Wall) reluctantly but necessarily give up children who can be rescued into the arms of middle-class, white, heterosexual couples who have calculated "the financial components of our decision because we want the limited dollars we have now and in the future to go as far as they possibly can." Opdyke unwittingly provides the first clue to why this calculation of desires and guarantees is a compromised prospect from the outset. His road runs *through* China and presumably back to him, making China one part of an ongoing circulation of resources and ideas that reproduce the family, and the adoption system. But this also means that the child and her new parents, as they move away from the Great Wall, carry with them not just the meanings of that moment of exchange but all the conditions that made it possible.

A Korean adoptee and friend has wryly suggested to me that perhaps all the factors that make adoption from China desirable make children from China the model minorities of adoption, or "model adoptees." But as with the Asian model minority rubric, this is a myth. And like all myths, it is powerful and revelatory, but it begs to be unpacked. Chinese children are not as easily rescuable/consumable, flexible, or baggage-free as dominant discourses of adoption would suggest—and not only because they individually come with their own quirks and needs or because the process does not always go smoothly. I have considered both senses of "why China" in this chapter—why parents choose to adopt from China and why, more generally, the practice has thrived—in order to open up the historical contexts that particularize it. I have looked especially at the racialized histories that impose themselves on adoptive choices. Imaginaries of flexible, rescuable identities take us *through* China and back to the exclusive desires of an American culture haunted by the fixations of race and market. The next chapter examines more carefully the a priori conditions on adoptive choices—the institutionalized, contested, and circulating parameters of normalized belonging that select and match children and parents.

CHAPTER **2**

Matches Made on Earth

Making Parents and Children for Each Other

> I think one of the reasons people go to China is there are a lot of stereotypic feelings about Chinese children? Definitely if they want a little girl, that's obviously the way to go . . . but it seems that with the children from China it's like you've got a real good chance of having, quote-unquote, a good experience.
>
> —Rita Jasper, adoption agency social worker

At the conclusion of his article "Chinese Orphans in America" (*Zhongguo gu'er zai meiguo*), China-based journalist Li Yamin (2000) writes, "We also have to ask, who is rescuing whom?" (*You gai shuo, shi shei zhengjiu shei?*) Coming on the heels of a text extolling the virtues of universal love, Li's question hints at the exchange of affective and material values that mutually produces children and parents. Indeed, the universalized wholeness promised by adoptive kinship relies on a vision of parent and child uniting in a linear movement toward each other. As a worker at the CCAA told me, she disliked it when parents played the part of savior for pitiful children; the best and most honest reason parents could give for wanting to adopt a child was that they needed one. A balance of mutual need could then be struck. But to expand our vision to the broader political economy of transnational adoption is to qualify even this narrative (of dyadic, bidirectional transformation of parent and child) in two important ways: children and parents are produced for each other even before they meet, and this is accomplished through a series of institutionalized but contested practices that distinguish among differently valued parents and children.

This chapter examines the institutionalized practices that produce American parents and Chinese children for each other—practices that anticipate the conditions of their kinship and reproduce the global political economy of adoption exchange. The selection and preparation of "adoptable" children in China and "able-to-adopt" parents in the United States may seem to be separate processes, but they are intertwined by means of the ideologies, images, and resources that circulate before parents physically cross the Pacific to meet their children. These symbolic and material flows tend to value, discipline, and link abandoned children and those who care for them in particular ways. I trace these circulations by moving back and forth between the preadoption paths of children in China and parents in the United States, as they are first selected/recruited into and then prepared for adoption itself. The images and bodies of Chinese children are the "organizing" principle around which adoption practices are standardized and particularized, but also contested, in orphanages and agencies.

One of my starting points is that market and care, or capitalism and humanitarianism, are not necessarily antithetical or mutually distinct (Haskell 1985a and 1985b). While it is naïve to understand China/U.S. adoption as a purely humanitarian dramatization of the global village, it is equally simplistic to paint adoption as a crass market in which American parents are the demanding consumers, Chinese children the commodified objects, and agencies and facilitators the entrepreneurial brokers. Rather, it is in the analysis of how human agents engaged in sometimes contradictory practices of care perceive and interpret them that power relations are understood (Sevenhuisen 1998). A globalized market of adoption allows new possibilities for intervention in the welfare of marginalized children, even as such techniques also have the effect of reproducing hierarchies. American monetary donations shape orphanage care; images of the flexible Asian female generate interest in adoption; adoption professionals and bureaucrats question the suitability of lesbian parents in the "best interest of children."

Analyzing preadoption narratives and practices on both sides of the Pacific brings to light the ways in which marketized and caring practices together not only distinguish among but produce subjects valued for migration (Anagnost 2000; Lowe 1996). As discussed in the previous chapter, parents choose to adopt from China in part because of the imagined transformability of children's identities, made possible through legal and social "clean breaks" from birth family and birth country. These transformations are enacted by a political economy of material and symbolic values circulating through agencies, orphanages, officials, and facilitators. But this is more than a specific way to reproduce *the* child, *the* parent, or *the* family. It produces children valued in particular ways for parents who are also valued in particular ways. And so it must entail exclusions, or the threat of exclusions, pointing the way back to the conditions of global exchange. I show in this chapter, for example, that abandoned Chinese children who come into the transnational adoption system are given "universal" value and meaning by being distinguished not only from an earlier stage of their own biographies as marginalized abandoned girls but also from children who do not enter that system (e.g., special-needs children in China or children of color in the American welfare system). Stories of destiny and magic help facilitate the production of unique children and parents, meant for each other.

The reproduction of social and familial relationships occurs through unequal sacrifices and the exclusion of "wrong" values. Children might not be directly commodified, yet the dominant demands of adoption reproduce desirable children, and do so through gendered hierarchies of caregiving labor. This does not mean that institutions and actors in the United States, or American adoptive parents more specifically, dictate terms and conditions. To borrow from Lydia Liu's (1999) elegant argument about transnational acts of exchange and translation, we can observe in the process of selecting and producing parents and children for each other a certain degree of *coauthorship* between Chinese and American actors. Transnational projects of reproduction, as exemplified in the case of China/U.S. adoption, are hegemonic projects that bring seemingly separate intranational relations of power into the same international web of movement of people, meaning, and resources (Lauria-Perricelli 1992).

Standardizing (the Fulfillment of) Desire

When social worker Rita Jasper said that China offered a "good experience" for parents, she referred not only to the desire for unattached, culturally interesting, and healthy infant girls but also to the standardized processes by which children and adoptive parents are produced to fulfill those desires and made legally and culturally to belong to each other. Indeed, the first decade of the China/U.S. adoption story was one of increasing standardization and regulation; as one social worker put it at a focus group in 2001, "The bugs are worked out. Everyone knows how long it takes, and how it goes." Parents and professionals alike tend to contrast the "transparency and predictability" of China/U.S. adoption to other domestic and international adoption programs—where lawyers' fees might be variable and unstable, where laws allow birth parents to reclaim children, where trafficking might be more likely, where governments create stringent rules about who may adopt, or even where the "culture" of a country might be seen as opaque and untrustworthy. The China program's trustworthiness is further reinforced by way of comparisons to its earlier self, when in the early 1990s it was another "frontier" of international adoption *and* ostensibly of China's path to globalized modernity—when so-called pioneer families ventured to China amid decentralized and uncertain adoption policies.[1]

Such unpredictability, as well as its accompanying tropes of adventure and backwardness, has faded with increasingly standardized regulations and procedures for *selecting* and *preparing* children and parents in the China/U.S. adoption process. Many of my informants suggested that little was left to the imagination, as the spectacle of "getting paperwork right" is now of top priority. Facilitator David Lee,[2] who worked for an agency based in the Bay Area, remarked that when he helps families prepare for application to the China Center of Adoption Affairs (CCAA), "the end product is a neatly printed out dossier, very professional looking . . . so every family, when they submit the dossier, we have some recommended format, a half-inch binder." On the Chinese end, bureaucratic practices discipline the movement and handling of both files and bodies. Procedures for orphanages to submit child referral information to the CCAA are controlled by quotas and institutional standards, and procedures for placing children with families have also become increasingly uniform across provinces.

The convergence toward predictable standards is appealing for a Chinese welfare system trying to lessen its burden of child care and increase its income via transnational adoption, for parents entering the uncertainties of transnational adoption, and for agencies wanting to place children and attract business. Yet for all these parties, with the relief and promise of predictability comes a complex set of unequal needs and desires at the nexus of child and parent, of sending and receiving nation. Mr. Xin, a former administrator of the CCAA, told me that when the government decided to legislate international (and domestic) adoption in the early 1990s, some government officials felt China could not take care of all its abandoned children, "so why not let foreigners do it?" while others felt this was "like selling off children to foreigners." For this reason, he emphasized, increasing standardization of paperwork and procedures—the *jiji de taidu* (attitude of vigorous implementation) the CCAA takes pride in—was to ensure both foreign and domestic observers that families were carefully selected in rational, systematic ways. In the particular mix of latent socialist sloganeering and globalized expressions of efficiency that characterizes political rhetoric in China, the CCAA has announced its model status as a site of "innovation of theory, system and technology" (http://www.china-ccaa.org, accessed September 2004). But as I demonstrate in the pages to come, such standardized practices occur through particular images of nation and family; uneasiness remains about placing Chinese children with "not normal" (meaning, usually, not married or not straight) families, and about placing "not normal" (older and special-needs) children with American families.

Ensuring desirable families *and* desirable children entails exclusions, especially as they are produced for each other through the standards of market and care. At various times agency administrators in the United States have expressed to me a discomfort akin to that offered by Adoption Links director Lynn Besky, who said she sometimes felt her agency was becoming "China R Us"; they seemed to slip into competition with other agencies for the business of parents who want the "best" children rather than concentrating on the placement of children most in need. Lynn posed a dilemma that haunts the process: it should not be or seem that parents go out and acquire a child, yet parents request—and agencies push—particular countries or types of children through a program that promises choices, services, or sometimes guarantees. This process reproduces expectations of the particular kinds of children that will fulfill needs and desires. But standardization also means that certain kinds of families are increasingly excluded, which bothered some social workers and relieved others. As for parents, their uneasiness with standardized practice takes various forms, including a wariness of bureaucratic control and inflexibility. Some parents advocate "consumer protection" measures on adoption industry practices, arguing that international agreements such as the Hague Convention serve the interests of adoption business more than those of adoptive parents and children (see, for example, the Adoption Agency Checklist at http://saradave.tripod.com, accessed summer 2004). Chinese facilitators of adoption migration, meanwhile, step in where standardized policies cannot reach, beyond the spectacle of "getting the paperwork right"; they buffer the unpredictable and contradictory practices that inevitably occur at national and cultural border crossings.

The exclusions and disciplinary practices of the increasingly universalizing and standardizing claims of a "clean, pure program" are fleshed out in the sections that follow. My argument centers on the ideas, resources, and practices that "select" certain children and parents into the transnational adoption process and then produce and prepare them for adoption migration. In an attempt to mirror the multifaceted circuits of value, I start with the forces that select children into the international adoption system in China, move to the selection and preparation of parents in the United States, then return to the everyday practices of producing children in Chinese orphanages and foster homes for adoptive placement abroad.

A Baby Is a Baby Is a Baby? Selecting the Child-Client

Claims to universal forms of childhood and child welfare—celebrating the individual and equal worth of children and articulating their rights and interests as such—are articulated in China by everyone from foreign philanthropists to Beijing officials. The same CCAA official who emphasized the importance of an "attitude of vigor" in international adoption told me that, in keeping with the UN Convention on the Rights of the Child and the Hague Convention,[3] to which China had just become a signatory when we talked in early 2001, the bottom line was that every child had the right to a family, that abandoned children had the same rights as birth children, and that domestic adoption should be given priority over international adoption. Indeed, officials and administrators often refer to this discourse of international norms. But as some of them hinted to me, such international norms of universal childhood coexist in some disharmony with other national displays of development. For example, family-planning policies in China, meant to produce a "quality" population for rapid development in the global economy (Anagnost 1999), produce abandoned children but also have precluded the promotion and support of domestic adoption.[4] And globalized human rights discourses, such as that proffered in the 1995 Dying Rooms exposé, incite Chinese officials to examine care standards but also prompt them to favor children and orphanages that promote the proper modern image of the nation.

Claims to universal children's rights are challenged by transnational adoption practices, which rely to some extent on distinctions among children. An overabundance of children, a constrained flow of resources, and a labyrinth of perceived needs and interests distinguish among children's eligibility for revaluation as adoptable. As abandoned children enter the orphanage system in China, how do some of them end up as a file of photos and documents that will go to international, and more specifically U.S., families? How are they selected as appropriate clients, given the ideals of "the best interest of children"? While it is impossible to explicate all the various routes by which Chinese children enter the adoption system, there are salient examples of transnational influences; we might trace Chinese foster-home routines to the advice of U.S. social workers, or link the CCAA's handling of child referrals to the expressed needs of adoptive parents.

In the first decade of the China/U.S. adoption program, practices that informally distinguished among children became increasingly and more formally institutionalized. On the one hand, the children placed in the arms of the pioneering families of the early 1990s were more likely to be in weak health than they are today; uncertainty about the health of the child and the outcome of the bureaucratic process was understood to come with the decision to apply for adoption from China. Parents usually became (and still do become) attached to whatever child was presented to them. On the other hand, an unregulated system meant that Chinese mediators (orphanage officials, agency go-betweens) could and sometimes did offer to "switch" to a more desirable—healthier or cuter or younger—child; "I can get you a better one if you are not satisfied," some facilitators are reported to have said to parents (and sometimes still do). In other cases, either American or Chinese mediators would, in an act of triage, "handpick" children who were healthy enough to be adoptable by U.S. families. With the introduction of more money to at least some orphanages through international adoption, children are increasingly in better health; and through an increasingly regulated system of child placement, parents can indeed expect to receive a relatively healthy child (unless they have asked for a special-needs child, which some do). But with regulated and standardized procedures, parents can also expect that they will need good reasons not to accept the referral given them.

The image of the desirable child has thus become embedded in the stages of the process that produces children for international adoption. A transnational transfer of money and care standards helps shape the recognition of "proper" orphanage care and bureaucratic practice. From the perspective of adoption professionals in the United States, as Lynn Besky told me, "Some of the countries in which we don't really work, there are many children in need, but the process doesn't work. It's gotta be someplace where the process works. Because otherwise you're just taking people's money and it's not going to work out." But defining where the process "works" is in part a function of a competitive market that promises to fulfill parents' desire for a short waiting time, healthy infant girls, and a predictable process with a reliable outcome. A subtle articulation of the desirable child is inextricable from the right kinds of orphanage circumstances for producing such a child.

In China, the processes that distinguish children for adoption are further tied to the formal selection of orphanages that will become part of the international adoption system to begin with. The sensitive nature of adoption as an area of research in China means that I cannot claim to have obtained a complete picture of this process, but it is possible to piece together some of its key characteristics.[5] As might be expected, welfare institutions vary in size from dozens to hundreds of children, as well as in management styles, staff training, utilization of home-based foster care, and facilities and services available at the orphanage (some have schools and staff doctors and rehabilitation equipment, some have just basic living facilities). It is difficult to gauge the full range, in part because orphanages also vary greatly in level and manner of contact with foreigners, including those who adopt their children and help bring in resources. But it *is* clear that a minority of orphanages participates in international adoption, and that there is a correlation between participation and resource allocation. In several of the seven provinces I visited in 2001, only about one-fourth of the orphanages were sending referrals to the CCAA, and to become part of the system, they had to meet requirements of staff-to-child ratios, hygiene, facilities and equipment, and so forth. Aiqing, a Chinese adoption facilitator, understood this as part of the politics of displaying modernity on the global stage. Some orphanages cannot participate in international adoption because, as she put it, "whatever you do is not good enough" for a government office that is "the window of the country for adoption. If they do anything wrong, then a lot of foreigners [will point fingers]." It is difficult for orphanages to meet these externally imposed standards, since the state funds allocated to them are so limited. Those orphanages that are able to do so might already have had income from international adoption prior to centralized regulations, might receive income from foreign or domestic private charities, or might have been given provincial monies to become model orphanages.

Orphanages can become "distinguished" for international adoption through a kind of historical overdetermination of material and symbolic resources. They gain reputations as having the best conditions and there-

fore the "best children." Facilitator David Lee told me that although children are assigned to parents by Beijing (and the rule is "no picking"), he
encouraged prospective American parents to request particular provincial orphanages,

> because I know people there. I have some people who can help out
> when families travel there. And second is, I believe that the conditions,
> the health conditions, the orphanage conditions tend to be better. And
> that includes hygiene condition, health condition, shots, nutrition,
> that kind of thing. And most of the families do want to have a healthy
> kid!

Audrey Cass, who helped raise funds for a model care and education program for children at Wangjing Orphanage, said she was running into the
problem of parents who had heard of its success calling to ask how they
could get a child from Wangjing. The ebb and flow of an individual orphanage's involvement in international adoption depends, in turn, on
the kinds of children in its care. A veteran facilitator told me that in some
cases, small rural orphanages are indirectly articulated into the system
by sending their healthy infants to larger urban facilities that are "running low" on children—namely, healthy infants—for international
adoption. And the director of a large northern welfare institute indicated
that in the early 1990s only about 4 percent of the children in her orphanage were healthy infants, so they did not send many for international adoption; but a decade later about 10 percent were healthy, so they
were sending more for international adoption.

The question then becomes how children are selected from within orphanages for referral to international adoption. I asked the director of
Hongqi Orphanage (one of the largest in central China) this question, and
she said that the CCAA had certain *yaoqiu* (requirements): children as
healthy and young as possible. Almost all their healthy babies were
therefore sent for international adoption. On her desk sat a tall pile of
files being readied for posting to Beijing, each containing a photo and
medical information on a baby several months old. There were some
older children as well, and a few with special needs. According to one
Chinese social worker, some orphanages will even tell local Chinese fam-

ilies there are no healthy babies available, saving them instead for international adoption and the income it generates.

Not all healthy children are reserved for international adoption, however. The director of Wangjing Orphanage, a facility heavily involved in international adoption, explained that while the referrals they submit to the CCAA for international adoption are usually healthy young girls, they place a good number of children domestically who never officially enter the orphanage, or at least not for very long. Some children, he said, are adopted by the people who find them or by people they know. I encountered one such situation in the train station of a northern Chinese city. An older woman who cradled an abandoned infant boy she had just found in the station told me she would take him to her home village for her daughter to raise. Sometimes this occurs through formal channels: local officials will show up at the orphanage with a baby that has just been found *and* a local family that already wants to adopt the child. In other cases, older children are adopted by couples with grown children who want companionship in their older age. And while Chinese families adopt special-needs children, often they will adopt because they want at least one girl and one boy.[6] At Beigang Orphanage, I talked briefly with a new Chinese adoptive father of a baby boy; I recorded the conversation in my fieldnotes:

He was a 33-year-old chicken farmer with two birth daughters, and as he held the two-month old boy in his arms, the farmer told me he had paid five thousand RMB [about U.S. $600] to adopt this son, a sum he did not feel was too much since he made ten thousand RMB a year. When I asked whether the officials cared that he had two birth daughters and was now adopting, he said of course for the second girl they had to pay three thousand RMB or so, but now adopting didn't cost anything in fines. So why was he adopting?, I wondered. Well, because in the countryside, he explained, you had to have a boy. Not having a son just wasn't any good because when you get older, you need to have someone who can work and take care of you. So how did you find out about this child? I asked. Oh, he said, he knew one of the caregivers at the orphanage who told him there was a healthy boy available.

The paths that take particular children toward domestic, international, or no adoption at all are carved out amid the intersections of local and transnational practices and regulations. It is not easy for many Chinese families to adopt; as in the United States, it takes money, perseverance, and background checks. But these procedures are even more stringent in China. While 1999 changes to the adoption regulations allow Chinese families with children to adopt, domestic adoption is not actively or uniformly promoted. A young administrator at Xinzhou Orphanage told me that she thought the new regulation had involved a compromise: change the law to allow international and domestic families with children to adopt but do not promote domestic adoption. Chinese abandonment and adoption expert Kay Ann Johnson argues that, in fact, the new law may serve to curtail domestic adoption in China, which has usually been more informal than formal (interview with author, May 20, 2001). Indeed, local officials in one province campaigning formally to register domestic adoption told me that local adoptive families wanted to avoid entanglements with the uncertain repercussions of this official intervention. Families are accustomed to constant reminders of the state's ability to manage reproduction, such as public notice boards reminding local people that anyone who abandons *or* adopts a child outside the policy will be fined.[7] Desires for certain kinds of children—whether because of their sex, age, or health—become all the more poignant under the disciplining practices of the Chinese state.

Particular children thus become "right" clients for international adoption by means of a complex set of regulations, practices, and needs tied to domestic contingencies. "Who can blame us for sending children for international adoption?" one Chinese facilitator queried, citing the material benefits accrued by the cash-strapped orphanages and civil affairs offices and the political barriers to placing children domestically. At the same time, standardized practices are meant to ensure the availability of healthy baby girls for foreign adopters.

The exchange of meanings around special-needs children provides provocative illustration. While the adoption system's promotion of young, healthy children does not completely exclude older and special-needs children, it does depend on managing their routes of articulation into the political economy of adoption. This begins with the definition of "special needs," which includes children with medical and developmental problems but has also variously referred to "older" children, over three or four years of age. Such children represent an exception to the normalized desires of adoptive parents—desires that have become institutionalized. I asked orphanage director Yuan, who has been sending children for transnational adoption since the late 1980s, what she thought had been the biggest changes in the process. She responded that not only have the regulations undergone revision but the process has become more regulated and standardized. This is a good thing, she said, in that it helps prevent illegal adoptions; but it also means less flexibility, as in the placement of special-needs children, whom she thought were still left out.

In early 2001, when I talked to Director Yuan, the exclusion of special-needs children was fairly overt: a couple of officials told me placing special-needs children was bothersome (*mafan*), that the expertise was not in place to oversee it properly, and that sometimes the "heart" wasn't there to put in the extra effort required. There were even times when families or agencies in the United States asking specifically for an older child with physical or developmental needs were told that "there aren't any"—meaning that there were none being referred for adoption. (There are, in fact, tens of thousands of special-needs children in Chinese welfare facilities.) Changes to policies in 2002 were geared toward new efforts at regulating the care and placement of special-needs children,[8] but on both ends of the adoption process this remains a "special channel" of adoptive placement, distinguished from the main routes of infant and toddler placement. As Cartwright (2003) has pointed out in her analysis of adoption photo listings at U.S. agencies, children enter the system classified as special-needs, "laying out an imagined history of cultural and familial pathology—even before the child enters the home" (96). Special-needs children are on an increasingly specialized track within or between agencies, requiring creative incentives to offset the "risks" parents will be taking. One agency even offers "money down" on special-needs children, telling its online readers, "We place money on waiting children submitted to us by placing agencies in the hopes of getting potential families interested in the child" (http://www.brittanyshope.org, accessed August 2004).

Ambivalence over selecting special-needs children into the international adoption system is intertwined with what they represent materially and symbolically to both Chinese and American actors in the process. Many of my Chinese informants admitted they did not understand why anyone, let alone a foreigner, would want to adopt a child with obvious medical problems; they often came to the conclusion that such parents must either have suspect motives or be saints (religious or concerned, as all Americans seem to be, with "human rights"). Journalist Li (1999) titled his story of a single American woman who adopted special-needs children "Saint Ruth—The World Still Has Such Love" (*Shengnü Rusi—shishang hai you zheyangde ai*). Whether tapped into discourses of humanitarianism or consumptive harvesting (rumors of Westerners adopting children for use of their organs circulate in China, as they do in other sending countries), explanations for desiring special-needs children were inextricable from unequal transnational class positions. American parents were seen to have the material and ideological means even to make such a choice. In an orphanage in northern China that cares for hundreds of special-needs children, I talked briefly with a caregiver on the way out the door after her first half-day on the job. She was clearly shaken and told me she couldn't endure being around so many special-needs children. "Don't get me wrong," she said. "I have feelings for them. I just don't know that I can take care of them. *You* folks [foreigners] can take it."

This caregiver's statement speaks simultaneously to cultural, national, and class contradictions embodied in the identities of children selected for international adoption. Abandoned (and sometimes special-needs children) are "right" for transnational placement because they represent a burden on China that would not necessarily be a burden for those who have the material means and thus the choice to display the desire to care or consume. In other words, marginalized Chinese children can be transformed through the exchange values of adoption. Special-needs children, who are an exception to the regular channels of adoption, represent the fissures of commensurability. On the one hand, their selection for adoption allows the display of American national ideals of generosity. As a consular officer from the U.S. consulate in Guangzhou put it in an e-mail communication with me (February 7, 2001), "Not only is bringing [Chinese orphans] into the US consistent with the myth of the US being a safe haven and place that welcomes all the unwanted, an immigration policy that provides for orphans expeditiously also responds to needs of Americans to demonstrate that Americans care for others." On the other hand, special-needs children represent a potential "excess" of care beyond other kinds of value. A number of people in China expressed some discomfort at sending handicapped children abroad who did not properly embody the *suzhi* (quality) of a modernizing Chinese population. Modern cultural nationalism[9] is displayed not only through "good orphanages" but also "good children."

It is easier for *healthy* children to embody the right cultural stuff for imagined relocation from China to the United States. Freed of the marginalized status of abandonment—perhaps especially when they will not carry some kind of disability with them across the Pacific—adopted girls are free to be Chinese in affirming ways. I am suggesting here a nationalism that draws on both its "cultural" and "political" forms—a Chinese essence preserved in and made modern (ironically?) through the migrating body. The combination of love and material gain they are imagined to receive in foreign adoptive homes means that healthy Chinese girls can be claimed wherever they go as "connected heart and bone to the motherland and its people," as one Chinese writer put it (Zhu 1996:4). Some informants in China expressed national pride that American parents want Chinese children because they are smart and healthy and come from such a culturally (if not yet materially) rich nation. A 1996 article in the official magazine of the Ministry of Civil Affairs quoted CCAA personnel as saying that foreigners like to adopt Chinese children because they "revere Chinese culture, and consider Chinese children to be smart, beautiful, healthy, and with an innate feeling of loyalty; so they consider adopting a child with Chinese blood their finest choice" (Zhu 1996: 4–5). This rhetoric has not just nationalist but racialist implications, as biologized racial difference collapses into naturalized cultural character (see Dikötter 2002). One Chinese observer with whom I spoke went so far as to say that relative to Korean (too ruddy) and Japanese (too short) children, Chinese children were better looking.

As discussed in the previous chapter, these assessments of the cultural desirability of Chinese children to American parents are not necessarily off the mark. For a good number of American parents, the appeal of adopting from China is a combination of the availability of healthy young girls, China's openness to older parents and single parents, and the added bonus of Chinese culture—described variously as ancient, rich, unique, and exotic. This is indeed a racialized process, but one in which distinctions tend to be made in often oblique comparisons to the white and black children available through other adoption programs. Social workers get exasperated with the stratifications that lead parents to adopt Russian children who have special needs but are white, or that lead them away from adopting American children who have special needs and are not white. They warn parents about "issues" that Russian children have or argue, as Rita Jasper did, that race shouldn't matter since "a baby is a baby is a baby." Yet adoption professionals know that this stratification of children is enacted in part through the structures of competition in which they operate—the "China R Us" problem. Healthy Chinese baby girls are "needy enough" and "different enough," but not so needy or different that they are beyond desire and revaluation for white American families.

It is crucial to recognize here that the selection of particularly valued children into international adoption is inextricable from the needs and desires of their prospective adoptive parents, but that these parents are themselves valued in particular ways. As Berebitsky (2000) has argued, the professional brokering of the "best fit"—the most "loaded" children going to those with the most "buying power" (Lal 2002: 180)—is already half a century old.

A Family Is a Family Is a Family? Selecting and Recruiting the Parent-Client

Cultural and material representations and distinctions are important not only to the process by which children in China enter transnational adoption migration but also to the process by which U.S. parents are selected to adopt them. The selection of "right" children is related, in other words, to the selection and recruitment of "right" parents. Given the contradictions inherent in sending children across national and cultural borders, standardized procedures are meant to ensure good homes for children (or, as we have seen, for certain children). But among American and Chinese practitioners alike, an increasing regulation of proper parenthood emerges out of and through contested notions of who is positioned to make choices for children, of whether the client is parent or child, and of what conditions (for both parent and child) constitute a "good" adoption placement. In this section I briefly demonstrate the way global imaginings and forces work through these contradictions to select and recruit parents in the United States for adoption of children from China.

The new international adoption law that emerged in the early 1990s, as several Chinese officials told me, opened up the possibility of lessening two burdens on Chinese orphanages: too many children and not enough cash in the social welfare system. The material benefit brought to the system by adopters from wealthy nations has been a matter of interest within China from the beginning of the program, as Director Yuan of Hongqi Orphanage told me: "At the beginning, some orphanage directors wanted to charge just one thousand American dollars orphanage donation, saying this was for the children, but others said we should charge ten thousand because they can afford it!" So while factions within the Beijing administration have wrangled with each other and with international agencies over what kinds of families are suitable, the quintessential family from the United States is well enough off to afford to pay the various fees (including the required U.S. $3,000 orphanage donation) and to promise the kind of opportunities that Mr. Xin of the CCAA suggested help justify international adoption. The CCAA does not officially publish minimum income requirements, but agencies and facilitators know when they might have to put in an extra word of persuasion for applicants without comfortable salaries and respectable professions. (The U.S. Citizenship and Immigration Services, formerly the Immigration and Naturalization Service, requires that prospective adopters have salaries at least 125 percent of the federal poverty line.) Parent applications often include photos of a spacious home, of a potential child's well-groomed room, and of people and pets that will be part of the child's life as well, so that material and emotional well-being speak together for the best interest of children.

Definitions of well-being in adoption often begin but certainly do not end with money, as is evident in the vicissitudes of Beijing's regulations regarding prospective adopters' age and marital status. China's requirements initially allowed foreign parents up to as much as sixty years of age, as well as unmarried parents, to adopt Chinese children—unusually flexible regulations in international adoption. In the early years of the millennium, changes to adoption regulations in China have put in place more firm minimum and maximum age limits but also, more poignantly, regulations that limit the inclusion of unmarried parents.[10] Beginning in December 2000, international adoptive parents who were unmarried were required to sign a statement that they were not gay or lesbian, and beginning in December 2001, agencies in the United States were told that no more than 5 percent of their applicants could be unmarried. It is generally understood that the latter regulation is to further contain the placement of Chinese children with not just single but more specifically gay and lesbian parents.[11]

Norms and distinctions of parent selection in China are both heteronormative and racialized. I consistently encountered among officials and administrators of adoption in China an apprehension about families that were *bu zhengchang* (not normal)—with probing, I discovered that this sometimes referred to anything but white or diasporic Chinese heterosexual married couples. A few orphanage and CCAA administrators in China said they thought placing children with Chinese Americans was "more natural," and the CCAA officially expedites applications by overseas Chinese (*huaqiao*) and Chinese of foreign nationality.[12] My informants usually emphasized that of utmost importance was placing a child with a loving family. But again, this iteration of universal love could in practice be particularized to imply married and not black. One orphanage director, when I asked if he had met any parents with whom he felt uncomfortable placing a child, said, well, there had been an African American parent once; and one U.S. agency reported that the CCAA turned down an interracial African American and white couple that had applied for adoption from China. As Dikötter (2002) has argued, China's own national imagined identity has relied to some extent on discourses that reproduce blackness as primitive and/or sexually dangerous.

Contested currencies of "normalcy" in the reproduction of kinship— and of the adoption system itself—are, of course, not unique to China, and in fact depend on their transnational circulation. This is not as much a matter of federal regulation in the United States as it is one of state law and local practice; outside immigration and citizenship proceedings, there is no central set of policies regulating international adoption in the United States. From the beginning, a tacit "don't ask, don't tell" collusion between some U.S. adoption agencies and parent applicants—and perhaps even officials in Beijing who turned a blind eye—rendered China open to queer applicants despite official regulations. But this left a number of agency professionals in the United States torn between the ethical and pragmatic implications of placing children from China with gay and lesbian parents. (In some cases, agency policy excluded gay and lesbian parents to begin with, so there was no dilemma.) As Bay Area adoption administrator Rita Jasper put it, "Let me just pose this: what's better? 'Don't ask don't tell,' so you don't really know who's involved in the child's life? Or sort of just kind of torquing the truth to China? . . . You know, it's such a dilemma." Marjorie Sessions, director of the agency Family Foundations, did not find it such a dilemma. She said she thought that despite any feelings she may have about equity, it was just too risky to place children with gay and lesbian parents against China's wishes, because "they'll cut us off."

The relationship of parent selection to the fear of being "cut off" was perhaps nowhere clearer than in how agency administrators and social workers in the United States explained to me the new restrictions on unmarried parents announced by Beijing in late 2000. Impetus for the change was blamed on "outing" from various corners of the adoption industry's quietly open practices. Marjorie chalked it up to a commercial for John Hancock insurance, aired in the United States in the summer of 2000, that centered on a lesbian couple meeting their adopted Asian child at the airport. While some in the United States applauded the commercial's recognition of gay and lesbian families and others decried the overt trafficking of images of Asians for white consumption, the primary concern of adoption agencies was that such public recognition would cause China to shut its doors to all unmarried parents.[13] Other explanations for the 2001 revisions from the CCAA pointed to an "inside job"; a couple of social workers I interviewed were convinced that some conservative Christian agencies had tattled to Beijing about practices at other agencies that circumvented bans on gay and lesbian parents.

Whatever the reasons for it, responses to the revised policy demonstrate that the transnational adoption system and "right kinship" reproduce each other through a global circuitry of ideologies and practices, such that the moral problematic of distinguishing among parents is intertwined with market concerns and competition. This helps explain why many professionals were in part relieved by the new policy. Beijing's direct act of exclusion lifted the fear agencies had of being outed for placing children with subjects who sat at the margins of properly defined parenthood, and thus clienthood. Here is how two social workers at Midwest International Adoptions (MIA) put it, in somewhat coded terms:

> *Norma*: [The CCAA has] become more refined, or sophisticated, or specific as to what kind of families they want.
> *Carrie*: They've made our job somewhat easier by being so clear.

As with the selection of children into the adoption system, bureaucratic clarity and market competition spell the liminality and exclusion of particular kinds of parents. Terry Schlitz and Matt Landers, a gay couple, said to me that when they entered the adoption system, they got the distinct sense they were being steered toward special-needs children. As Matt put it, "The agency stuck us in a room of waiting children. I mean, those children need homes too, but it was like, 'You really should do this.'" Terry added that the agency seemed to be saying to them that yes, they could work with them, but "you might have difficulty . . . you guys have this little disability." A flip side to "right kids for right families" is thus the matching of marginal children with marginal parents.

Competitive interests in adoption practices are supposed to resolve themselves in service to the best interests of children. Yet keeping open the "general" channels of transnational adoption can require limitations on both parents and children, precisely because both are clients. Consider these uncertain comments from social worker Rita Jasper:

> I think our agency decided, we're sort of a vehicle to help people realize their dream. And it's not even about people we care about, it's about the *kids* that we care about, in order to get parents for kids. . . . What's best for children? What's best for children is to have families— a family is a family is a family. And we know that families can be comprised of many different types of people.

In one breath, Rita speaks of helping parents "realize their dream" but also of what is best for children. To accommodate both, she must then go out of her way to reclaim the universal family. But in reality, claiming both parents and children as "clients" tends to negate the universality of either, setting up a contradiction between "a baby is a baby is a baby" and "a family is a family is a family." Social worker Lynn Besky put it this way:

> It's a constant juggling of what's the best needs of the family, and the best needs of the child. We do want to find homes for children. I mean, that is our goal. But you do find yourself sometimes feeling like you're following the market as opposed to being the trailblazers out there.

Family Foundations director Marjorie Sessions bluntly told me, "We're *supposed* to say children are the clients," but it is parents that pay the bills, and because there are so many children, parents get to choose. MIA social worker Carrie Betts insisted that the child remains the primary client, but a kind of phantom ideal client: "[I]t's unknown to us, unmet, and maybe unborn." The (impossible) trick was to keep the child at the center of professional social work practice even as the parent, the "secondary client," was the one directly paying for services. Carrie continued: "My salary, and Norma's salary, is paid by a secondary client, whose goodwill we must maintain. And yet we may have to do things to this client that they don't like, that they're angry about, and that they may scream at us for." Carrie referred to the home studies and background checks parents must go through to meet health, financial, relationship, civic, and other standards set by the CCAA, state and federal governments, and individual agencies. The unknown and unmet child, meanwhile, is produced for adoptive kinship in a contradictory location between "primary client" and object of desire.

Parents, by contrast, are "secondary client" *and* active subject of desire. So just as orphanages compete to send children into the transnational adoption system, agencies compete to *recruit* or at least attract parents. Marjorie Sessions thought the reality was that parents "never see the agency as their advocate. We're advocates for children, yet it seems to them like we're trying to [compete to] find them a perfect baby." Some parents indeed look for what Rita Jasper called "the cheapest game in town, or the quickest game in town, or what sounds the 'best,' whether it's true or not." But my conversations with parents reveal everything from admiration to resentment of agencies' preadoption interventions in their lives, and some complain that it is agencies, competing with each other for their business, that make them into reluctant transnational consumers. Resistance to being both wooed and selected by adoption agencies might be heightened for parents who have experienced infertility and thus seek a path to parenthood that is as free of new obstacles as possible.

The recruitment practices of adoption agencies operate with *universal* visions of the needs of children and families who must nonetheless be made *uniquely* to belong to each other. At the Adoption Links orientation for prospective parents that I attended, the session leaders told parents, "Don't worry, there *is* a child out there for you." The promotional video for one agency I visited, called *Needing You, Needing Me,* concluded with the song "Somewhere Out There" over a montage of children's faces and their countries of origin, suggesting that borders can be elided to meet mutual needs. Indeed, images in the agency's international adoption brochure—photos of smiling children of color with white parents and an outline of the world in whimsical pastel graphics—slide across borders as easily as does the vignette that accompanies them. The description of a pitiful abandoned girl ("She has no family. She doesn't even have a name") segues into the description of a mother longing to adopt ("Since deciding on international adoption, she feels that the beginning of their new family is closer than ever. . . . Carol and her husband really like the name Christina"). The child in question not only meets her own as well as parents' (universal) need for a family but, more specifically, can be reimagined to belong to her new parents despite difference and distance.

Imagining belonging involves not just the elision but also the reinscription of difference, that is, the kind of celebratory American visions of China and Chinese children discussed in the preceding chapter. As Marjorie Sessions put it, "Most families are not global," meaning that they usually enter the agency having already fallen in love with a "particular kind of child"—maybe the adopted Chinese daughter of some friends or neighbors or the pictures agencies themselves circulate. Adoption magazines, agency brochures, and adoption Web sites begin to classify children already for parents. Photo listings on agency Web sites sometimes allow parents to sort by country, health, age, and/or sex of child. Through this practice, as Cartwright (2003) puts it, "the casual portrait becomes hard data on cultural identity . . . adoption photolisting is a historically recent example of physiognomic classification" (93). In adoption magazines, one finds an overabundance of ads and photos featuring Asian girls, some posed in silk Chinese dresses. When larger agencies work with a number of international programs, it is often Asian girls that serve as image front-runners. The child-client and parent-client are thus produced together and for each other as, respectively, object and subject of desire.

Preparing American Parents for Chinese Adoption

In the preadoption preparation of parents, racial and national difference might threaten to exceed the pleasure of global multiculturalism promised by Chinese adoption. So even as agency advertisements use images that promote cultural appeal, they tend also to manage the strange unknowns of China and of the child. Parents must be able to imagine difference within the possible horizons of, or perhaps at the edges of, white American middle-class households. This translates into anticipating parents' anxieties, as exemplified at the Adoption Links orientation:

> One of the orientation leaders tells the group of parents that they should feel free to ask any questions tonight, from "Can I ask for a particular gender or shade of skin?" to "Can I reject a child?" I feel a tension in the room, broken just a bit when one of the men directs a question to Susan, one of the adoptive parents leading the orientation—if when she had met her son in Colombia he had had a serious problem, then what? Are there stories of rejections? Susan says she doesn't know, but certainly you *do* have a choice.

For the China program more specifically, competition among agencies sometimes means almost guaranteeing the (right kind of) child, in part through promising to guide parents through an unfamiliar process. These provisions might end up reinscribing the very borders of race, nation, and kinship they offer to elide.

Preadoption "cultural training"—one among the professional steps that aim to prepare parents for transnational and transracial kinship—

exemplifies this curious balancing act between celebration and containment of difference, and between parent-client and child-client. While the general wisdom in the adoption world is that transnationally adopted children should know something of their birth heritage and that white parents should at least be aware of the racism their nonwhite children might encounter, the agencies I studied varied in the degree of importance they placed on such training: some kept contact with prospective parents at a bare minimum, while others required extensive preadoptive counseling, including some race and culture sensitization. Yet none of them wants to scare parents off with a lot of intervention; even those committed to thorough preadoptive training admitted they were wary of doing "too much" around race and culture issues at the expense of bigger risks. ("Risks" most often refer to the potential for both litigation and disruption of an adoptive placement and are not easily categorized as purely market- or care-driven.) As Norma Halliday at MIA put it:

> I think we've become much more focused on risks, and on developmental and background issues [of children]. We really have not focused more on race and culture issues. . . . The other stuff is almost more immediate. Ideally, I think it would be better to do race/culture things after placement [when parents are more ready to hear it]. . . . We need to have this stuff up front about risks.[14]

What parents are "ready to hear" speaks to the impossible contradictions of adoption: the desire for a child that can be reproduced to belong to a white middle-class American family despite difference, and the accompanying anxiety/knowledge that this might not happen—that racialized positions cannot be evacuated. The deferral of the need for race and culture knowledge might thus maintain the fiction of the young, flexible Chinese child, which in turn maintains the fiction of the universalized white American family. As Marjorie Sessions said, "You know, they're *babies* from China. This is not the same as adopting a five-year-old from Russia. With infants, parents move to normalize their family as quickly as possible." Rita Jasper suggested the opposite: "No matter how much they try to Americanize this child, culturize a child, this child is born in China." Yet both of these longtime social workers agreed that a lot of emphasis on adoption or on Chinese heritage could serve to make a child feel too different. Indeed, adoption agency administrators and social workers often spoke of the importance of parents—tacitly and in practice, white parents—doing "something" with Chinese culture, but not *too* much. What I want to argue here is that the professionalized emphasis on finding the "right" level of Chinese culture might serve to occlude the existence of too much *whiteness* and underscores its tacit normalcy.[15] Consider how Norma Halliday and Carrie Betts discussed the acceptable range of approaches to Chinese culture in white families:

> *Norma*: I have concerns about the families who become totally Asian.
> *Carrie*: Right.
> *Norma*: I think, don't they have any self-respect about their own background?
> *Carrie*: —or force it so much the kid feels weird. There is a "too much" line. . . . You need to meet needs, whether they are cultural or whatever. And it depends on the family; it's most important for the child to feel connected to the family.

At the same time, cultural imagery helps broker the fearful but exciting difference of the child, her country, and the process by which white parents will get her. The Web site of Great Wall China Adoptions, an agency based in Texas (http://www.gwcadopt.org, accessed 2002), announced the agency in both English and Chinese, with an image of the Great Wall and the statement "Pursuing cross-culture [sic] adoption can be challenging. You are faced with different customs and norms, plus a foreign language you probably have never heard before." China itself is made strange—even scary—but also culturally appealing. At a couple of agencies' orientation classes for parents preparing to travel to China to adopt, the friendliness of Chinese people was emphasized even as the sights, sounds, and smells of Chinese "street life" were made tantalizingly exotic. The promise of kinship formed despite and because of such difference is represented in parents and children who have already been through the process. At the MIA travel orientation, an adoptive mother narrated the trip for her eager audience of prospective parents with stories, photo albums, and the live presence of her four-year-old daughter Mei-mei. I wrote in my notes:

The agency coordinator asks Mei-mei where she is from, and she happily says, "China." Mei-mei, meanwhile, notices that the photo album chronicling her mother's trip to China has been passed around and has reached a man at the end of the row. She goes over and looks at the album with him. She points every now and again and says "Mommy," or "China," or "Where's Mei-mei?" The audience is charmed, not knowing whether to pay more attention to Mei-mei or the panel of speakers.

What strikes me about this scene is the bridging of preadoptive and postadoptive narratives, and thus of differences and borders, by means of the child herself—she who knows she is from China, who can point to her preadoptive self in the family photo album, who symbolizes the seamless possibility of creating a family "here" by traveling "there." This integration of past and future helps reproduce the adoption process itself, in part through the presentation of surmountable or harmless difference, embodied in the child.

Perhaps the most crucial way in which cultural imagery is managed in parents' preadoptive stage of preparation is through the presence and work of Chinese and Chinese American facilitators. The Great Wall Web site went on to say: "You certainly need people who are experts in intercountry adoption with well-established local contacts [in China]. Great Wall is such an agency with a team of knowledgeable Americans and bilingual staff." Differences of child and nation are bridged and brokered by transnational experts; Chinese facilitators working for U.S. adoption agencies offer access to government officials and orphanages, as well as an understanding of languages, propensities, and institutions on both sides of the Pacific. Indeed, administrators at several agencies told me that having a Chinese facilitator on staff was one way to distinguish themselves from other agencies in an otherwise standardized process. They could thus assure parents that people with the right kind of social capital would manage the uncertainties of adopting from and traveling to the strange land of China. I would further argue that the direct involvement of Chinese people tacitly legitimates adoption, quieting colonialist and consumerist accusations.[16] In this manner, preparing parents for adoption involves lifting some of the burden of cultural-historical knowledge work from parents, instead offering it to them as a service.

The work of facilitators begins in the preadoption phase of preparing and shepherding parents through the many steps of the process, in anticipation of crossing borders. For example, facilitators might provide to prospective parents an introduction to Chinese culture and history. Zhuli Pan, Aiqing Shu, and David Lee—associated with different agencies in San Francisco and the Twin Cities—all pointed to this kind of cultural education as important to their work; Zhuli said, "I just feel as a Chinese woman myself—I feel very good about my role as a coordinator because I see myself as a bridge, in a way." She and Aiqing spent time with families prior to their travel to China, trying to give them an inside look at things such as the Cultural Revolution and everyday relationships in Chinese families. Chinese facilitators also provide inside information on the unofficial side of official Chinese policies and practices. Aiqing, for example, told me:

> If [CCAA staff] don't trust you, they . . . can just tell you, "Hey, look at the Internet, that is our new policy." But the new policy won't give you enough information to help you, to screen your families, which one is good, which one is not good. But if you have the trust, then you can understand the policy better, understand their assessment better. So that will reduce the risk for our families.

This was Aiqing's way of saying that the China/U.S. adoption process is in some ways not as standardized as official discourse indicates, and it is usually Chinese facilitators that buffer and negotiate the contingencies and unwritten rules on behalf of adoptive families.

Like agency administrators, Zhuli and Aiqing expressed feeling torn sometimes between working on behalf of the Chinese child-client and being paid by the American parent-client, a tension crosscut by their roles as both cultural and economic brokers. Zhuli told me:

> I think the majority of families are very reasonable and they do it with their heart. Just sometimes with a few families I find it is kind of difficult, when they say they want a child really, really young, and it's not possible. You know, if I have a client who is really demanding, that makes me uncomfortable, when they tell me, "Well, I want my child to have this shape face, or that shape eyes." Or "Oh, I don't want my child

to have very dark skin." You know, that kind of talk. That's not very common, but it does exist.

Zhuli took pride in being a "midwife" of adoption, as she described it, and more particularly a midwife for Chinese girls who, she felt, were getting a new lease on life through adoption into the United States. But this role was curtailed by risks of its own: the extent to which her desire to educate parents could go was determined in part by the dictates of the "right" kind of child, whose imagined belonging was constructed at the juncture of race, gender, kinship, and nation.

Preparing Chinese Children for International Adoption

Given the circuits of value in adoption, facilitators also play an important role as brokers in the other direction, informing orphanages and officials in China about the needs and interests of families and agencies in the United States. Facilitators thus help produce commensurability between preadoption practices in both nations. One key domain in which this occurs is that of the kinds of care given in Chinese social welfare institutions to children who will be adopted abroad. I argue below that these caring practices demonstrate (1) the stratified articulation of children, as well as the organizations and agents of their care, into the transnational adoption system, and (2) the ways in which capitalist and humanitarian processes together particularize the meaning and value of individuals, institutions, and nations. I explore how circulations of money, ideas, and practices in the transnational adoption system are enacted locally.

Practices of care in Chinese orphanages are shaped and governed by particular flows of resources, which in turn inevitably shape particular styles and notions of care. In the process, Chinese facilitators sometimes become transnational agents of styles of practice originating on the receiving end of adoption migration (from which also originate in the U.S. many of the material resources). This is demonstrated in the description Zhuli gave of her role as a bridge between Chinese orphanages and officials, on the one hand, and American parents and agencies, on the other:

I tell families a lot of cultural issues they should be aware of when they go to China. What they should expect, what they should not expect, and those kinds of things. And then with the Chinese, you know, the orphanage itself—I talk to the orphanage directors a lot, and I let *them* know the expectations of families here and what's better for the children and for the families, what they need, those kinds of things.

When I asked Zhuli for examples of the messages she conveyed in both directions, she said she had to explain to parents why their eight-month-old might not be crawling yet (children are bundled up tight in winter, and orphanage floors are sometimes cement), or why their baby's head might be shaved (to help keep them cool in hot summers). But while American parent-clients were asked to "be aware" of these Chinese practices—to put up with these temporary signs of a particular and peculiar form of child care—in the other direction, their needs and wants were translated back to China as expected standards of child care.

Zhuli discussed a number of specific practices she has asked orphanages to institute on behalf of American families, among them the process of naming children. Adoptive parents in the United States sometimes balk at the Chinese names given to their children by orphanages, in part because the names do not seem individually meaningful to parents or are meaningful in ways that uncomfortably connect the child to abandonment and institutionalization. For example, in some orphanages all the children found in the same year are given the same family name, their given names perhaps including a Chinese character that reflects where or when they were found. Zhuli found herself asking orphanages to employ naming practices that would seem beautiful and unique to adoptive parents—signs that their children were cared for as valuable individuals (a "universal" quality) but imbued with a Chinese flavor (a "unique" quality). Parents' need to know their children are being cared for as unique and valued individuals, as signified in particular naming practices, is translated as children's need to be treated as such.

Children in Chinese orphanages are thus produced for adoption through a cultural economy of practices and meanings that anticipate their migration to the United States and other Western countries. A number of agencies promised prospective parents that as soon as a child was matched with them, she would be put in foster care for the several weeks or months before placement. Proper care is also signified on the body of the child in ways made recognizable to the consumer culture of American parents. Consider the experience of Patty Lou, whose daughter was selected for adoption, and thus for particular signs of care, in 1996:

> We found out later that [the agency representative] had sent American formula over there [to China] before we came, to get the babies used to it. And he sent diapers. 'Cause she had on Pampers, or Huggies, or something when we got her, which surprised me. I thought she would just have cloth diapers. But then we found out he had sent everything for them. So they were in excellent shape.

Since the late 1990s, formal foster-care programs and other signs of professionalized Western micropractices of care in Chinese orphanages have become more routine, mediated by transnational facilitators, agency social workers, and various U.S. and European charitable organizations. The offices of the child welfare institutes in Dayang and Hongqi, both of which send hundreds of young children for transnational adoption each year, were stacked with American-brand formula and diapers purchased with funds donated through international adoption. The photos of foreign adoptive families on the office desks and walls were a testament to the production of care at the juncture of subjects and objects of desire.

What is striking about this scene is its place in the transnational adoption system in relation to other people and rooms in the orphanage, to other welfare institutions in China, and to overseas adoptive families and organizations. Orphanages, or at least some of them, have become access points and transnational nodes (for both Chinese and Westerners) for the importation and display of market and welfare ideals. They are spaces where the needs and desires of actors and institutions in two different nations come together around signs of modern efficiency and care—signs required by American parents and agencies and then reflected back at them by Chinese orphanages and caregivers. Adoption-related funds are brought into China's welfare system from both the donation of U.S. $3,000 required of adoptive parents and the many charitable projects organized by adoptive parent groups[17] and adoption agencies. Orphanages and welfare bureaucracies, in turn, display practices and images that reflect their articulation into this flow of material and symbolic resources. (There are quite literally signs of this articulation—plaques hanging over doors to rehabilitation rooms or near orphanage playgrounds, acknowledging U.S. and other foreign companies or organizations, including those formed by adoptive parents, that have donated resources.)

While there are many donations that go to a wide variety of people and services in Chinese social welfare institutions, my interest is in the inescapable links between adoption-related funds and the reproduction of the international adoption system. Because the donations of money and goods received from adoptive parents and adoption-related charitable organizations are so precious and inadequate to a resource-poor child welfare system, how and under what constraints that money gets disbursed deserves some scrutiny, especially as it has implications for the care of children who are and are not part of the transnational adoption system. Displays of care, including at the site of the child's body, are signs of the constraining *and* productive power of these resources (Foucault 1991b).

Constraints on the use of the donation money required of foreign adopters come in part from the skepticism of American and other foreign adoptive parents and agencies that the monies do not reach their intended destination, namely, the care of orphaned children. While there is only limited direct evidence of corruption,[18] a number of adoption practitioners expressed concerns that, as one facilitator put it, "some money is stopped in the middle" by local civil affairs officials. She pointed out that administrators work hard on behalf of the children for whom they are responsible and officially don't get any extra pay for this, "but some people are getting cell phones and nice cars." As a result, Chinese officials and orphanage directors have become extravigilant. Cognizant of precious resources, Director Yuan of Hongqi Orphanage said she was especially careful to demonstrate accountability: "You should be clear about how that money will be used, and then have photos and receipts and such to show that it has been used as promised. If you don't do this well, like some orphanages, then your sources of money will be cut off (*mei le*)!" Director Yuan spoke to the imperatives of meeting certain standards in the use of transnational resources, for the simultaneous goals of keeping the needed supply of money coming and of demonstrating and practicing proper care for children. This imperative was heightened after the *Dying Rooms* exposé of 1995, which might also have further funneled funds from abroad into model orphanage programs.

The many effective efforts to improve conditions for orphan children in China cannot be denied (for examples, see Johnson 2004; Evans 2000). But given the pressure to comply with international norms and limited resources to do so, it also behooves the Chinese social welfare system to constrain the display and practice of care according to what Aiqing called its "window of the country" for "foreign eyes," namely, transnational adoption. Indeed, the desire by the Civil Affairs Ministry, its branches, and the welfare institutes under its supervision to reflect some version of the expectations of modern, Western care—and thus the preparation of adoptable children—is evident in official public images. Orphanage and government office materials published in English and Chinese create an image of surroundings suitable for nurturing adoptable children. A Wangjing Orphanage brochure is full of photos of brand-new buildings, doctors caring for children, and office workers putting files away and is plastered with child-friendly graphics; it boasts that modern facilities and park-like surroundings make it "an ideal place to adopt children." In similar fashion, the colorful lighted billboard in one provincial adoption affairs office has two sections side by side: the left side announces, "Children's Welfare Services under Supervision of Hunan Civil Administration Are Prosperous," and the right side proclaims, "All We've Got Are Good News from Abroad about the Adopted Babies." Photos on the left of new orphanage buildings are balanced by photos on the right of foreign adoptive families, suggesting that happy adopted babies and good child welfare require each other in a circular process. Together, these pre- and postadoption stories narrate a national modernity directly related to the expectations of foreign adoptive parents, portraying a win-win managed migration of adoptable children. Given reports of some local protests against sending children for international adoption, the display might also reassure Chinese observers.

Resources are thus somewhat constrained toward reproducing a particular circuit of exchange: adoption funds are used to produce child-care practices that the transnational adoption system recognizes as good enough to produce adoptable children. One Chinese social worker told me she was disgusted by a foreign-supported orphan home that had an agreement with their local civil affairs office to place children for international adoption, with 70 percent of the donations going to the orphanage and the other 30 percent going to the Civil Affairs Ministry. She called this *lingshigong* (contract work) and thus an example of the market forces that help shape the reproduction of internationally adoptable kids. The use and display of modern care is its own fluctuating currency in this process, even among and within those orphanages that send many children for international adoption. Especially in the wake of a spate of media coverage on poor orphanage conditions in 1995, only a limited number of "model" orphanages were made open to foreign visitors. At Beigang Orphanage, the front gate displays neat placards in English and Chinese welcoming visitors to the "family" of Beigang but reminding foreign visitors that they must have special permission to enter. Beigang, in fact, provides a poignant example of the extremes to which the spectacle of care can be taken. The entryway to the orphanage is dominated by a sign that reads, in both Chinese and English, "Thank you for taking care of our orphans." But immediately beyond the lobby, shiny new rooms labeled "Dental Clinic," "X-ray Room," and "Occupational Therapy" sit empty and unused. One lesson to be learned from Beigang is that the inflow of material resources from foreign sources (mostly from the United States and Europe but also Hong Kong) sources magnifies the ideological imperative in China to perform value and care for all children—sometimes, ironically, to the detriment of children.

It is understandable that funds might be more concentrated in "model" rehabilitation centers, living quarters, or education programs, but they have also tended to be stratified *within* orphanages, where transnational adoption resources are *productive* of the very kinds of children valued for international adoption. Social worker Yan Wei visits orphanages that run the full gamut of small to large and rural to urban, and it seemed to her that often the money received through transnational adoption went back into improving standards of care for healthy infants, the ones "who can bring more kids." She pointed especially to the differentiation of facilities and children within orphanages that are part of the transnational adoption system: many of the disabled children she saw were in a "second facility" where outsiders do not and usually cannot go. Yan had recently visited an orphanage where the difference in care was stark. I, too, spent time in a couple orphanages whose facilities for healthy babies and toddlers were cleaner, warmer, better staffed, and

more geared toward developmental activities than those for older and
handicapped children. At one of them I met a local social worker evalu-
ating special-needs children in the back section of the orphanage. When
I asked her why she thought these facilities were poorer, she hesitated
and said she'd think about it. Later in our conversation, I happened to
mention that prospective parents (both domestic and international) usually wanted healthy children; she smiled and said, "There's the answer to
your question." The "triage" described earlier in this chapter, whereby
facilitators in the early days of adoption picked out children most likely
to survive and be healthy enough for foreign adoption, has become
somewhat standardized through the differentiation of resources. A local
adoption expert in Beigang even referred to the two separate facilities for
special-needs and healthier children as the "Chinese" and "foreign" sections of the orphanage.

U.S.-based adoption administrators might be more likely to perceive
transnational adoption and the material and symbolic capital it brings as
a vehicle for inculcating in China a spirit of valuing all children, sometimes echoing the zeal of missionaries and businesspeople for instilling
modernity in China (Madsen 1995). Marjorie Sessions, director of Family
Foundations, put it this way:

> Care in Chinese orphanages used to be abominable; children were *as-
> sured* neglect and starvation. With the realization that adoption brings
> in money, now the children are better cared for. The child is "upped in
> the food chain." Adoption puts a price on children that makes them
> more valuable . . . valuable to rescue and valuable to take care of. . . .
> I am starting to see that people in China understand that those aban-
> doned girls need nurturing. Adoption has made six of those seven
> girls *valuable*.

Marjorie's exaggerated estimate of the percentage of children "revalued"
by adoption (we cannot be sure that even *one* in seven children in the
Chinese welfare system is placed for international adoption) is meant to
underscore her point that *the* child is valued more because of adoption—
that market demand nurtures the valuing of life. Several Chinese facilitators professed a similar transformation in Chinese orphanages as a result of the intertwined material and ideological facets of adoption work.

As David Lee put it, "One way to improve things for children in Chinese orphanages is to have more adoption! We have a few American families who donate heavily, mm-hm. One family donated about ten thousand dollars. The money went to four orphanages, and they purchased a lot of things, badly needed stuff. And the other thing is, when more adoption goes on, then the orphanage becomes more open to the world! And it helps to improve their work." Zhuli more strongly connected this performance of care to the circulation of adoptive desires and demands:

> *Sara*: Do you think the orphanages you're working with have undergone any changes since they started placing children in Western homes, and if so, how?
>
> *Zhuli*: I think so. I think they are probably more aware, just by interacting with adoptive families for that short time, they are more aware that children need a lot of love and holding and those kinds of things.
>
> *Sara*: You don't think they know that already?
>
> *Zhuli*: They know that, they know that. But [sigh], how should I put it? [Pause.] You know, I think in China, the orphanages have so many children, and I don't think a lot of orphanages have enough staff members. Just for practical purposes, they want to make sure these children are healthy when they are adopted. You know, that will serve the purpose of the children receiving good care. For the orphanage, they don't want the families to go there and find that this child is so sick she can't even travel.

As Zhuli describes it, transnational adoption disciplines/motivates Chinese workers into providing care that will benefit children and thus, in turn, the parents who will adopt them. And as we have seen, claiming children as valuable can mean the power to write their value in particular ways.

Although they occupy a separate track of China/U.S. adoption, special-needs children are not outside its flow of resources and the signification of care; they therefore occupy a telling ideological space somewhere between the universal valuing of children and the particularizing value of adoption. At Beigang, Dayang, and other welfare institutions in China, the efforts of American and European charity groups to provide direct care to groups of special-needs children[19] become ways to demonstrate the value of marginalized children despite their "extra" needs. Even though, and perhaps because, they are not as valued in the adoption system, special-needs and older children are the placeholders of true care—a site for modeling the value of all children equally. In a couple orphanages, for example, I witnessed a kind of tug-of-war between orphanage staff and foreign charitable groups over claiming special-needs children as their "own" object of care and belonging. Special-needs children might, as objects of adoption, require an excess of rescue and care, but they nonetheless become valuable for the display of care.

Transnational adoption groups and organizations increasingly help direct resources toward children who will not be adopted; but it can sometimes happen that things work the other way around, so that caring "even" for these children has symbolic currency that can be good for the particular needs of adoption agencies. Aiqing alluded to this two-way tension in her job as a facilitator, where she strived to promote simultaneously in China the valuing of marginalized children and of adoption. Aiqing emphasized the importance of her agency's charitable programs for children who were *not* the object of adoption, such as training foster families for the care of special-needs children and providing donations to a very poor rural school. She argued that her work on behalf of all children in China built upon the American spirit of voluntarism by inspiring local Chinese people to do something for otherwise neglected children. Breaking into a combination of Chinese and English, she told me: "*Zemme shuo? Shi jingshen shangde; bushi shuo neige* money. *Jiu shi zheige* spirit, or mental support." (How should I put it? It's about consciousness; it's not the money. It's that spirit, or mental support.) Aiqing went on to tell me that the CCAA administration had made it very clear that the humanitarian efforts by American adoption agencies should not be motivated by the desire for "getting priority for getting more kids or getting some special treatment or credit." But then she continued:

> Okay, I'll be very honest with you. If I do this and tell [the local people] I have no intention to place these kids with American families, they won't feel that I'm going to take those children away. I want to convince them that I have come over to help the orphans. If they can trust me, maybe they will learn more and more and eventually they

will *help* me to do international adoption, [especially in central China where] the people's mind is not very open at all. They feel like, why do we have to send the kids out.

It didn't hurt, she pointed out, for the CCAA to hear about her agency's aid projects. "So, when you are working with them for your international adoption, because of the respect they have, I think they believe you, they trust you, which benefits your adoption program. But we're not doing this *for* that."

As Aiqing suggests, resources earmarked for the care of prospective international adoptees can exacerbate resentment about local/global inequities. Orphanages and caregivers, too, were not always willing or able to put extra effort into caring for marginalized children, let alone do it in ways imposed by foreigners—especially given their own socioeconomic status. Many of my conversations with *ayis* (caregivers) at Beigang and Hongqi orphanages in 2000 and 2001 revolved around their low salaries and long work hours. They and other caregivers I met at orphanages across China were paid U.S. $50 or less per month, and many had come to this work after being laid off (*xiagang*) from China's reforming state enterprises. All were women. Some simply did their job as minimally as possible, and some pointed out with more than a hint of irony that these orphan kids lived in better conditions than their own families. And there was some resentment at their lost labor, abstracted and fetishized in children sent abroad. I think of the caregiver who, upon hearing someone say how lucky children were to be adopted internationally, snapped, "They're lucky to be in this orphanage!" As Director Jin of Beigang Orphanage put it to me, "International adoption is important, and of course we welcome it. . . . Those children get good education, knowledge, and love. But of course it's important that they not forget where they came from, that they started in this orphanage. *Yinshuisiyuan*—don't forget about the source of the water you are drinking." Aiqing summed up well the jarring inequities and everyday acts of resistance that arise in the relationship between a struggling Chinese social welfare system and American expectations of care:

[American] parents just don't understand the situation in China—not even the social worker who once said to me, "Just have the orphanage

drive over to get the child some X-rays to send to the parents." What
do you mean, drive her over? Who is driving? What car? And even if
they have a jeep, it's four hours from the city. One orphanage directly
told me [in a terse tone], "Okay, we'll do another lab test, but just to let
you know, they're not using disposable needles." They just try to scare
you away, so you're not asking them anymore! [She chuckles.]

At the same time, however, caring regimes can themselves be acts of
resistance, especially as they are productive of Chinese modernity.
Proper valuing of the *child's* development becomes a symbol of *China's*
development, relative to both domestic backwardness and international
progress. Several of the large orphanages had adopted routines and sys-
tems of care based on scientific theories of child development, techniques of rehabilitation, and other "modern" knowledge of child care.
For example, the suite of baby rooms at Hongqi was run by an older
woman who had been specially trained by World Alliance, an American
adoption agency. Under her watchful eye, young Chinese nurses cradled
and fed babies one by one, recorded formula amounts and times on the
chart that hung from each crib, and kept a schedule of diaper changes.
Director Yuan proudly showed me the standardized forms, developed
with the resources and expertise of World Alliance and printed in both
English and Chinese, used carefully to track the monthly physical and
cognitive development of the many children in foster care. But Director
Yuan also emphasized that the orphanage administered the program
without foreigners running around the grounds of the welfare institute
(which is the case at some other large orphanages). One day as we talked
about ways in which American child welfare programs interacted with
Chinese ones, Yuan said, "Sure, help us, but don't tell us what to do.
These are our kids; we are the ones taking care of them, not you (*women
dai tamen, nimen bu dai tamen*), and they are our responsibility." Her sentiment echoed that of a social welfare professor working closely with
Beigang, who told me that international adoption exposed a delicate matter of national pride: China needed resources from abroad to enact a modern social welfare system but could not ideologically afford to let foreigners manage it.
   Producing national modernity for external consumption requires internal distinctions, one of which comes in the form of the "backward"

rural element in China from which most children are presumed to come. Ironically, pockets of abandoned, marginalized children are the objects of some of the same kind of Western child development expertise now being marketed to middle- and upper-class urban Chinese one-child families. In the winter of 2001, for example, I noted a growing number of shows and commercials on Chinese television hawking consumer goods (e.g., tactile toys) and techniques (e.g., play therapy) for measuring and enhancing "your child's development." In this context, orphanages such as Hongqi became transnational nodes of differentiation between modern (urban) and backward (rural) approaches to valuing children. Director Yuan distinguished their orphanage methods from traditional rural care, telling me that children in rural foster homes aren't doing as well as in the city; rural folks measured the quality of their children's development by things such as strength and height, rather than the range of activities and knowledge covered in Hongqi's evaluative practices.

As sites for preparing children for adoption in the United States and other Western countries, and thus for displaying modern standards of care for the benefit of both domestic and international eyes, the orphanages most involved in transnational adoption are in an intriguing liminal position. The material and symbolic resources that flow in and out of them give them the power to claim children and their care not only vis-à-vis ignorant rural families (the same ignorance blamed for the abandonment of children to begin with) but also vis-à-vis potentially interventionist American and European actors. In ways reminiscent of the tension between "let foreigners take care of them" and "we're selling off our children," there is space at the crossroads of care and consumption to claim Chinese modernity in particular ways.

Concluding Remarks

I once remarked to Director Yuan that I had heard members of American Christian organizations working in Chinese orphanages talk of being inspired to save individual children. Yuan became animated, pointing around the room: "Yeah, suppose she's an orphan child, and so am I, and so are they, and you save *her*? What about me, and them? So God is 'sending' you to go save one child and not the rest?" Not all children can be placed for adoption, and not all parents can adopt. But then by what principles do certain children get "saved"? Who make appropriate parents for them? And how are parents and children made recognizable to each other? All this happens by means of a transnational circuit of ideas and resources that revalue subjects in particularizing and increasingly standardized ways. I have tried in this chapter to foreground the ways in which preadoption practices rely on universal principles yet work to discipline people in relation to "normal" ways of being and doing (Foucault 1991b). The series of exchanges within the political economy of China/U.S. adoption that produces parents and children for each other echoes and foreshadows certain disciplinary forces of power: heterosexual, middle-class kinship; managed cultural and racial difference; modern nationhood; and techniques of individualized care.

Systemically, the complex circulation of ideologies and resources in adoption can feed on itself. I have included in this chapter the voices of actors located in institutional nodes of the adoption process in both China and the United States, and several expressed fears of being "cut off." A Chinese orphanage director worried that if she did not carefully account for her use of funds, the lifeline of foreign resources to the orphanage would be cut off; American agency administrators worried that knowledge about orphanage conditions or gay adoptions would cause Beijing to cut off the placement of children. The very reproduction of the adoption process thus depends to some extent on a set of exchanges fraught with exclusions and particularizations. But then again, possibilities for creative transformation are opened up: transnational benefits and resources often reach more than quintessentially adoptable healthy children and can underwrite local claims to modern care.

Why should it be contradictory for both parent and child to be clients of the caring practice of adoption? Part of the answer clearly lies in the market competition of adoption that creates values of exchange between desirable children and desiring parents; children are supposed to be the *sacra* outside of commodification, yet material and ideological resources are concentrated toward selecting and producing them for particular kinds of parents and kinship. As Rachael Stryker (2001) argues in her study of relationships between Russian orphanages and American adoptive parents, "the commodification of children and the emotional reconciliation it requires to do it have taken their toll, and this manifests itself in the exchange practices" (23). Ultimately, the tendency to naturalize the "universal" bond of kinship can blind us to the social contestations—whether racialized, gendered, or classed—through which "proper" parents and children are made. Yuan asked what social conditions make one child more adoptable than another, but this question is inextricable from what social conditions make one parent more able to adopt than another.

I thought of Yuan's question again the next day when I sat helping feed babies in the clean, bright, and efficient suite of rooms set up by World Alliance at Hongqi Orphanage. A group of American adoptive parents, some of whom had just adopted children from Hongqi, came through on a quick tour of the facilities. They stood out in the hallway, having traded their outside shoes for slippers per the regulations, and looked in at the babies and caregivers through the doors and windows. The caregivers and I went about our business, but I was aware, with them, of being on display; there we were, demonstrating good care for children who were marginalized enough, but not so much that they couldn't be revalued for a future with families that looked a lot like the ones looking in at us from the other side of the window. One extroverted woman in the group of American families teared up as she told me she realized what a nice facility this was, but it made her so sad to see all these babies without families. She then said aloud to the room full of babies, "There are families waiting for you in the U.S.," and, to express her thanks to the caregivers, proceeded to pass out postcards of American scenes stamped with the big block letters "USA." In this small scene, parents and children were naturalized for each other as *particular* parents and children. Modern and professional practices of care make Chinese children for American parents and produce the developing Chinese nation; the investments of the adoption system in this transnational philanthropic process make American parents for Chinese children and enact the already modern American nation. Other kinds of parents and children, as well as other forms of meeting children's needs, are perhaps too easily lost in this process.

The transformative possibilities of transnational projects—the potential for undoing national, class, gender, and racial hierarchies—begin with recognizing the unequal and particularizing practices, meanings, and claims through which subjects are interpellated into the process. Transformative possibilities also lie in recognizing the ways in which symbolic and material capitals fuel each other in the selection and preparation of adopted children and adoptive parents, constructing each in anticipation of a future imagined in overly narrow ways. But there is a diversity of possible futures and interests, made a bit more visible when the multiple locations of the adoption field are brought simultaneously into view. The multiple identities attendant on the child and her kinship become increasingly apparent as prospective parents receive their referral information and travel to China.

CHAPTER 3

Picturing Kinship

Do they deal them out
like face cards in a deck?
Baby pictures in adoption workers' hands . . .

. . . Official documents neatly stacked
link up waiting babies with waiting parents
in a two-step march:
baby   baby   baby   baby   baby   baby   baby
family family family family family family family

. . . Pictures shuffled, files shifted and the deck becomes Tarot.
These dealers must connect fates.
They grope for texture, seek skin and scent
beneath these papers to whisper "yes."

—Mary Cummings, adoptive mother[1]

The referral packet on a child that has been matched with particular prospective parents usually consists of a small photo and some basic health and background information. Yet this humble set of papers is a tipping point in the transnational adoption story. It is for parents what Jon Telfer (1999) calls "a vital perceptive and transformative moment" (148), especially coming as it does after the long haul of meeting with social workers, filling out paperwork, and perhaps mourning the pain and disappointment of infertility. It suggests the passage from mundane bureaucracy to magical bonds, from abstract, "nameless, faceless" child to individual child with unique features—to "our child." It is the first solid, readable sign that the emotional and material exchanges that have occurred thus far in the process will make good on their promises.

The "matching" of children in the Chinese welfare system with prospective parents in the United States—and some twenty other countries—is largely a mundane, march-step affair done by workers in Beijing. Files of parents and files of children work their way through various departments in the offices of the China Center of Adoption Affairs (CCAA), meeting in what is called, predictably enough, the "matching department." The political economy of kinship desires, but also of particular networks between overseas agencies and Chinese orphanages and officials, has already determined how some of that matching will go. Meiming, a woman who works in the CCAA offices, tells me it is fairly bureaucratic and straightforward: parents and children are matched in bunches by order of entry into the system, depending on such factors as age and location. (Special-needs matching goes through a separate process and is by necessity less mechanical.) But then Meiming gets animated and wonders out loud, how are we supposed to know we are matching the right child with the right family? How do we know the family will like the child matched with them? Of course, she adds, all those American parents want young, beautiful, smart children—like any parent would want. I commiserate with her about the strange role of matching children and parents across oceans and bureaucracies, and she smiles and says that even so, parents will ask her and her colleagues, "How did you know she was just the right child for us?" Bureaucratic process can and perhaps must be constructed as a conduit for fate.

The centerpiece of the package sent from Beijing to waiting American parents, which includes limited health and background information on the child, is the photo. In the first decade of the program it was usually a passport-size shot of a child's head, poking out from layers of clothing. Photos have become an increasingly important piece of what Cartwright (2003) calls "adoption image culture"; they serve as advertisements, family artifacts, and medical diagnostic tools. But what is so crucial about the referral photo is that it performs these functions around the individual child that a family will adopt. Along with the sparse information accompanying it, the photo is scrutinized and fetishized as a dense matrix of potentially fulfilled expectations. Is this the child we expected? Is she of the health status and age we hoped for? Can we imagine her as *ours*? Much of the work of fulfilling these expectations happens, as described in the previous chapter, through the trans-Pacific exchange of resources that produces particular kinds of children and parents for each other even before they are matched. But those general assurances of a kinship that will work for both parents and children are now translated into *a* child, into "the one."

The referral photo equally, and paradoxically, grounds parents in the reality of their adoption *and* magnifies the fantasy of connected fate: the magical whisper of "yes" of which poet Mary Cummings writes. These are both at work in the stories parents tell of the phone call they first received from the agency about the child referral, of their mad rush to go pick up the photo, of the mixture of anxiety and anticipation that surrounded opening the package of materials about the child. Some women likened these mixed sensations to those of pregnancy, as did adoptive mother Eileen Kretz:

> I felt like all of a sudden I was pregnant. It was like, we get this picture, and it's like, "Aagh!" (laughs) I really did! I felt like—actually it felt that way the whole way through, except the procedure was so slow, and then all of a sudden you have this baby waiting for you.

As with ultrasound images, the referral photo makes the child *real*. But a decision must also be made about whether to accept or deny a referral. This often means scrutinizing the photo and the scant medical information for signs of trouble. In fact, agencies encourage parents to have the information looked at by a physician, while making disclaimers about the possible inaccuracies of information sent by China—a real and notorious possibility, especially in the early years of the program. Josh and Gretta Peterman had expected a healthy toddler but were worried when the head circumference readings they received were quite small. After much agonizing consultation with their physician and some initial ire from Chinese officials, they turned down the referral and were assigned another toddler. Such scrutiny is also about other forms of belonging: the photo might be screened, however innocently, for ethnic desirability (Cartwright 2003) and for a sensibility of "right fit." And as with parents who admit they did not feel the expected bond with their birth children, a few adoptive parents told me in confessional tones that they had not

felt the proverbial connection to the photo they were sent; Josh Peterman said he had not felt especially bonded to his daughter until several
months after they went to China.

While sometimes the child in the photo is not the right child, the
adoption photo is invested with an intoxicating, almost supernatural
power to bond parent and child. So agencies also sometimes suggest that
prospective parents not look at the child's photo until after consulting
with their doctor, lest they find themselves split between love for the
child in the photo and uncertainty about the (same) child on paper with
medical problems. This is what Telfer (1999) refers to as asking parents to
put "head" before "heart." A child has been made for its prospective parents through bureaucracy, and so the match must be double-checked.
But the power of the photo takes over; if a child is to be theirs, something
more fantastic must be happening. Christy Kinsler and Debra Fine got a
medical report and photo for a child whose reported head and height
measurements "would have made her like, a bowling ball." But, added
Christy, "I looked at the paper and thought, this is our kid. And a number wasn't going to persuade me one way or the other. And it, it spoke to
Debra." Columnist Ellen Goodman expounded on the enchantment of the
photo in an Independence Day column in the *Boston Globe:*

> Just six weeks ago, Cloe was halfway around the world in an orphan-
> age in China. Six weeks before that, my stepdaughter and her husband
> got her photograph in the mail. It put a face—her face—on what had
> been a stack of papers, a mound of red tape, and, of course, a hope.
>
> Psychologists, neurologists, "ologists" of every variety may say it's
> impossible to bond to a photograph. But we connected to Cloe before
> she was named Cloe. We connected to her before she had any idea we
> existed or that there was a world outside the orphanage, outside the
> province, the country, the continent. ("Cloe's First Fourth," July 3,
> 2003: A13).

The referral photo marks the possibility of the child becoming real to
her parent(s) across the layers of geography that separate them. As some
families described it to me, the photo allowed them to let go of the haunting fear that they might not actually ever have their child. Constructed

under a theme of waiting and reprieve, it "signals the imminence of shared history" (Telfer 1999: 149). Many parents then begin to imagine and act on that history. They might launch into fully decorating the nursery, buying baby clothes they estimate will be the right size when they arrive in China a few months later, and telling family and friends. Here the photo often becomes fetishized as a sign of imminent kinship. Enlargements of the tiny photo are faxed or e-mailed to family and friends, laminated and hung around parents' necks like talismans, or put on Web sites chronicling adoption journeys and stories. One single mother made a mock magazine cover that featured her daughter's photo surrounded by headlines about the mother's impending trip to China to meet her. These rituals of using images to call kinship into being sometimes work in both directions, so that prospective adoptive families send photo albums of themselves to their waiting (usually older) children—"this will be your room, here is your new brother playing with the dog. . . ." Fred and Cindy Coombs imbued with special significance the substitution of human contact for the preadoption exchange of photos, when an acquaintance got to see their child in the orphanage prior to their actual trip to China:

> *Fred*: This was a time of thrilling tears.
> *Cindy*: This was a time when people had no information.
> *Fred*: A human being that we were communicating with had touched
> our child.

Preadoption "contact," especially in the form of the referral photo, takes on a life of its own that continues even beyond the adoption. As the first and one of the few pieces of tangible evidence of a child's life before adoption, it becomes emblematic of that preadoption life. But perhaps most important, the referral photo becomes a memento that links and invites comparison of the child's past and future. It is a piece of identity narrative that kick-starts the compulsive search for coherence between there and here, then and now, and in particular ways (Wheeler 1999; Hall 1996a); it produces history as a way of making sense of what has happened in both continuous and comparative terms. Many times when I visited adoptive families' homes in San Francisco or the Twin Cities, out would come life books and photo albums of their adoptive journey. And quite often, the referral photo was displayed early in the book as a solemn representation of the life that was. In some cases, it was folded into a fuller story of the history that connected the child to both China and the United States. In other cases, it served as a comparative "before" picture to the improved new life displayed in later pages of photos. Parents would then sometimes tell me, with a mixture of sadness and joy, "I can't believe she's the same child." Making such comparisons requires that she be, in some fundamental way, the same child. But with this mix of continuity and dislocation comes its own set of uncomfortable, ghostly presences of inequitable racial, familial, and national splitting—borders that are produced and made more visible with the migration of the child. The child is transformed, but *never completely,* and the next step in the process—the trip to China—helps reveal why: she is object and subject of multiple sets of social relations, making her many things at once.

CHAPTER 4

Client,
Ambassador,
and Gift

Managing Adoption
Exchange

> [E]xchange produces a set of social
> relations, communicates a cultural or
> symbolic value . . . , and secures routes
> of distribution and consumption.
> —Judith Butler (1997: 275)

Amid the pleasant buzz of a com-
fortable hotel lobby in a coastal Chinese city, an adoption facilitator spoke
to a white American man holding a little girl he had adopted just days before: "The officials want to know if you are satisfied with your new baby."
The facilitator was one of scores of mostly Chinese nationals who escort
American adoptive families through the two-week process of adopting
children in China, through a series of hotels and government offices
wherein is enacted the legal and social transfer of children from orphanages to adoptive families, from China to the United States. From parents'
perspectives, the trip usually looks something like this: travel to the city
where the child resides or nearest to where she resides; within the first
couple of days, meet the child in the hotel, a government office, or sometimes the orphanage reception area; visit several different government
offices to finalize the adoption legally; in between, spend some time in
the hotel or out in markets and tourist sites; and finally, travel to Guangzhou to get the child's medical check and visa at the U.S. consulate.

Actors and practices in these various spaces manage the fate of "shared history" between parent and child, imparting both material and symbolic legitimacy to transnational adoption exchange.

As suggested by the scene in the hotel lobby, this is serious business and delicate work, for while temporary and transitional, the adoption trip to China entails intense interactions between people with varying relationships to the child—foster parents and orphanage caregivers, adoption officials and professionals, adoptive parents, and even casual observers on the streets of China. The transfer of the child thus takes place in an overdetermined space between the past and future, here and there (Bauman 1999; Bourdieu 1990 [1980]) of the adopted child's life. Ambiguous and multiple meanings surround the child as she is disconnected from and relocated in two different families, nations, and cultures. It is a moment, on the cusp of migration, when it is uncertain whether she "belongs" to one, both, or neither. Her transferral unsettles the relationship "of a nation to 'its' citizens, a parent to 'its' child, or a person to his or her 'nature'" (Yngvesson 2002: 232).

The child is many things but cannot be all of them—she must be made to belong to her adoptive family, despite and because of difference. As I have thus far described the political economy of Chinese adoptions, institutions and ideologies in China produce girls who cannot be kept; institutions and ideologies in the United States produce parents who can and want to adopt them; and transnationally circulating resources and discourses operate to produce them for each other. But in the phase of the adoption process when this linkage is most direct, namely, when parents travel to China to meet and adopt their children, the contradictions that produce adoptive kinship come close to the surface, threatening exposure. For when a practice of exchange is put into conversation with the productive activities that precede and anticipate it, its attendant inequalities are revealed (Butler 1997; di Leonardo 1993; Perrons 1999). Because of the multiple people and places with preexisting attachments and claims to the now-migrating child, the question arises of whether and how the social relations of exchange that must finally seal adoptive kinship will be reciprocal or inequitable. The traces of abandonment and orphanage life meet the traces of the adoptive life for which the child has been prepared, begging us to ask "through what mandatory exclusions the sphere of reproduction becomes delineated and naturalized" (Butler 1997: 273–74).

The intense two weeks in China when facilitators, bureaucrats, and parents manage the production of adoptive kinship entail the elision and reproduction of a globalized order of nations (Malkki 1992, cited in Yngvesson 2002: 245) that is both gendered and raced. To understand this process, we must look at the double-sided distinctions that make adoptive kinship in the moments when child is transferred to parents. What is being produced, and what does this in turn tell us about what or who is being excluded or contained? And how do these exclusions and differences make exchange possible even as they are all the more exposed? In short, what must be managed, and why? Marilyn Strathern (1988) suggests that the answers to these questions must start with *representations* of exchange. She asks, "If one relocates the question of production as the production of social relations through circulation (of items, food, women, children, and men), by what mystifications do people represent these structures?" (153) We might also frame this as a question of the *symbolic capital* by which the exchange of other forms of capital is legitimated (Bourdieu 1987).[1]

This chapter considers three particular tropes that help legitimate the exchange of the child: she is variously constructed—or mystified—as *client, ambassador,* and *gift.* Each of these representations of the migrating child positively produces adoptive kinship, even as it simultaneously might exclude or negate (1) other possibilities for giving meaning to the process and (2) particular actors and practices through which the exchange process is even made possible. Perhaps most powerfully, these three ways of imagining the child do the labor of taming and circumventing commodification. As Anagnost (1997) points out, "The anxiety that the child might be a commodity is aroused by the incontrovertible fact that as the child moves from one site of nurture to another, money has to change hands; agencies are established; 'baby flights' are chartered; tour packages are assembled" (8). These facts come to a head, around the child, during those two weeks in China.

In this chapter I unpack the tropes of "client," "ambassador," and "gift"—individually and in relation to each other—to examine the legitimating, exclusionary, but also transformative power of what Butler suggests exchange does: produces social relations, expresses value, and secures routes of circulation. But it is also important, Butler reminds us, that these practices of exchange are powerful not just because they persist but also because they are changeable and multifaceted; the multiple meanings given to the adopted child might reproduce dominant forms of power but can never do so completely. As we see in placement practices in China, exchange produces new relationships around the migrating child and may enchain people in broader layers of social relations (Yngvesson 2002).

Travels with Charlie and Sheila

The experiences of one white couple—Charlie and Sheila—whose travel group I accompanied during part of their trip through China, help introduce the multiple and uncertain meanings, uneven relations of exchange, and emotional tugs that mark the transfer of kinship. As with other parents from the United States who travel to China to adopt their children, Charlie and Sheila suddenly found themselves face to face with the child whom they had only known through a small photo and an unfamiliar name:

> The dozen or so parents sit on sofas and chairs in a waiting area of the hotel in Fudao, listening to Harry, their Chinese facilitator, tell them they will meet their children in just fifteen minutes. In fact, he tells them, the children are already downstairs. People look around as if caught off guard, and some mutter that they need time to go back to their rooms and get their cameras. Charlie and Sheila run to get theirs, handing me a video camera. A titter goes through the room and I turn to see three babies in padded yellow outfits come off the elevator in the arms of Chinese women who look both expectant and wary. People kind of stare and then urge forward a bit, asking which orphanage the kids are from. "Jinlong" echoes through the room. "Oh, that's us!" says one couple, as everyone surveys the little group of babies. A single mom asks for names and when an *ayi* says a child's name she takes in her breath and says, "Ahhh, that's me!" Soon Sheila is standing next

to me with her new baby. She says, "I just knew when someone said there were some babies in yellow downstairs that our baby had arrived. I just knew it!"

The moments when parents and children meet can be constructed as both magical and mundane, caring and commodified. On a more literal level, they are constructed by adoption officials, travel facilitators, and orphanage caregivers who with varying degrees of visibility facilitate the translocation of children from one family and nation to another. Along with adoptive parents, these actors put labor into legitimating the historical and cultural conditions of the exchange. Harry was one of scores of Chinese and Chinese American facilitators who work full- or part-time, independently or with travel or adoption agencies, to take parents through the process; they book hotels, make appointments at Chinese government offices, check and recheck paperwork, translate, share cultural information, arrange tours, and facilitate the transfer of U.S. dollars to the appropriate offices and organizations in China. The caregivers come from orphanages small and big, near and far, or from foster homes affiliated with those orphanages. In this case, the women that stepped off the elevator included two orphanage *ayis* and one foster mother who had traveled for about seven hours and would stay for one more day—long enough to be present at the adoption ceremony—before returning to their small city. Local bureaucrats are a third category of important actors who manage the legal and financial transactions of transnational adoption.

At the front of the Civil Affairs Office meeting room, a Chinese official lines up small black-and-white stuffed pandas in neat rows on the desk, China's national flag hanging behind her. When she is done with this task, and Harry has explained what will happen next, the young official calls up each family by their child's Chinese and English names. Charlie and Sheila sit nervously with their daughter; they are missing an important piece of paperwork and Harry is still working with local officials for final approval. In practiced English, the Civil Affairs official quietly reads each family their adoption certificate and then hands over the certificate and a toy panda. Charlie and Sheila are finally called up. They come back to their chairs and sit close, looking at their certificate, crying quietly, while the official calls up the next family.

Facilitators and officials regulate and manage the procedures of adoption across borders in response to, or in spite of, an uncertain terrain. It is uncertain in part because of a myriad of bureaucratic requirements[2] that have become increasingly standardized and rigid since the mid-1990s but also because the abandoned and adopted child comes with a history that attaches her in palpable ways to two different families and nations, and to the exclusions of race, gender, and class that make the relationships between them. These uncertainties are extenuated by the work of facilitators but also by the safety and familiarity of the spaces through which facilitators escort parents: comfortable Western-style hotels and restaurants, government offices increasingly outfitted for adoption (e.g., stuffed pandas and English-speaking officials), tourist sites, and the minibuses that shuttle families from one to the other. But not all can be contained, and when parents venture out of the buffering effect of these spaces or the uninitiated wander into them, the multiple categories of belonging that circumscribe kinship come to the fore.

> I sit in a restaurant with Charlie and Sheila and their ten-month-old baby of three days, who contentedly sits in her new mother's lap. Her parents are eager to connect to both their child and this country, Charlie digging into his noodles and singing a Chinese children's song he has memorized. People around us are amused, watchful. An older woman walks by, stopping to look with puzzlement at this Chinese baby with white parents. With Charlie and Sheila's consent, I explain to her that the child is adopted. "*Bu xiang(3) tade mama ma?*" she asks. Doesn't she miss her mother? I explain that she has been in an orphanage since not long after birth. "Mmm," she says, thinking. She looks at Sheila and the baby and says, "*Bu xiang(4) tade mama.*" She doesn't look like her mother.[3]

Later Charlie and Sheila tell me how strange they feel about taking their daughter away from China. I ask why, and Sheila says because it feels "like a new form of imperialism, at least ideologically." But still, she says, she knows it's probably good for everybody involved.

The "good" of adoption lies in tension with the "unnatural" kin and colonial relations it simultaneously recalls. This tension is heightened by the proximity of American parents, Chinese children, and Chinese observers during the trip to China, when looking different becomes a clue that a chain of relationships of belonging is out of joint.[4] Even after several years of spending lots of time with transracial and transnational adoptive families, I too was startled the first time I walked into a hotel restaurant in China and saw about twenty Chinese babies in the arms of white Americans and Europeans. The work of constructing value and legitimacy takes on particular urgency in transnational and transracial adoption processes because family is an important site of gendered and racialized national reproduction that, as Sheila implies, has an unsettled imperialist history (Balibar 1988b; Stoler 1997; McClintock 1995). That children are supposed to be immune to commodification further necessitates a narration that counters the notion of a global market in children. For all these reasons—the symbolic sacredness of children, histories of unequal transnational exchange, and assumptions of natural belonging—public and private acknowledgments of difference ("she doesn't look like her mother") call for engagement with the conditions that connect individuals and families to national and global histories, namely, to their political and cultural economies. Constructions of the child as client, ambassador, and gift point to those conditions precisely because they serve to manage them.

Clients, Ambassadors, and Gifts

On July 4, 2001, Immigration and Naturalization Service (INS) Commissioner Doris Meissner visited the China Center of Adoption Affairs (CCAA), China's headquarters for overseeing international adoption. The CCAA gave special recognition to this unusual visit on its Web site, devoting space to photos of the commissioner and CCAA director Guo Sijin shaking hands and to the texts of their official remarks. These remarks used all three representations of the child, as client, ambassador, and gift, to praise the transnational relations produced by and through adoption. Director Guo's remarks included the following phrases:

The point of departure of our work is to take into consideration the best interest of the children. . . . [W]e are convinced that the children . . . will certainly become the people-to-people friendly ambassadors between our two countries.

And then came words from Commissioner Meissner:

[T]hanks for a foreign adoption program that is renowned for its transparency and predictability . . . each child is a gift from China that will shape our country for generations to come. . . . [We] look forward to enhancing further such cooperation.[5]

As used in state and popular discourses, these tropes speak to interconnected emotional, social, political, and economic forms of value. "Client," "ambassador," and "gift" have the effect of characterizing adoption exchange as a service-oriented practice that, through the figure of the child, facilitates meaningful relationships among nations and peoples. In other words, they accomplish the tasks of exchange invoked by Butler: producing social relations, communicating value, and thus reproducing adoption in particular ways.

In everyday practices and understandings of exchange during parents' two weeks in China, all three of these representations converge around legitimating adoption across borders. One particularly poignant example of this is the increasingly common practice among American parents of carrying a small card, mimicking the size and look of a business card, that can be given out to people they meet in China. The card explains in both English and Chinese why they are in China and what a Chinese child is doing in their non-Chinese arms. One version displays a photo and name of the child on one side, and on the other, this explanation (in Chinese and *pinyin,* as well as English): "I come to China to adopt a little Chinese girl. I will always love her and will teach her about beautiful China." In one stroke, a recognizable symbol of contractual exchange becomes a vehicle for communicating emotional exchange; it signals adoption as a trustworthy act of care on behalf of the client-child, whose cultural ambassadorship will be preserved by her adoptive mother, who in turn is grateful for the gift of the child. It communicates a universal personhood for the child, albeit in reference to a Chinese past and an American future.

That a business card explaining adoption is even necessary or desirable indicates that the ambiguities and contradictions of China/U.S. adoption invite and require intervening narratives. The goal of formal and informal adoption proceedings—the creation of a permanent relationship between child and parent—must particularize an excess of meanings. In this way, invocations of ambassador, client, and gift are a response to class contradictions, cultural imaginings, national inequalities, and gendered exclusions. At the same time, they construct forms of global kinship that might creatively reckon with new ways of belonging; the woman observing Charlie and Sheila could, if somewhat hesitantly, acknowledge Sheila as *mama*. There is enough uncertainty in the exchange to undermine automatic reproduction of naturalized ways of being, but it is precisely because of this uncertainty that the process demands narratives and practices of legitimation.

In the pages that follow, I analyze each of the three representations of client, ambassador, and gift in turn. I first look at their idealized meanings and the particular kinds of adoptive kinship they are meant to produce, then turn to examine the ideas, actors, and practices they occlude and exclude. I conclude with the implications of the three tropes, considered together, for the reproduction of the adoption system itself.

Distinguishing Clients: In the Service of Kinship

To narrate the child as client echoes an increasingly international discourse of children's best interests, which usually conjures "client" in the sense of a beneficiary of social care and welfare. At the same time, "client" conjures up efficient and, as Commissioner Meissner used it, transparent bureaucratic practices. Both senses of the word are often at play in the discourses of officials and facilitators in both China and the United States. The display in one provincial civil affairs office speaks simultaneously of "multiple functions of nurturing, medical care, recuperation and education" and a "modern administrative system" in the management of orphan adoption. The U.S. consulate in Guangzhou, where all American parents must go as they exit China to pick up their children's immigrant visas, also uses both meanings of "client." The Web site of the consular unit handling adoption visas depicts a smiling Chinese baby girl who is declared "A happy client!"[6] The "best interest of children" thus smoothly incorporates pastoral care and the disciplinary governing of individuals (Foucault 1980).

We know from preadoption practices that there are two clients in this process: parent and child. And it is during the two-week trip to China that they are most closely held up together as clients. Here, the work of facilitators, officials, and caregivers contributes to the creation of kinship through the personal, cultural, and bureaucratic services they provide. Eddie, the Chinese facilitator for a large adoption agency based in the United States, narrated his work of transferring child to parent as a combination of the business of serving parents and the business of caring for children. As we sat and talked on a bench in Guangzhou—Eddie dressed smartly in a casual suit, answering cell-phone calls, and checking his watch—he described a kind of circle of benefit whereby his group of assistants worked hard for both parents and children. He told me, "American people are good. If you work hard for them, they give back" (meaning, in the form of tips, which his agency tells parents are expected in China). Later he added, "I don't mind to change diapers, being a kind of nanny for the families." Many facilitators echoed Eddie's assessment of their work as both a business opportunity and a labor of care. Jane, another facilitator, put it this way: "At first I thought of it as only a business, but now I do it for the babies and families, because I can feel the love between them."

But we also know that as practices of exchange work to produce a social relationship between parent and child, the multiple symbolic values of the child may be in tension with the necessities of securing routes of distribution. Some meanings given to the child, and to her exchange, are at odds with the needs and desires of the parent-client—the client who, as social worker Carrie Betts put it, pays "my salary . . . [and] whose goodwill we must maintain." It is here that the meaning of "client" undergoes a double splitting between parent and child, market and care. Eddie's "circle of benefit" is driven to a certain extent by the cash that comes from parents' pockets. Both he and Daniel, another facilitator I met in Guangzhou, told me they thought that market competition between facilitators wasn't necessarily a bad thing, since it meant more children would be placed and facilitators would be motivated to provide more caring service. But in practice, this abstracted exchange of economic capital for symbolic value distinguished between clients; material exchange naturalized differentiated needs. Daniel told me, "Some wealthy guys [meaning parents] will pay more to get more intensive care . . . different people have different needs, and we just satisfy them." The differentiation of care along material lines intersected with national-cultural distinctions—Arthur asserted that some facilitators figure, "Americans have money, so hey, we can charge more." When I asked Daniel about tipping, he said he depends on tips from parents, but it can't be the most important thing since some Europeans don't tip. Then, with a smile, he added, "You can't assume you'll have Americans every time!"

So why even bother calling the child being adopted a client? Parents themselves would rarely, if ever, refer to their adopted children as such, yet (caring and competitive) brokers of adoption go out of their way to confirm that the child is the "ideal client," the representative of what is good and right about the exchange, and the ultimate recipient of the tour and adoption services paid for by parents. Even as U.S. consular staff in Guangzhou spoke of adoptive parents as political clientele well-situated to shape the quality of their service, they made a point of telling me that protecting the soon-to-be-citizen child's interests was central to their job of processing adoption immigration. The child becomes a client of caring practices, but *through* the power of the parent as client of marketized political practices. As the facilitator I overheard in the hotel lobby put it to a parent, "The officials just want to know if you are satisfied with your new baby."

Abstracting the child as "ideal client" thus serves to manage, among other things, the threat of commodification. It is not just children but parents and the adoption system itself that must be buffered from commodification, in order to keep intact the symbolic value of the exchange. And it is often facilitators who serve as buffers, juggling the various kinds of capital exchanged in the process. Veteran Chinese facilitators have learned to absorb contradictions, even when they are personally uncomfortable.[7] For example, Arthur told me that local administrators, knowing the powerful symbolic value of the children they are placing for adoption, sometimes add extra charges at the last minute that he then has to figure out how to explain to parents. Larry gave me the example of disgustedly but quietly watching an orphanage director who knew nothing about the children in his own orphanage count out the donation money from adoptive parents, then hold up the crisp U.S. $100 bills to ask semi-jokingly, "Are these fake?" Larry and Arthur would never relay these experiences to their direct clients: parents who in the vulnerable moments of exchange need (pay?) to be protected from signs of a commodified child. Larry understood that in these moments, multiple kinds of value hovered around the child; when I asked him if he thought transnational adoption in general was a marketized process, he threw the question back at me by responding, "If you think so, you think so."

The child must remain client for yet another reason. Adoption exchange, if done according to transnationally circulating standards of both caring and contractual service, suggests the more equal, modern relationship between China and the Western world desired by many Chinese and expressed in state nationalism. The combination of transparent business practice and humanitarian individualism serves, in turn, to legitimate the system of China/U.S. adoption itself, assuring its continuity. So while individual parents and children are only temporarily clients of adoption facilitation, clienthood as a discourse is perpetually reproductive of modernity for China, of the political economy of adoption, and, more immediately, of the jobs of people who labor to make it happen. Once again, the costs of absorbing the contradictions of the process can fall on facilitators. A Chinese facilitator named Lana found herself stuck between the client services demanded by marketized adoption exchange and the social services no longer provided under a marketized Chinese economy. She wept during our interview, which came after several long days of helping a rather demanding U.S. couple visit cultural sites and shop the city, beyond Lana's expected duties. Lana depended heavily on tips to care for her own family—her parents had been laid off, her grandmother was ill, and there was little of a social safety net for either—and these particular adoptive parents gave her nothing for her extra work. The travel agency Lana worked for paid a low base salary, and the U.S. adoption agency had not informed this family that tips were expected. Lana begged me not to tell anyone, afraid that her complaint might cost her her job.

This is not to downplay Jane's point that it was the love between parents and children that made her impassioned about her work. The benefits to children who are adopted, to the parents who adopt them, and to those who get meaningful material and symbolic rewards from facilitating the meeting of child and parent cannot be denied. But the above examples point us toward the inequities that necessitate the discourse of the child-as-client. Making her "right" for parents entails making distinctions among clients that ideally are not commodified yet in reality threaten to be. This is perhaps no more evident than in those intense moments when the idealized, abstracted child-client—the object of parents' desires, made only partially real in a photo—finally emerges as a flesh-and-blood child. Parents sometimes face situations where a seemingly irresolvable contradiction arises between the ideal and real child, throwing into question the compatibility of care and market. There are very difficult cases, for example, where parents arrive in China to find that a child healthy on paper is very ill in person. Aaron Kretz described watching a parent in his travel group decide she couldn't keep the child assigned to her because the baby was so sickly and said, "That was pretty difficult. Because from the moment we had the photo we were clear this was our daughter."

Such situations complicate the relationship between "parental choice" and a "choice child"—a relationship that preadoption practices were supposed to take care of. Suddenly, parents must make a choice impossibly situated at the juncture of care and market. In almost every one of these cases that I know about, agencies and facilitators have emphasized that parents have a choice, and parents have usually chosen to keep the child. But in those uncertain hours or days of indecision, services of both care and efficiency are put into high gear—doctors are brought in, calls are made back to social workers in the United States, the possibility of adopting another child is looked into. And once again, facilitators absorb and buffer the uncertainty of the exchange. Arthur said that these kinds of cases were one of the hardest parts of his job, as he had to supply emotional labor to supporting parents as clients of care *and* supply a choice to them as business clients; meanwhile, the client status of the child hangs in the balance. Yet he once quietly told me that in some cases he did not know what he would do if the parents decided not to take the child: what would he tell the officials and the orphanage, whose good graces were crucial to securing routes of adoption? As Aiqing put it, orphanage directors "want to please the parents so that we won't say anything bad about the orphanage. . . . If we complain that their child is not raised well, and has malnutrition, those orphanages are going to be in trouble. Because then you are making [the director of the CCAA] lose face, and making China lose face."

Yet parents almost always make the real child their own ideal child. Sean and Diane Scott were given a different child than had appeared in their referral photo but felt very strongly that they had received the right child. "I even thought she looked like me," said Diane (who is Chinese American), laughingly admitting that the resemblance wasn't necessarily there, but it felt that way. But this process of making a child your own—distinctly yours—is more than a mental leap of faith; it entails ongoing practices of particularizing kinwork. In the short two weeks in China, this happens in very tangible, physical ways. Over breakfast or shuffling between offices and cultural sites on the bus, adoptive parents compare notes on children's rashes, bites, coughs, neck control, head shape, and such. Much is made of children's rapid progress after placement; the first time a child smiles or clings to her new mom is a sign that a child is becoming one's own. These micropractices around children's bodies start to distinguish between a child's Chinese past and her American future. It is sometimes difficult to acknowledge both simultaneously. A few days into one adoption trip, a couple parents remarked to me that their children still smelled like the orphanage; one mother said that at least Johnson's Baby Wash was beginning to take over, and now it was just her daughter's bowel movements that still smelled "like sauerkraut or something." And a number of parents have changed their girls out of their smelly orphanage clothes as soon as they can, with the babies appearing at the next meal in the hotel restaurant in fresh, crisp Baby Gap outfits.

However, remaking a child's symbolic value in the social processes of adoption exchange is not a straightforward process. Judith Butler (1993) asserts in *Bodies That Matter* that "bodies never quite comply with the norms by which their materialization is impelled" (2). She argues that the very attempt to fix the body is what opens up the possibility for other articulations. Indeed, some parents later have deep regrets about shedding the outfit their child was wearing when they first met. Several years after adopting her daughter, adoptive mother Joan Spencer cried as she told me how much she regretted throwing those clothes away, because at the time they would have carried a familiar smell and feel to her daughter, and now they would be a precious piece of her sketchy preadoption history and a tangible connection to China. For these reasons, one well-respected facilitator makes a point of suggesting to parents that they not be so quick to whisk their children off for a bath and a change. The transformation of the child does not need to happen so quickly. In fact, it cannot, because the multiplicity of gendered, raced, and national meanings around the child prevents attempts to affix new identities, especially when parent and child are still in China, surrounded by the strange newness of each other, of Chinese landscapes and cityscapes, and of the curious picture they paint for those who observe them.

Ambiguous Ambassadors: The Cultural Brokerage of Kinship

If the child-as-client discourse does the work of softening the marketized power of the parent-client and producing the child as object of care, then the child-as-ambassador discourse does the work of softening the globalized power of adopting nations and producing the child as subject of cultural exchange. This is especially apparent from the perspective of Chinese people observing the transfer of Chinese children to foreign families and nations, and of transnational adoption officials in both China and the United States who wear its public face. In this case, adoption is read as creating positive relations between nations and cultures that might otherwise be rightly suspected of reproducing a global order of nations. The discourse of "little ambassadors" manages this uncertainty by making children culturally specific subjects of a universal process of belonging. In other words, it suggests an embodied cultural and national representation and the promise of goodwill across borders. Many Chinese facilitators spoke of children as cultural bridges and said that part of their job was introducing new adoptive parents to Chinese culture, or at least to the city and province of their child's origins; some spoke idealistically of how these children might come back to China someday to help it develop. And a number of observers of adoptive family groups on the street would give a "thumbs up," sometimes saying how lucky these girls were to go to the United States, sometimes indicating they were proud that foreign parents would want Chinese children.

In the historical context of this study, ambassadorship is especially potent. In the 1990s, a confident cultural pride was on the rise in China, "given form by nationalism as a way of talking and thinking and seeing the world" (Calhoun 1997, quoted in Guo 2004: xiv). Not only do various versions of Chinese nationalism both envy and resent the political, economic, and cultural power of the United States in particular (Guo 2004; Madsen 1995), but official relations between the two countries are continually strained because of forms of border crossing much more threatening than adoption. In 2001, when INS commissioner Meissner visited the CCAA and praised the diplomatic power of adoption, a U.S. spy plane crashed on Hainan Island, China detained several Chinese American scholars, and China joined the World Trade Organization (WTO) amid protests of human rights violations.

In constructing adoption as an arbiter of equitable social relationships between different nations and cultures—with Chinese children and their American parents acting as proxies—ambassadorship contributes to securing the reproduction of the adoption system and its routes of distribution. From the perspective of both official and nonofficial Chinese actors, then, the child takes on value as social capital for the nation. This social capital translates into an ongoing circuit of "cooperative" processes, such as mutual visits by official adoption delegations, families, and other exchanges inspired by the generosity of cross-cultural understanding. An exchange program for Chinese high school students to the United States, for example, regularly contacts adoptive families as potential hosts; more powerfully, Chinese television broadcasts and print-media stories tend to report not only how well children are doing in the United States but how committed their parents are to teaching them about Chinese culture.[8]

The quality of the ambassadorship of the child thus relies, somewhat problematically, on the goodwill of parents to "adopt" Chinese culture. Their two weeks in China expose parents directly (many for the first time) to Chinese culture (however they might interpret it) but also are a crucial opportunity to make their children their own. As with practices of hygiene and clothing, practices of naming children illustrate, first, the limbo of the child's cultural and national identity and, second, how that uncertainty is tamed and managed.

> The morning after the children are transferred to their new parents' care, I ask adoptive parents Paul and Ling what their daughter's name is and they say they haven't chosen one yet. When I say they might need one today for official paperwork, Paul looks a little surprised. Later at the Civil Affairs Office I slip over to see how their paperwork is going, and look down to see a capital "M" under the question, "Will your child have a new name? Please write it below." I chuckle and ask if that's as far as they've gotten. "So what do you think of the name Melody, and how would you spell it?" asks Paul, showing me a little scrap of paper on which he has written two different spellings.

While almost all parents assign their children a "new name," there is a brief period of uncertainty in which parents do not know quite what to call them. I noted that for the first few days of the trip, the children were often just "the baby" or "she." This is something we might expect from any new parent, but in transnational adoption the exclusive relationship between parents and children is forged across differences of language, race, culture, and parentage. As adoptive mom Barbara told me one morning in our hotel, her one-year-old woke up crying in the night, saying, *"Baba, mama"* (asking for her foster mother and father in Chinese), and "didn't even recognize me." This limbo can be unnerving for both child and parent and begs for clarification of the different "parts" of a child's identity. Later, in the hotel dining room where adoptive families from different travel groups often ran across each other and shared experiences, another American woman asked Barbara what her baby's name was, and Barbara replied, "Her name is Brigitte, but she also answers to Qiu Qiu, her Chinese name." Indeed, I heard most parents respond to this question with their child's new name (usually a Euro-American name) and then add "and her Chinese name is . . ." How quickly the adopted child's new identity is formed, in spite of, or in response to, the ambiguous space of the exchange. It must be noted, however, that toddlers and older children are harder to detach from names and people and places.

That a name belonging to a child just a few days previous can become an afterthought clouds the mission of the child-ambassador. The child's Chinese history is not necessarily lost with her Chinese name, but it is read in particular ways—sometimes as backward or exotic. The renaming of the child as American (and thus tacitly more universal) subject is in some cases built through a cultural and material particularizing of China as a place that cannot or will not take care of its children, especially its girls. For some parents, this means putting China "behind" them and hence jettisoning a child's Chinese name. In other cases, however, the appeal of a child's Chineseness can lend magic to her unpleasant history. One new American mother, Jan, expressed delight that Chinese friends in the United States had told her the character for her daughter's name meant "orchid." But while she was in China, Jan found out in a short conversation with the orphanage director that actually it was the name of the small town where the orphanage was located. This was disappointing for Jan—a mythical and exotic history was replaced by a much less interesting fact.

But these less interesting facts are what make up children's histories. In fact, their "old names" point to a host of other histories and people that bring parent and child together: the policies that shaped their abandonment, the places they were found, the orphanage caregivers who named them, the bureaucrats who recorded their information, the foster mothers who rocked them to sleep. Renaming a child may begin to write a new history for her, but the necessity of assigning her a new name and handing out a business card to explain her adoption demonstrates the power of these unwritten histories.

The ambiguity of children's representation—what they represent to people in China and the United States, and how those people represent them—becomes especially apparent in the ways that Chinese and Americans read each other through just-adopted children. Children's bodies become the object not only of their parents' attention but also of scrutiny by Chinese people they encounter in shops, on the street, or even in the hotel lobby. Chinese responses to children's dress are predictable enough to have become a kind of joke among adoptive parents and agencies (in one travel group, adoptive parents would wryly speak of the "clothes police"). As I traveled with parents in the winter months, shopkeepers and random passersby would cluck at how little clothing the children were wearing. Any area of exposed skin was cause for teasing and scolding directed at parents. Some parents handled this good-naturedly, but others retreated, upset at the scrutiny given to their children and to their parenting. "Cultural difference" explained but did not necessarily alleviate the discomfort of being between cultural spaces, as my field notes attest:

> Adoptive mom Tasha and I are chatting in the lobby about her shopping adventures. She tells me with a mixture of humor and exasperation that in one store the female clerks had remarked on her daughter's thin socks. They kept trying to put shoes or slippers on her baby's feet for her to buy, and finally Tasha firmly but gently pushed people away, saying, "No." "I'm sure they think I'm so rude," she said, "but . . . ," as if to say hey, there are limits to my cultural tolerance when it comes to my kid.

The point of relating these simple encounters is to connect them to a larger context of ambiguity about the ambassadorship of children. As Chinese people read transnational adoptive families, and as adoptive families read China, contradictions arise that expose the limited reach of national and cultural representation. And as suggested throughout, racial difference becomes an especially salient touchstone for histories of familial, national, and cultural difference. Many times as we walked through markets or traversed airports, our group of white adults with Chinese babies stimulated responses from Chinese onlookers that varied from delight to consternation. "She looks Chinese," many people would remark about a child. And when I would confirm that she was, conversations were often marked by the twin responses of skepticism and admiration.

> On the plane to Guangzhou, our last stop before the families head back to the U.S., I sit with Barbara and her one-year-old daughter Brigitte. Soon the gentleman across the aisle is leaning forward to engage me in conversation, and surmises the child must be adopted. He nods kind of slowly and thoughtfully as he watches Brigitte, and says he has seen several families like this before. He asks where we are from, and I tell him the United States. "Mmm," he says, "this child will have good opportunities." I venture to ask this man what he thinks about

international adoptions, and he cocks his head in thoughtfulness and says, "*Women juede qiguai*" (We think it's strange). But then he adds, raising his eyebrows and forcing a little smile (as if to convince himself as much as us), "*Aixin meiyou guojie*" (Love has no borders). Yes, I say, these parents do love their children. "Most of them do, don't they," he replies. When I ask if he thinks these children are still Chinese, he glances over at Brigitte sitting and playing on her mother's lap and says, "Well, we hope they will know where their roots are." I translate this conversation back to Barbara, who says yes, of course she will teach her daughter about China.

This observer's mixed response raises a specter of unequal historical relations between China and Western nations that I encountered repeatedly in China. When people spoke of "little ambassadors," they sometimes accompanied this with a little laugh of uncertainty at its idealism. Conversations with taxi drivers or fellow train passengers revealed that international adoption invoked collectively constructed memories of experiments on Chinese children in the 1930s by Japanese colonial occupiers (Japan is usually included as a "Western power"). And it invoked ambivalent reminders of China's "lag" relative to the United States, a nation both envied and despised as a world superpower. One memorable conversation with a Chinese worker who sat across from me on a long train ride turned from platitudes about the benefits of adoption for "relations between our two countries" to a critique of American intervention in world affairs. But as often as Chinese people wondered if maybe Americans adopted Chinese children to harvest their organs or use them as domestic labor, they would humorously add, "Is she going to the U.S.? Can *I* be adopted?" One Chinese professor told me some friends had also jokingly asked if he could help them "abandon" their children and then make sure they got to a home in America. Adoption thus serves as a reminder of the dream of migration to the United States, but also of its unattainability for most people. Child-as-ambassador is a tenuous and necessary response to such contradictions.

Adopted children can certainly symbolize and represent China, but they do so by standing both inside and outside it. And, however ironically, abandonment might serve the cause of ambassadorship. While the practices that sever legal and social ties to birth family and nation facilitate the transformation of the child-client into a member of adoptive family and nation—for example, the changes enacted on her body, described above—they simultaneously and perhaps paradoxically serve to facilitate the potential transformation of the child-ambassador into cultural and political representative of the Chinese national family. Abandoned children are marginalized and somewhat shameful symbols of China's quest for a modern, disciplined population (Anagnost 1999). But by leaving the nation, and perhaps only by leaving the nation and becoming part of another one, the children can represent China positively, stuffed pandas in tow.

Chinese observers did not always agree about the "Chineseness" of abandoned and internationally adopted children, but one particular sequential reading of the children seemed to prevail: through birth they inevitably carried a certain cultural and historical essence in their "Chinese blood"; abandonment loosened this essential tie and curtailed full national citizenship; but then, adoption suggested a restoration of identity, if tenuously Chinese. When I would explain to chance acquaintances in China that the children in the arms of these foreigners were from orphanages (i.e., not bought or stolen, as some wondered), and that the parents who adopted them often were not able to have children by birth, their discomfort was often visibly allayed. In other words, that these were girls already outside naturalized routes of biological and social reproduction helped legitimate their exchange, as they took on value they could generally not have as marginal citizens in the Chinese context. This point is further illustrated by the deeper skepticism reportedly expressed toward foreign families who adopt healthy boys (why would a boy be available?) or who are accompanied in China by their birth children (why would they want to adopt if they can have children of their own?).

In other words, adoption promises to transform abandoned children's status as symbols of exclusion from the Chinese national family into symbols of global inclusion for both child and nation. A Chinese journalist who covers international adoption said to me, with some moral indignation, "Abandoned children in China are children without a country," but then, in discussing international adoption, said, "Love has no borders." Constructing children as ambassadors thus does the tenuous narrative labor of erasing the problematic material and symbolic burden of China's orphans and easing their translocation through adoption. It also helps resolve the tension between the image of China as, on the one hand, a modernizing, globalizing nation and, on the other, a backward nation that produces so many abandoned children. Adoptive ambassadorship thus fends off the kind of critique leveled at China in an October 2003 cartoon in the *Milwaukee Journal Sentinel* (http://www.jsonline.com). Published at the time of one of China's celebrated space missions, the cartoon depicted little Chinese girls in space outfits, marching two-by-two into a government rocket; the government cadre looking on says, "Ah, Space! It not only enhances our image, it solves the problem of what to do with all those excess females." Not surprisingly, some online adoptive parent groups called for a letter-writing campaign to the *Sentinel* for its insensitivity to "Chinese girls and to the many American couples who have adopted Chinese infant girls," as the *Journal Sentinel* wrote in an editorial response (October 22, 2003). The cartoon uncomfortably displayed the other side of adoptive ambassadorship, displacing the image of children getting onto planes in the arms of their new adoptive parents with a less palatable form of departure.

From the perspective of many Chinese observers, ambassadorship is made possible, and qualified, by the socially unnatural circumstances of both abandonment and adoption. These same circumstances allow American parents to think about their children as optionally Chinese, or at least Chinese in select ways. Abandonment loosens perceived ties to country and culture, opening the door to ambiguous ambassadorship and to a level of Chinese culture chosen by adoptive parents. Barbara assured the man on the airplane that she would teach her child about Chinese culture but later told me she and her husband had been attracted to the China program because children were unequivocally available, and without birth-family ties.

The trip to China and the process of handing over the child might suggest Homi Bhabha's (1994) "third space" of hybridity—a process of signification at the border spaces between cultures where meanings are "appropriated, translated, rehistoricized, and read anew" (37). Yet even as we might pose ambiguous ambassadorship as full of transformative possibility, it must also be understood as materially wrought through the dislocation of child from birth family, and as unequally produced through the labor of participants in the exchange. Adoption facilitators in particular manage adoption exchange and cultural ambassadorship in the messy space between, in response to a multiplicity of voices, and as brokers of potentially threatening hybridity. Their job requires constant translation, selectively expressed to their clients. As managers of exchange processes, facilitators have ongoing contact with all key players and must know the needs and desires of all parties. In this position, they absorb and buffer conflicts and inequalities, translating back and forth what must be said to keep the exchange going smoothly. Adoptive parents are often quite unaware of the extra gifts and favors traded on their behalf, just as officials may be unaware of the demands made by parents. Countless times I have watched or heard about facilitators who did what they thought they had to do as *zhongjianren* (middlemen and -women), smoothing ruffled feathers or omitting offensive translations. This does not mean that all facilitators do things the same way or agree on what's most important, nor that everyone always walks away happy. Compromises must be made.

One especially informative area of facilitation and translation is the brokerage of cultural representation, where Chinese facilitators convey sound bites of Chinese culture to American parents. All facilitators I interviewed agreed that getting paperwork right was the most important part of their service to clients, and that introducing parents to Chinese culture (however it was fashioned) ran a close second. Indeed, as I toured with adoption travel groups between hotels and offices and historic cultural sites, I watched facilitators relate the local history, explain foods and eating habits, and sing Chinese children's songs. Several facilitators added that it seemed especially important for parents to be introduced to the history and culture of the specific city or region their child was from. However, facilitators also recognized that the ambassadorship of children was not by any means automatic but instead filtered through adoptive parents. As Larry put it, a big part of his job as bridge was "letting the people who are interested know about Chinese culture, since these families will also be a bridge." Larry conceded that this most likely meant an abridged, "secondhand" version of Chinese culture, but at least adoptive families might have one or two pieces of Chinese furniture or paintings or something in their home to help other people understand about Chinese culture. But then, for ambassadorship to be parent-dependent is for it to be somewhat market-dependent as well. Some adoption travel agencies in China, for example, offer two different packages to parents: the cheaper of the two leaves out visits to cultural sites and local restaurants.

Facilitation practices at the juncture of market demands and ideals of cultural ambassadorship thus have the effect of dislodging bounded and authentic notions of Chineseness, pointing instead to culture itself as made through a dialogic process of exchange (Bauman 1999; Hays 1994). Chineseness is reproduced and performed around the body of the child through the labor of facilitators—and not just for the consumption of adoptive parents who expect to learn about "beautiful China" but also for facilitators themselves and for local Chinese who witness the exchange. Facilitators might find themselves juggling the contradictory feelings of Chinese observers, as Larry and Jane indicated to me in a joint interview:

> Jane says Chinese people are of course very curious about seeing this adoption happen, and will ask what so many foreigners are doing with Chinese children. Larry agrees that he hears people in every big hotel asking this, shaking their heads in bewilderment. He interprets this as a kind of pride in being Chinese, in Chinese children being good at so many things. Jane disagrees, and says these observers feel anger and embarrassment that foreigners are adopting Chinese children. Jane tells me it is different for them than it would be for me when I travel with U.S. parents; she and Larry are Chinese, so other people still say bad words to them about these parents, and thus about their work in facilitating adoption. "They don't understand our work," says Larry; Jane adds, "We need to protect families, *and* protect Chinese feelings."

So as much as I felt compelled in my role as participant-observer to explain adoption to Chinese onlookers, Chinese facilitators feel even more compelled. They are all the more aware of the ambiguous meanings of foreigners adopting Chinese children and must try to buffer these contradictions.

While facilitators legitimate adoption exchange for several audiences, ultimately they are paid to legitimate the transfer for parents. This may mean that facilitators subordinate ambassadorship to client demand, silently absorbing the contradictions of their position "in between." Lin, a facilitator for a travel agency, said she would never tell a parent what she told me: "Most of the families are pretty wonderful, but some of them don't seem to care about Chinese culture. I asked a mother from Holland why she was adopting from China, and she said because she had no other choice. What a strange reason!" Even Eddie, who championed good public relations for adoption, expressed disappointment at the occasional family who asked him not to speak Mandarin to their child because they thought it might "confuse" her (thus presumably obstructing the parent-child bond). And Larry, who was passionate about wanting parents to know more about Chinese culture, was deflated that the group of American parents he was leading didn't seem to care about the history and culture of the province. As I accompanied this weary new group of parents on the bus to the notary office, they looked out the windows and half-listened while Larry shared historical anecdotes from the front of the bus. But when it came time to fill out the official adoption application forms at the notary office, and parents had to answer the question "Why do you want to adopt from China?" they dutifully obeyed as Larry slowly dictated the words they were to write: "Because I love Chinese culture and the Chinese people." Just as it takes emotional labor (Hochschild 1983) on the part of facilitators to legitimate adoption as a form of ambassadorship, so it might take emotional labor for some parents to show interest in Chinese culture, especially during the whirlwind two-week adoption trip. In the process, the notion of cultural ambassador might slip easily into a symbolic gesture of legitimation, akin to the pandas handed to parents along with their adoption certificates.

The Gender of the Gift: Confronting Impossible Reciprocity

Parents themselves do not often refer to their children as ambassadors of China or Chineseness, even as they may understand them to have visceral ties to China via birth family and cultural history, marked in race. Neither do they refer to their children as clients, even as they expect their own resources to be put into the well-managed care and transfer of the child. Rather, parents are more likely to refer to their children as "gifts."

The discourse of gift giving legitimates and resolves the contradictions of exchange somewhat differently than ambassadorship. Where the latter suggests that the child has been entrusted to carry intact the cultural representation of one nation to the other, the discourse of the gift suggests an ongoing and more intimate relationship between giver and receiver, the child having been freely entrusted to new parents (and new nation). The gift further serves to offset the discourse of the client, that is, the "placement" practices of the adoption profession and, more important, the commodified relationships of the contractual market.[9] As Rayna Rapp (1999) argues, transnational adopters use "gifting discourse to elevate the value of their child-centered exchanges, and in that process, resist utilitarianism through state and market value claims" (xvii).

Rapp goes on to problematize the distinctions gift discourses try to make arguing that the gift economy is nevertheless "imbricated with state and market, simultaneously resistant to and reproductive of its productivist biases" (xvii). So, as Yngvesson (2002) argues with reference to Bourdieu, the child-as-gift evokes "two opposing truths": the "clean break" from a birth mother and nation that give her up, signaling a completed transaction, and at the same time the relationships created through adoption exchange, signaling an ongoing chain of reciprocities. This places the identity of the child in a complicated position between forms and locations of belonging. As with the trope of the little ambassador, imagining the adopted Chinese child as gift serves to "doubly deflect" what these two truths together suggest: historically embedded exclusions make children available as particular kinds of gifts.

Gendered relationships of inclusion and exclusion, particularly those among differently located women, belie the contradictions of the gift. Children are produced as Chinese girls, by Chinese women (both birth mothers and state-employed caregivers), for American women. The dislocation of the gift-child promises a revaluation of her marginalized gender status, but this is in turn accomplished through the gendered exclusions that have made her available for adoption. As Strathern (1988) shows in her work *The Gender of the Gift,* the creation of new value in exchange does not necessarily signal alienation of actors from that which is produced and exchanged. This is comprehensible only when we understand the identities of both individuals and the things they produce as multiple rather than unitary and as given value in social relations. So rather than labor to make clear distinctions between commodity and gift, I focus on how the discourse of the gift both relies on and resists commodified relations among women, which is a way of exploring the relationships of power that link exchange and value (Appadurai 1986; Bourdieu 1990 [1980]).

The multiple determinations and meanings of gift exchange in adoption come to light when we ask, "What is the gift, and from whom and to whom is it given?" The child is usually the gift, but not always; sometimes she is the recipient of the gift of family. Birth parents and adoptive parents, as well as the nation, are also variously constructed as giver and recipient. For example, some adoptive parents and adoption agencies speak in terms of the birth mother providing the "gift of life" to the child, not just through birth (thus saving her from abortion) but also by "placing her somewhere where she will be found" (thus saving her from infanticide or from not being found at all). In this case, the gift is given to the child but is also for the adoptive parents, who are in turn indebted to a sacrificial birth mother. Chinese journalist and radio personality Xinran uses this narrative in her sentimentalized stories of birth mothers who explain the abandonment of a child in terms such as "I promised I wouldn't let my girl have such a hopeless life."[10] This construction also segues into adoptive parents as able givers of love and life; Xinran quotes another birth mother as saying, "I am very pleased for a rich person to take my daughter; she has a right to live a good life." Many times, people in China would remark to me how "big-hearted" parents are to adopt these unwanted children. And some parents, like the Cooks, felt that adoption was a giving of their gifts. Nancy described how Chet had put it to her as they contemplated adoption: "You know, the last few months I've really been feeling that we should do more with our God-given gifts—financial, emotional, spiritual, etc."

But then, the child might also be understood as a gift to American parents and the U.S. nation from China, which has done the right thing by the child by finding a good home for her; this recalls Commissioner Meissner's assertion that rather than "just another new immigrant," the child "is a gift from China that will shape our country for generations to come."[11] Or (or rather *and*, since these are not mutually exclusive renditions of the gift) the gift—of the child, of parenthood—may be from God or destiny. When parents were told by Chinese observers how big-hearted they were or that their children were so lucky, they would often ask the facilitator or me to translate back, "No, no, *we're* the lucky ones," thus suggesting that they had received the gift of parenthood through fate. In a seamless enactment of the mutual imbrication of client, ambassador, and gift, facilitator Eddie sometimes takes his travel groups to a local Buddhist temple for a "blessing ceremony." A bureaucratically authentic blessing from the state is reinforced by a culturally authentic blessing from Chinese gods, legitimating the gift of kinship to both parents and children.

However the gift and people's relationship to it are rendered, the discourse of the gift manages the dislocation and commodified alienation of the child that haunt the process: for instance, she is not "freely" given by birth parents; the Chinese state gets monetary resources in return for "giving" her (using some part of this to pay minimal wages to caregiving women); and gendered policy structures as much as fate have shaped the conditions of her availability. All these contradictions are to some extent resolved in rendering the child as recipient; she is given and received in *her* best interest and thus may be understood as unencumbered by direct reciprocal obligation. The potential for adoption to become a commodified transaction or an endless cycle of reciprocal relations is further warded off by the giving of other kinds of gifts. The U.S. $3,000 orphanage donation (even if required) is the most obvious example. Parents are also encouraged to bring small gifts to give to caregivers and orphanage directors as a token of good relations and thanks. At the same time, foster mothers and orphanage caregivers will sometimes give to children the parting gift of a jade amulet or other token of good wishes that connects them to the child, and the child to China, while simultaneously sanctioning her departure.

This dangerous duo of crass marketization and obligation-laden gifting is further resolved in the discourse of adoption as destiny. Here, fate proffers the gift of balancing out lives. In some parents' narratives, fate gestures toward the equalization of losses and gains. Women who have experienced infertility, along with agency social workers, will sometimes speak of the "balance of losses" by which their child came to them—the birth mother has lost a child, the child has lost her birth family, and the adoptive parent (usually figured as the mother) has lost the chance to have her own child. (In the case of straight single parents, a similar scenario might point to the loss of the opportunity to have a child by birth because of the absence of a different-sex partner.) Through adoption as gift exchange, then, everyone seems to gain, gratitude is expressed in multiple directions, and what is meant to pass has passed. Fate's gift transcends not only the instrumentality of human transactions but also the hierarchies of reproduction that might make adoption socially inferior to "natural" routes. Likening it to drugs used in biological organ transplantation, Donald Joralemon (1995) asserts that gift ideology inhibits "cultural rejection of transplantation and its view of the body" (335, quoted in Layne 1999: 3).

Fate is indeed one of the most powerful forms of gift ideology. Within a few days of receiving their children, many parents remarked that they got "just the right child"; I, too, found myself having a hard time imagining any child being with a parent other than the one they got. And a number of facilitators, even as they worked behind the scenes to smooth the transfer by giving gifts to the right officials at the right times, melted a bit when speaking of the *yuanfen* (something preordained) that brought parents and children together.

Gender relations are crucial to the making of the gift. The sex of the child can, on the one hand, be rendered as a positive sign of fate's gift to girls, on behalf of her birth family—girls rescued from the oppression both they and their Third World mothers experience and then given the gift of (a better) life by adoptive mothers.[12] On the other hand, the sex of the child casts doubt on narrations of predestination by standing as a testament to the material structures that shape abandonment. I would therefore argue that the language of fate tends to suppress the histories of patriarchy and state policy that loosen girls from the "giving" birth family and that make them gifts *un*freely given. The counterexample of families who adopt healthy boys underscores the point. It is much harder for both Chinese and Americans to speak of boys as gifts, since it is harder to explain why they were given (up). A couple of families have reported to me stares and glares from people in China who found out they were adopting a boy; one family was surrounded by interested women on the street who wouldn't believe their child was a boy until they had pulled down his pants to check.

To fully acknowledge the gendered divisions of reproductive practice that make the gift possible is to expose the fiction of the gift—or, more accurately, to expose the exclusions that make the language of the gift necessary. Yet such exposure is exactly what threatens to occur when the trip to China brings into temporary proximity the Chinese birth families that must give up their children, the orphanage workers who care for those children, and the American parents who have come to adopt them. When a Chinese child is literally handed over to American parents, her value is multiply determined in the social relationships among those who could not care for her, have cared for her, and will care for her. Importantly, these people are mostly women, but women in divergent social positions of stratified reproduction (Colen 1995).[13]

Physical and emotional interactions during the adoption trip are strained by the transfer of the child from one caregiver to another—from the Chinese *ayis* to the American women who desire and strive to "become mother." I witnessed many subtle conflicts between the desire to connect to a child's history and the desire to transform her primary relationships and identity. While this is most observable in American adoptive parents' interactions with Chinese orphanage caregivers, it is equally palpable in their felt proximity to absent-but-present birth parents—what Derrida (1994) calls "others who are not present" but who can exert a force on the here and now of the child's body and birth country. This stirs a host of emotions that unsettle positive constructions of the birth mother's gift. As one couple put it, it was strange to walk around the city where their child was abandoned, knowing/sensing that one of the women they passed on the street just might be their daughter's mother. A few of the mothers in the travel group told me they thought they saw looks of longing or pain on the faces of some of the Chinese women they passed and wondered if those women might have had to give up a child. They related these stories with a mixture of empathy toward birth mothers and resentment toward the patriarchal structures under which those women felt forced to give up their children. Under such circumstances, adoptive parents must labor to create the gifting relationship.

The contradictory emotions of American adoptive mothers toward Chinese birth mothers—who are so crucial to their children's histories— were heightened by closer encounters. Nan Heinman, a single adoptive mother, told me she kept every single piece of information about the people and places in her child's preadoption history in case her daughter wanted to search for her birth mother some day. But then she related the following story about a possible encounter with a birth mother or relative, her tone quiet and pensive:

> *Nan*: You know, the morning after I adopted her, we were in this little
> hotel in this tiny town. And there was this tap on the door, and I
> look up and there's a young woman, a young Chinese woman stand-
> ing in the doorway. And she hands me a piece of paper. It was a let-
> ter. And it was written in English, and Chinese—one side was Eng-
> lish, one side was Chinese. And it said, "I would like to correspond
> with you; will you write to me." And it was very strange, because
> she came to this hotel, [found my room,] . . . and then she handed
> me this letter. And there was this part of me that just shivered,
> thinking "Could it . . . ? Is it possible?" You know?
>
> *Sara*: Have you corresponded with her?
>
> *Nan*: No, I couldn't do it. I couldn't do it. I was just . . . there was some
> part of me that thought if there's any chance that that's her mother,
> I don't think I can do it! Or [maybe it was] someone who knows her
> mother, who was there as a sort of ambassador, so they could fol-
> low. . . . It was very strange. [I had] an incredibly strong response.
> I remember I had, and actually I still have it while I'm talking about
> it right now, like I'm tightening all the way up, all the way through
> my chest. . . . And every time I read the story of, like, these people
> who have adopted domestically and they stay in touch with the
> birth parents and there's, like, reciprocal visits, I don't know. . . .
> You know, people are constantly saying to me, "You and Faith are
> like two peas in a pod. You're so, like, you couldn't have gotten a kid
> who suits you better."

Nan's inability to respond to the reciprocity demanded by this encounter exposes the boundaries of the exchange relationship and the particularity of the gift. The gift Nan had counted on came "free" of an actual birth mother; the potential appearance of one showed the gift to be less free than imagined. The demand for shared history put Nan in a seemingly impossible situation. Nan desired a connection with Faith's past for the sake of her daughter's possible future connection with her birth mother but also felt that this connection posed a threat to her close relationship with her daughter. These contradictory feelings are experienced as well in relation to foster parents, who sometimes form close bonds with the orphans in their care. Lisa Walker described the surreal discomfort of having people recognize her daughter Pan Pan as they walked down the streets of her hometown in China, where Pan Pan had been in a foster home for a year. Like Sheila, Lisa said that she felt in those moments like she was "stealing" her daughter away from her roots.

Given the political and economic inequities between mothers, the discourse of the birth mother's gift is made possible by imagining the sacrifices she makes: first by laboring to birth a child and then by "freeing" the child to be adopted. When it comes to orphanage caregivers and foster mothers, however, it is rarer to run across the language of the gift, except perhaps to acknowledge the care they have shown the child *in transit* from abandonment to adoption. This differentiation of birth mothers and orphanage workers is reminiscent of the differentiation Ragoné (1999) has found between traditional and gestational surrogate mothers; in the case of the former, who supply ova and not "just" the (seemingly more instrumental) service of carrying a child, gifting language is more often used. Because they are paid and do not sacrifice a biological link with the child, Chinese foster mothers and orphanage *ayis* are situated within the political economy of production and consumption, mostly outside the discourse of the gift. From this position, they provide the labors that convert material resources (including the orphanage donation) into the gift of the child.

And so Chinese caregivers often sit in the shadows of adoption exchange, their emotional and physical ties to children subsumed to their role as paid laborers. Caregivers do regularly get attached to the children they care for, in some cases taking them home on weekends and even forming kinlike relationships; in other words, some of them feel they potentially lose a part of themselves in the exchange and do not wish to be alienated from their labor. They might more readily understand the children they have cared for as gifts if their emotional and physical attachments were recognized. Remember the occasion when a caregiver insisted that children were "lucky to be in this orphanage." I read this as protesting the notion that the child is without care and a specific history until she reaches her foreign family. She and other caregiving women expressed in a number of ways a desire for that history to be recognized.

When I asked an *ayi* how she and her coworkers got the children ready to meet their adoptive parents, she explained that they washed and clothed them, but then lamented that they often didn't even know ahead of time which children would be leaving and did not always get to accompany them to the meeting. She said she guessed she was happy the children had families, but it was *nanguo,* "hard to take," to see them go. Once when I was present during the chaotic and brief moments when children are handed from Chinese caregivers to American parents, one foster mom pressed me to make sure that the adoptive parents knew she had just given the baby a bath and put new clothes on her. Another foster mother urged me to remind American adoptive parents to send photos; she had not heard anything from a family that adopted a child she had fostered for more than one year. Parting gifts from foster mothers and caregivers to the child thus serve as reminders of their part in producing the child-as-gift, and of the history embodied in the child. It is perhaps precisely because of this attachment that the women who have directly cared for a particular child are sometimes barred from directly delivering the child to the adoptive parents—a moment laden with the emotional labor of making the child a gift.

In her study of Russian adoption exchanges, Stryker (2001) concludes, "Deprived for so long of their rights to parenthood by infertility and bureaucracy . . . [parents] are now fueled by the overdue fantasy of bringing the children from the public to the private, from the collective to the individual, and from deprivation to indulgence" (23). Under such circumstances, the welfare institution and those who work in it must remain outside the gift exchange. This is not to say that adoptive parents are oblivious to caregivers; Lisa Walker may have felt like she was stealing her daughter, but she also said she felt deeply the pain of the caregivers who had to let her go. She echoed the sentiments of a number of parents with whom I talked. Yet economic conditions differentiate possible emotional relationships to the child.[14] Adoptive parents from the United States and Europe have the economic resources even to think about adopting from China, while the gendered class position of orphanage caregivers would normally prevent them from stepping inside the four-star hotels where they hand over the children, let alone formally adopting one of the children themselves (which a few told me they wanted to do). While the people into whose arms the caregivers pass children are also usually women, they are women who can afford to pay for the services that reproduce and legitimate kinship exchange across borders and who have an investment in making children part of themselves.

When parents and caregivers come face to face in the first day or two of the trip to China, their interaction is limited by language differences and the everyday requirements of the process. Caregivers must get back to work, and parents must be whisked to various government offices to process paperwork; with the limited time and translation service available to them, parents use this time to ask practical questions about allergies, eating habits, sleep patterns, last diaper changes, and the like. But it is also an occasion for contemplating the strangeness of the child's past or future, with both caregivers and parents nervous about the child's transition. I watched in hotel rooms and government offices as children were passed back and forth between adoptive mothers and foster mothers, each quietly sizing up the other's care practices. American mothers raised their eyebrows when a foster mother let a ten-month-old gnaw on a whole apple; Chinese foster mothers muttered to each other when an adoptive mother let a child cry herself to sleep.

These divergent claims on the care of the child sometimes reached a highly emotional pitch, signifying the incongruous relations through which the magic of adoptive kinship is constructed. A story from my field notes illustrates:

As we sit in a government office waiting for paperwork to be completed, Josh and Gretta Peterman ask me to translate a few questions to the foster mother. Gretta is visibly tired from a night of little sleep. Their toddler Madeline has cried much of the night, further upset in Gretta's estimation by a surprise visit from the foster mother to their hotel room the evening before. Gretta is weary of foster mom hanging around, weary of handing over to her an unsettled and unhappy child, and escapes across the room from where we sit, Madeline in her arms. The foster mother then tells me with tears in her eyes how hard it is for her and her family to say goodbye after caring for this child for more than a year. She repeatedly asks Josh to promise to send photos and letters, and asks for their address, which Josh reluctantly hands over to her. Finally, the foster mother asks me to ask the Petermans if she could stay with them throughout the day and hold Madeline. Josh, smiling tightly, says he'll talk to Gretta, and crosses the room to do so. The foster mother watches, and when she sees Gretta break into tears, quickly says, "*Mei guanxi*" (It's okay, no problem) to me. I relate this to the clearly relieved couple, and as we leave the office, they and foster mom say strained goodbyes. Gretta says later she could not stand to keep watching Madeline scream for her foster mother every time they said goodbye. Josh says he knows how hard it must be for foster mothers, but . . .

These moments of transition are difficult for both adoptive and foster parents, whose own social identities are entwined with the past and future of the child—a past and future that remain mostly unknown, in the present, to one or the other. Ultimately, however, the social, legal, and economic determinations of this moment are weighted in favor of adoptive parents. Caregivers might end up absorbing its excess of historical inequities and multiple meanings.

It also falls to facilitators to broker the impossible contradictions that arise: legitimating adoption exchange as a special gift sometimes means subordinating the needs of caregivers to those of parent-clients. Daniel told me that before his aunt became a foster mother, he just thought of himself as a tour guide: "I thought only of the adoptive families, and not the other side." But now that he was part of a foster family, he realized how attached people got to the foster child. I asked him if he thought adoptive families realized this as well. Daniel replied that some did and some didn't, pointing out that they were sometimes afraid to visit foster homes for fear the child would reenact attachments to her foster family. "Not all of them are willing to go to the foster care home and visit, afraid the child will not come back to them and will suffer 'emotional feelings.' But I encourage them to go, because this may be the only time here, and it is so meaningful. They *should* experience this." Later in the interview I asked Daniel if he ran into conflicts in trying to serve the needs of both child and parents. He said yes; in trying to satisfy adoptive families in the first few days they are in China, he felt he had to "sacrifice the rights of the foster families. . . . Sometimes I take the foster families elsewhere so they won't see the kids [even though they want to]." But then, Daniel added, there are also those foster families, especially in poor counties, who are doing this because they need the money and sometimes ask him for extra. "I have to try to avoid this," he said.

As Daniel's last statement indicates, emotional and material needs among a variety of actors complicate the job of legitimating the child as gift, and threaten the symbolic capital of adoption exchange. The management of the contradictions of these multiple needs and desires is essential to the production of the adoptive parent-child relationship. Indeed, brokers of adoption face a delicate balance between providing caring labor on behalf of the child and doing so on behalf of the parent. Caregivers are sometimes caught in the middle, not exactly alienated from their labor but subsumed in the transformation of child into gift. Facilitators, meanwhile, broker gift giving that solidifies the routes through which transnational adoption occurs. Their management of gifts (including tips) during the exchange process in China serves to reproduce a smooth system by which the child herself can be made gift.

Conclusion: Reproducing Adoption

The needs and desires of adoptive parents certainly help shape exchange processes, but as I have argued above, parents do not make adoption exactly as they please. And while their experiences are diverse, in some ways they must give themselves over to a political economy compelled, as Butler (1997) reminds us, toward particular kinds of social relations, values, and routes of exchange. The sharpening coherence of systemic practices in China/U.S. adoption is evident in the kinds of social exchange that take place in the "safe spaces" of hotel rooms, offices, and tour buses. In the early years of the program (the early 1990s), parents actually went to orphanages to meet their children, and the time it took to go through the process was less predictable. Now there is more distance between the "productive" (e.g., orphanages) and "consumptive" (e.g., adoptive families) locations of the process, more institutionalization of abstracted caring labor, and more professionalized management of the practices that transfer child to parent. This is evident from the moment Americans enter particular hotels in China—at least, white American women. The hotel in Dayang does a lot of business with adoption groups, and when I first walked up to the front counter to check in (just me, with bags and no baby), the young Chinese desk clerk looked at me and asked, "Will you be needing a crib?"

The social relations and values around the everyday practices of transferring children to parents help reproduce this coherence, the system itself, and its attendant inequalities—although never completely. Constructions of client, ambassador, and gift are signs of that incompleteness, not only because their invocation is even necessary to the labor of legitimating adoption exchange but because together they reflect and produce multiple and ultimately untamable processes of identification. I take them as evidence that adopted children's subjectivities push beyond most attempts to name them. This is especially evident during parents' two weeks in China. In other words, the very discourses ("ambassador," "client," and "gift") that labor to legitimate adoption point us to the exclusions they labor to forget.

In the winter of 2001, I went with a group of new adoptive parents to visit the orphanage where some of their children had lived just a few days before. I share this encounter in some detail because it encapsulates many of the contradictions and connections that characterize the transfer of children to adoptive parents:

> As our mini-bus winds its way through suburbs and then countryside, some parents tell me they are eager to see Nanshan orphanage, while others tell me they are nervous. Perhaps it is the uncertainty of a return to what had been home for their children, when parents already have their sights on returning home to the U.S. But they also know it is a rare opportunity that their facilitator has used his connections to arrange. When we pull up to the orphanage, we gather in the courtyard and are greeted by Mr. Zhao, a kind-faced administrator who apologetically informs us that regulations prevent us from actually going into the orphanage building. It's not that the building is shabby; it actually looks pretty new. Zhao tells me that they have been able to make improvements with the donations that come from international adoption applicants.
>
> Parents snap pictures of the outside of the building, the garden, and some of the playing children. I ask how many children live here at Nanshan and Zhao says, "There are ninety—oh, and then there are the handicapped children, and another ten who are school-aged." Some of

the ayis come out to join us, and there are awkward smiles and silences on both sides as they stand with the families whose children they had cared for. One adoptive mother calls me over and with tears in her eyes says, "Please tell her how thankful I am for taking care of my daughter."

Meanwhile, Tina, a seven-year-old in our group who was adopted as a baby from a neighboring province, skips right into the orphanage with a couple of the older orphanage girls she has met on the playground. Some in the group joke that Tina has passage inside because she's Chinese, but that when she returns she can report to us foreigners what it's like in there.

These moments when the otherwise disparate subjects of adoption—children who both are and were orphans, American adoptive parents, caregivers, and adoption professionals—momentarily come into close proximity are dense with the uncertainties and desires of belonging. They bring into view the two-way relationship between the political economy of adoption exchange and the everyday encounters of people with links to the child, who is client, ambassador, and gift. Who is client in this moment? Certainly both parents and children are, as the facilitator arranged this visit as a special part of the journey for parents but also for the children whose histories they do not know. But there is also the reminder that certain clients are "right": Zhao names the number of children who might be considered adoptable before tacking on the special-needs and older children. We might also see China itself as a kind of client of globalizing modernity, its bureaucrats protecting against being labeled "backward" under the foreign gaze. Zhao's role as gatekeeper of the image of modern care and his delineation of adoptable children are shaped, in the case of adoption, by the circulation of monies that come through the gifts of foreign donations. These resources make possible the construction of the child as gift, although as parents stood face to face with caregivers and nonadopted children in Nanshan's courtyard, it struck me that such encounters might help defetishize this gift. In this vein, I consider Tina's movement across the densely configured border between the inside and outside of the orphanage. She has been dislocated from China and her orphanage home through adoption, and yet it is she who can "pass" into and back out of them and, in doing so, refigure imaginaries of national, cultural, and racial kinship. In the circumscribed encounters between parents and orphanage, and in Tina's movement between them, there are hints of the "enchainment" in new kinds of social relations that the cultural economy of adoption can promote (Yngvesson 2002).

Indeed, the months and years since my research trip to China have seen the reproduction and creation of new forms of client, ambassador, and gift. Adoptive families are becoming more permanent clients. Not only has the CCAA increased its requirements for postadoption reports on the well-being of children, but both public and private entities are making longer-term clients of adoptive parents and their children by putting in place services ranging from counseling to adoption-related consumer items to "homeland tours" back to China. One provincial office I visited had recently established a *shouyang fuwu zhongxin* (adoption service center), which, according to a civil affairs official, was formed to help manage foreign donations, provide facilitation of the adoption process, train orphanage directors in management, and put cultural programs in place for adoptive families who come back to visit on what are commonly called "homeland" or "motherland" tours. And the contradictions of the gift of the adopted child have prompted parent groups in the United States to embark on ambitious fundraising campaigns independent of the formal adoption system; some specifically designate those gifts for the special-needs and older children who form the "constitutive outside" to their own children's identities. New relationships are being constructed between adoptive parents and people in China's welfare system.

The multiple ways of identifying children as gift, client, and ambassador do not resolve themselves when parents leave China to return to the United States but rather continue to surround the process of remaking the child as social and familial citizen. They expose, to some degree, the inequalities that produce the child and haunt the undetermined construction of her cultural and racial and gendered identities, *within the family*, upon return to the United States. In the following chapters I examine how the inequalities of exchange considered in this chapter are transformed across borders and in the context of American social citizenship. But first I make a quick stop on Shamian Island, locale of the U.S. consulate in Guangzhou, and the last stop for all American adoptive families before they head home.

CHAPTER 5

Shamian Island

Borders of Belonging

When you venture off of Shamian Island,[1] it is probably best to leave your stroller behind. A stroller may work on the quiet tree-lined boulevards and riverfront walkways of Shamian, but it is rather unwieldy when negotiating the steps of the pedestrian crossovers that lead up and over the congested avenue that separates the island from the rest of the bustling seven-million-person city of Guangzhou. You might just get brave enough one morning to carry your child of two weeks into the busy market across the avenue, where raggedy little boys beg for coins, housewives bargain for fish and dried herbs in tone-rich Cantonese, and fashionable young people shop for shoes. But you are probably tired after nearly two weeks in China with a new child, so you stick close to the hotel, pushing or carrying your child around this pleasant little island, taking in the river boats, nodding at the elderly men and women that sit under trees and talk, and watching kids play badminton on the broad boulevard. Maybe you stop in some of the shops to buy some last-minute mementos. The shopkeepers will happily offer to have the likeness of you and your child etched into a polished stone, or help you pick out a pint-sized silk jacket. As you explore this small island, you run into other adoptive families at every turn who stop to trade information about ages and rashes and orphanages. And when you get back to the hotel room, you can call out for pizza and settle in with CNN.

Shamian Island is not technically an island.[2] It is a flat chunk of sandy soil about a half-mile long and three hundred yards wide that hugs the banks of the Pearl River in Guangzhou (Canton) on the southern coast of China. A small lighted sign at the main entrance to the island briefly tells its history: the island was ceded to the British and French in 1842 after the Opium War but then returned to China in 1945.[3] Perhaps it is fitting that after it reverted to China, Shamian's old colonial trading houses and elite homes became Chinese government offices and multifamily dwellings; but now, as the sign will tell you, its colonial villas are being restored (in 1996, Shamian was declared a protected historical space) "for the benefit of the people"—at least, for the benefit of domestic and overseas tourists and those local Chinese who can afford to move into the refurbished apartments. There is scaffolding on many of the villas, some already repainted and regentrified; a tennis club stands by the river's edge. This is genteel urban renewal, compared to the twenty-three giant construction cranes I counted on the Guangzhou skyline from a vantage point on the twentieth floor of Shamian Island's White Swan Hotel. That Shamian, and Guangzhou more generally, is a borderland that enacts and produces different forms of Chinese belonging is evident at the international church there. Its bulletin announces that, following Chinese regulations, it is not open to Chinese citizens—except for "Chinese engaged or married to foreigners and Chinese being adopted by foreigners."

Amid the testament of the villas on Shamian to its unfolding history stand small businesses advertising translation and immigration services for local Chinese visa applicants, intermingled with tourist shops chock full of little silk dresses and diapers for adoptive families. This seems an odd combination until one notes that these businesses cater to the immigrant hopefuls brought to Shamian by the U.S. consulate, a large nondescript office building that sits in one corner of the island. The paths of local Chinese and foreign adoptive visa applicants rarely cross, except when they both enter the consulate, and even then, they are easily distinguished. As adoption facilitator Lana told her little group of weary families when they embarked on the last step of their journey in China, "Don't worry about your paperwork. It's easy to get your visa. But not for me!" Indeed, I will never forget walking right into the U.S. consulate with a group of adoptive families, past at least a couple hundred

Chinese adults who stood in tight lines behind signs that bore the hour ("8:30–9:29," "9:30–10:29," etc.) in which they had their two-minute chance to make their case before a consular officer. One adoptive mother looked at this crowd of prospective immigrants and said she felt kind of guilty just marching right in; later she told me she had been shocked by this scene. Meanwhile, we went to the consulate's special visa unit for adopted children, a pleasant room where adoptive families waited on comfortable chairs, photos of adoptive families and a quilt with an adoption motif hung on the walls, and facilitators milled about with paperwork. This room and the visa application process that takes place in it[4] are the focal point of parents' trip to Guangzhou, and the raison d'être of the businesses around it that directly serve the process—the medical office where children get the required checkup, the shop that takes the small photos that will be affixed to visa forms, and the stores selling Chinese dolls and American-brand diapers.

American adoptive parents come to Shamian Island along with yet another set of border crossers, namely, international business and diplomatic elites, sharing the space of the swank hotel that stands next to the consulate, the White Swan. Ask any parent in the United States who has adopted a child from China, and they know the White Swan Hotel. According to Pierre, one of its foreign managers, their "dumb luck" in being next to the consulate means a brisk business in housing adoptive families for several nights at a time; the White Swan provides rooms for more than four thousand adoptive families a year. To their upscale shopping and dining services they have added over one hundred cribs, extra supplies of baby food and diapers, a babysitting service, and a special room just for adoptive family meetings. It is not uncommon to see a waitress or clerk in the hotel carrying or playing with an adopted child while her parents eat or shop. As adoptive mom Monica Johnson put it, "We feel like we're at the Shangri-la. So much for roughing it in China!"

But Pierre also noted that while service to adoptive families is good business, they must practice a kind of "containment" to keep their other clientele happy. International business guests have complained about everything from crying babies in adjoining rooms to adoptive families changing diapers or playing with their children in the area around the front desk. Some have even complained about the unseemliness of children from local orphanages being delivered to adoptive parents right there in the hotel lobby. So there are rules about the use of space: no sitting on the lobby floor, adoptive families are to be housed on particular floors if at all possible, and facilitators must arrange for Chinese caregivers to bring children to a private room to meet their parents (in cases where parents adopt children who reside in and around Guangzhou). Foreign adoptive families thus disrupt the relationship between local and transnational spaces. The rules at the White Swan suggest that ordinary Chinese, and more specifically local Chinese children who cross into transnational spaces in more than a fleeting way, violate the boundaries of global professional decorum. (Local Chinese families come as day tourists to the hotel, to take photos by the large fountain or eat in one of the restaurants, but then they leave.)

Pierre was the first to admit that this is delicate business, catering to different kinds of transnational elites. Providing special services to adoptive families and containing their activities were two sides of the same business coin. He gently laughed when I asked if the hotel viewed its service to adoptive families as an act of generosity outside the usual business purview; their needs as clients required adjustments, he said, but not a new ethic. In fact, Pierre suggested that the White Swan, by competing with other local hotels and service agencies to attract the business of adoptive families, had the opportunity to reinforce a "proper" Western business ethic. Pierre told me that in the late 1990s, adoption facilitators with connections to competing hotels floated a rumor that the White Swan did not like dealing with adoptive families. These facilitators, he said, were upset that the White Swan would not play the pricing game that gave facilitators a cut of the action, a common local business practice Pierre clearly found distasteful. In a similar vein, facilitators might have relationships with specific shopkeepers on the island, sometimes receiving kickbacks for taking their groups of adoptive families to those shops.

Shops on Shamian have adjusted dramatically to the needs and desires of this newest group of tourists, their practices straddling care and market at the nexus of client, ambassador and gift (as discussed in the previous chapter). Shamian is to many adoptive parents the last opportunity in their trek to China to buy gifts and connect to China in some tangible way. The White Swan, the waterfront, and the relative peace of the small island make this consumption a pleasant experience. One shop even has a corner shelf of "free stuff" where parents leave their extra bibs and left-over jars of baby food for other adoptive parents who pass through. And the gender of adopted children and of the parent usually shopping for them is not lost on these retailers. A couple of upscale shops attached to the White Swan sell, almost exclusively, toys and clothing for little girls. China Doll, a shop up the street, sells little embroidered shoes, zodiac animal mementos, folk paintings, and, yes, China dolls with braided black hair and silk *qipao,* the traditional Chinese dress. (Almost any adoptive parent can also tell you that it is very hard to find an Asian-looking doll, let alone one without blonde curls, in China.) In 2003, the White Swan Hotel got in on the action when it started giving adoptive families "Going-Home Barbies": blond Barbie dolls with "unmistakably Chinese" babies in their arms.[5]

Such items are the standard fare in shops on Shamian, but some shops stand out from the rest and have acquired almost legendary status in adoptive family circles, for example, a shop across from China Doll called Sherry's Place. I walked into this small, overstuffed shop to find Sherry behind the counter at her computer, e-mailing one of a number of American adoptive parents she has befriended over the years. Sherry said sure, this kind of contact was good for business (her name pops up every now and again in Listserv chats), but she also just liked keeping in touch with these families. Sherry enjoyed serving as a Chinese godmother of sorts to families who didn't really know any Chinese people besides their facilitator. Enter Sherry's Place, and you might gain not only a silk or embroidered memento of China but also a Chinese friend—two activities Sherry felt served the same goal of keeping adopted children connected to their homeland. I later noted that Sherry appeared in a number of the pictures of adoptive families hanging in the window of the photo shop around the corner. There is something touching but ironic about Sherry's ambassadorship to American parents, whose sights at this point in their journey are turned homeward.

A less visible shop on the other end of the island is geared toward not only taking a bit of China with you but simultaneously leaving a bit of the West behind. This shop, a ten-minute walk down the street from the cluster of businesses around the White Swan, dubs itself "Guangzhou's first charity store." Called A Gift from China, the shop was started by a few European women who wanted to give gifts *to* China. As indicated in

Figure 3
View of
Guangzhou
from Shamian
Island. Photo
courtesy of
Joe Molon.

Figure 4
Colonial
architecture
restored.
Photo courtesy
of Joe Molon.

Figure 5. Mother and daughter try a hat at a Shamian shop. Photo courtesy of Deb Kane.

Figure 6. Sherry's Place. Photo courtesy of Joe Molon.

Figure 7
Mother and
daughter
greeted while
strolling on
Shamian.
Photo courtesy
of Brian Reilly.

Figure 8
"Going Home Barbie,"
available only from the
White Swan Hotel.
Photo courtesy of
Rebecca Mathers.

its brochure, profits go toward giving children living in orphanages "the opportunity to receive surgery and rehabilitation that will increase their chances of being adopted by a local or international family." One of the shop's founders told me, however, that they really wanted to help older and special-needs children who would most likely not be considered "adoptable" but who could still become productive members of Chinese society. As the name of the store suggests, these gifts to children in China depend on gifts *from* China—the items adoptive families will purchase in the store and carry home as expressions of their children's cultural heritage. The unique items sold in the shop are meant to appeal to Western tastes (they are mostly designed by a Western woman) but are made by local Chinese artisans using Chinese motifs and materials (brocades, silks, bamboo, etc.).[6]

The border-straddling position of A Gift from China makes it the object of both mistrust and emulation. When the European women who founded it approached the local tax office about the idea, they were met with incredulity; only after the office had sent observers did it approve this novel charity. Similarly, the staff told me, shop owners from the other end of the island were sometimes suspicious of the nonprofit entity, even as they visited the store to get ideas for their own shops about what American adoptive families liked. So A Gift from China has become an erstwhile transnational teacher of Western consumer tastes and service (the practice of providing a "free shelf" of goodies for adoptive families started here). The women who run the shop explicitly express the desire to be a model for China—of both a proper business disposition and a proper ethic of care. They have trained and turned over the operation of the shop to a young Chinese woman and have hired local people with disabilities as cleaners. A Gift from China thus straddles the Chinese border, intent on serving domestic needs with Western notions of modern humanitarian and market practices. American adoptive parents make the perfect clients, spending the last of their cash as they pass out of China with their material and symbolic gifts. Practices at A Gift from China and Sherry's Place link the inside and outside, here and there, of China/U.S. adoption. In their processes of exchange, they give particular meaning and value to this multiply determined borderland.

Educational and disciplinary practices at the borderland are equally evident in the work of the U.S. consulate on Shamian. Staff at the adop-

tion visa unit told me that parents might sometimes see them as a bureaucratic obstacle; after all, consulate workers do have the power to
deny a visa to an adopted child if paperwork is incorrect or if they have
reason to believe a child is not a "true" orphan.[7] But they also construct
this job of protecting the orphan and the law as "an education process,"
as one consular officer put it—education of families, agencies, and the
China Center of Adoption Affairs. The consulate staff described their
work with the CCAA as a process of coaching Beijing toward a professional level of transparency and proper legal handling of adoption
affairs, even as that sometimes meant tussles over who had what kind of
claim on the process and the children themselves.

The question of who has the power to claim children in transition and
of the proper way to manage their exchange is related to the issue of who
exactly is or should be client and citizen. The "premium service" the
consulate provides to these parents, as consular officer Ted Gong[8] told
me, is necessary to ensure that "the child belongs where they should belong." Their careful work is thus understood as in the best interest of
children, to ensure their proper citizenship (i.e., American, if all the
right paperwork shows they are legally severable from birth parents and
birth country). But this is also a matter of the political and economic
power of citizen parents, who, for example, can and do contact their con-
gressional representatives about snags in the process. China/U.S. adoption is thus unique as a form of migration, Ted Gong told me, because
there is a very big "American citizen component" and because it appeals
to the myth of American humanitarianism. I quote extensively (with his
permission) from an e-mail Ted Gong sent to me in February 2001:

> The priorities our procedures allow for [adoptees] seem out of propor-
> tion to what we allow for other regular migrants . . . for orphans, there
> are two factors to explain the priorities afforded them: 1) a very artic-
> ulate, and well organized middle and upper class that advocates on
> their behalf 2) the inherent humanitarian character of an orphan adop-
> tion. . . . The last couple of immigration reforms [created] more em-
> ployment and investment based categories. . . . On the other hand, the
> myth of a purely altruistic immigration policy continues. Refugees and
> orphans fall into this area of humanitarian hopes . . . an immigration
> policy that provides for orphans expeditiously also responds to needs

of Americans to demonstrate that Americans care for others . . . and it supports the American myth that America is the land of hope and solutions to the problems of the old worlds.

Material and ideological forces collude around the adopted child to make her a worthy migrant and potential citizen who is obviously an exception to the usual routes of migration and citizenship. I chuckled with one adoptive parent as she sat in the White Swan Hotel, reading part of the INS visa form for her child; it indicated that the "immigrant applicant" should not be involved in criminal activity, belong to the Socialist Party, or be involved in or likely to be involved in prostitution. We could laugh because we knew adoption migration was largely outside the purview of this standard bureaucratic form, not only in the manner of exit from China but also in the manner of entry to the United States. Children leave Shamian Island and enter the United States flying above and beyond Angel Island, the immigration station that once processed or turned away many Chinese immigrants. It is a different era, but one nevertheless haunted by the way this racialized national history meets the disjointed histories that travel with the child from China. Constructing belonging for the new migrant adoptee, especially within the white middle-class American family, becomes a tricky business of navigating the "both-and" promises of adaptable multicultural identity and the "either-or" requirements of racial desires, national and class imaginaries, and exclusionary gendered structures of kinship.

CHAPTER 6

Storied Origins

Abandonment, Adoption, and Motherhood

We'll ask her, "Do you want to hear a story?"

And she'll say, "Yeah, China."

So we tell her the story about China:

We lay her in bed and we say our prayers. And we tell her a story about how mommy and daddy wanted a little girl named Katya so they asked baby Jesus for one, and we waited and waited, and she didn't come, so they started asking everybody, "Where's Katya? Where's Katya?" And then we asked our social worker and she said, "I'll bet she's in China because a lot of girls go to China on their way down from heaven and forget to come home." So mommy got on a plane and went to China, and sure enough, there was Katya.

—Teresa Huang, American adoptive mother of two-year-old Katya

Korean adoptee Tonya Bishoff begins her poem "Unnamed Blood," "i was squeezed through the opening of a powerful steel bird that carried me far away . . ." (Bishoff 1997: 37); the trans-Pacific airplane that "thrust me into soft, white fleshy arms" symbolizes both the silencing of her previous life and the painful birth of a new one. Airplanes also figure regularly in China adoption stories, but Beijing requires that parents travel to China to meet their children. This is why, as in the story Teresa Huang told her daughter countless times, it is possible for airplanes to become not so much vehicles for birthing a child into waiting parents' unfamiliar arms as vehicles for taking parents to a child who is waiting to be safely delivered "home"—to activate the full citizenship promised by an already partially accomplished kinship.

While some adult Korean adoptees have remarked on the importance of adoptive parents traveling to their children's birth countries, one recently told me she wasn't sure it was such a good idea that white American parents went to China to meet their children. Some of them, she said, seemed to think that just those two short weeks gave them license to speak for and about China with some authority, to shape the memories that would connect China and the United States for their children. My own research shows that parents take on the mantle of imagining China and their children's relationship to it with widely varying degrees of confidence and temerity. But in light of Teresa's diminution of China to a kind of way station in her daughter's origin story (even if, in their family shorthand, it is known as "the China story"), it would be wise to heed this Korean adoptee's cautionary tone. Having returned from China to their national and familial home, how do adoptive parents "make sense" of their children's adoption stories, for both themselves and their children? How do these stories construct the disparate desires and choices and imaginaries that took parents to China and made children available to them? How do they respond to multiple frames of belonging and reflect the identities imagined for both parent and child?

The answers to these questions often circle around motherhood, and more specifically the (im)possibility of "psychic space for two mothers" (Eng 2003: 3). Tonya Bishoff's birth is allegorized *between* two mothers. Teresa Huang's story seems to contain no birth mother, and if she is there, she makes only a fleeting appearance from her permanently immobilized place in China. And yet, when we remember to think of her, her absence is loud. Indeed, much of adoption discourse in both China and the United States is about the specularized absence or presence of a mother's love and the contradictions of journeying between two mothers juxtaposed by class, nation, and race. This is why scholars have increasingly recognized that adoption remakes the agency and meaning of motherhood in divergent ways (Solinger 1994; Telfer 2000; Gailey 2000). Importantly, those narrations of motherhood do the work of realizing fuller citizenship for both child and mother. Stories of adopted children's origins are thus what Anagnost (2000) calls

> a realm of affective labor still culturally identified with "the maternal," lying within the deep interiority of family life but also often externalized as a practice of display. The importance of this affective labor perhaps becomes more urgent the more the link to the child appears to be tenuous and needing support. . . . But their being more highly charged, the practices of adoptive mothers can speak to those of middle-class mothering more generally. (391–92)

Because it wrestles with multiple motherhoods, the affective labor of creating an originary identity for the child tells us how blood and culture speak to each other, through gendered kinship, racialized fantasies, and national imaginaries. Origin narratives begin to show how "international and group histories of gender, race, poverty, and nation [are] managed or erased within the 'privatized' sphere of the domestic" (Eng 2003: 2). The fetishizing of the abandonment story in particular makes motherhood the centerpiece of identity and kinship. Narrations of abandonment are thus a key to motherhood itself; their construction of biological dislocation exposes kinship as "basically the reification and naturalization of certain forms of belonging" (Weston 2001: 151).

A different kind of adoption story, from early Chinese history, helps open up these questions. In December 2000, I was in the office of Professor Huang Banghan, one of few scholars in China studying both domestic and international adoption, when he pulled out a handwritten copy of a story he said contained the earliest reference in Chinese literature he knew of (it is from the Zhou period, 1100–221 BC) to two important words: *qi* (abandon) and *shouyang* (adopt). The story, Huang told me, goes something like this:

> A mother left her boy on a small path because she thought he was not a normal child. But then, as she watched, she saw that passing animals stepped around the child. She then moved the boy to the forest, and placed him on a frozen stream. But then a bird flew down and covered

the child with its wings to keep him warm. The mother then realized that the boy must be a magical being. So she adopted (*shouyang*) him and named him *Qi* (left, abandoned).

This mythical story shares elements with origin narratives in contemporary China/U.S. adoption—the weaving of magic around the "chosen child," the knotty suspense of mother-child relationships, a desire to reckon with separation, and the hopeful need to believe that abandonment can lead to a better life (O'Donovan 2002). But unlike many adoption stories it readily sidesteps the foundational injury of abandonment. It tells of one mother, almost but never separated from her child, who averts the biographical rupture of biological and social identity. While her initial rejection of the child suggests that motherhood is denaturalized and socially created, we never have to find out what the fullness of that revelation might mean for both her and her child. The internal bonds of family are publicly tested and restored, the child permanently claimed by the mother who bore him.

Unlike this Chinese tale of abandonment and adoption, contemporary stories of Chinese children adopted into U.S. homes often lack a sense of completion. While the magical language of the "chosen" child is still sometimes used, it is destabilized by the dislocation of children from the material and symbolic, raced and gendered ties of "natural" kinship. (And a dislocation the child is aware she did not volunteer for; one five-year-old, who was an infant when she migrated, protested to her adoptive mother, "But I didn't want to go!") Rather than being rechosen by a birth mother, adopted Chinese children are seemingly unchosen by her and then matched with new parents—and not just coincidentally but through a legally sanctioned process of exclusive kinship and motherhood. Such clean-break adoptions leave melancholic holes, read off of the child, that parents both fear and long to fill; the questions of why a child was abandoned, by whom, and under what circumstances remain mostly unanswered.

Several months later, Professor Huang and I sit in a living room in Minneapolis, where we are together interviewing a white couple with a five-year-old girl adopted from China. The Erdahls ask Huang about the birth families he has researched in Anhui province, then listen with tears in their eyes as Huang tells them that most birth families seem to miss the children they have abandoned very much, and wish they knew something about where their birth children were or how they were doing. Later, as we prepare to leave, Carl begins to cry again as he thanks Huang for sharing information about birth parents. He says, "It helps make me feel a little bit . . . closer."

Abandonment and adoption are two sides of the same coin; it is separation and rupture that make adoption possible. This is why what might first appear ironic is in fact a crucial dialectic: many prospective adopters choose China because they will be free of involvement with birth mothers, yet that very "freedom" is later often mourned and experienced as a lack. Amid such contradictions, adoptive parents must try to narrate who their child is and how she got from China to the United States. As we shall see, parents, and mothers in particular, construct stories of their children's origins in relation to their children's bodies and behaviors, to unknown birth parents, to each other's experiences and stories, to imaginings of Chinese culture, and sometimes to magical portents. The affect and content with which parents fill a child's biography thus reflect the tangled succession of historical contingencies that gather around the child from the past, the present, and the imagined future. By considering a variety of such stories together, I hope to approximate the histories of girls abandoned in and adopted from China—not their individually specific histories but the social histories through which their identities and memories can even be imagined.

Holey, Haunted Stories: The Problem of Getting It "Right"

It says in her documents, "forsaked, was forsaked . . . her parents could not be found to this day. . . ." There's some hard words, some hurtful pieces to that.   —U.S. adoptive mother

Stories of kinship and origin—including not just verbal or written texts but also the photos, objects, and activities through which stories are socially transmitted—are meant to bring coherence and unity to identity, call people into being, explain where they came from and how they got to where they are, and make sense of what has happened to us and to others (Widdershoven 1993; Denzin 1990; Wheeler 1999). These identity narratives are the locus of the dialectical process by which history not only shapes us, but we shape it (Somers 1992; Maynes 1992). Yet there is an inherent tension in narrative formation; Foucault reminds us that while agents have the power to select particular versions of a story, social conditions foster particular stories that come to be taken as true (Rice 1992). In the case of China/U.S. adoption, then, it is instructive to ask which identity narratives about children are taken to be true and "right," *especially* in the midst of many biographical unknowns.

In most cases, children arrive at orphanages with no information on birth families or the circumstances of relinquishment. Stories of their identities and ways of belonging thus wrestle with the problem of narrative cohesion and closure. Memory, which Sturken (1997) argues "provides the core of identity" (1), must be created out of disparate pieces of information, such as the tidbits about birth families that Professor Huang passed on to Martha and Carl.[1] It isn't as if nothing is known about the general circumstances under which children in China are left and found. In the introduction, I provided an overview of the structural factors scholars and adoption experts think variously combine to lead to abandonment: the stringencies of the family-planning policy, cultural and economic gender relations that "necessitate" having a son, rural or urban poverty, stigma and lack of resources for special-needs children, and lack of social and legal support for single motherhood. But it is difficult to know which of these factors come into play in individual cases, with what frequency, or in what ways. Neither is a national survey of Chinese birth families or the discovery of circumstances in individual cases very likely. No matter how much information one has about abandonment in general, there is rarely if ever enough to be definitive about a specific child's history.

Adoptive couple Joyce Cousins and Marion Frank expressed the frustration felt by many parents at the lack of specific information; that they focused especially on the unknowns of relinquishment was not uncommon in my conversations with parents:

Joyce: That, I think, is the only thing that bothers me about adopting from China—that it's so hard to know.

Marion: The idea that Corrine [our daughter] will never get to know, that's the part that's hard to me.

Sara: What parts especially would you want to know?

Marion: I would want her to know what the circumstances of her being given up were, so we can effectively deal with it instead of us trying to guess whether it was a second child, or an unwed mother, or . . .

What ensues is a delicate balancing act, for both parents and researchers, of "choosing" the right story, or at least a story that partially satisfies the desire to know while leaving room for other possibilities. Explaining abandonment and adoption *to* a child catalyzes this dilemma, as adoptive mother Jennifer Bartz pointed out:

It's like the sex question. You sort of dread them asking it. But in fact, the "How come they didn't keep me?" is a great question. And you have to preface it by saying, "I don't know. I can only guess. What do you think, and what do you imagine? Here's three or four things I imagine, or I've been told. What do you want to construct?" I can tell her, you know, what sometimes just seems like the facts, and what sometimes seems sort of propagandistic, depending on who's telling you. You know [in a sing-song voice]: "They couldn't keep you because of the one-child policy, but you're still really valuable, dadada. . . ." It's like, I've encountered all that . . . that's a historical force. There's some part of that that is an historical truth, there's a reality to it. And it's, *it's how you invite her to tell it back to herself, or how you invite her to explore it, that really is compelling.* [Emphasis mine.]

How is one supposed to know how to feel about a child's abandonment, let alone explain it to a child so that she, too, can make sense of it? Jennifer points out that her daughter's history is constructed and therefore all the more weighty. She recognizes that storytelling is an act of social reproduction that lies at the uncertain juncture of individual experience and collective knowledge. She expresses what we might think of as a sociological insight—that narrative formation is social, evolving, and historical, striving to provide coherence to identity through a retelling of the past in order to make sense of the present and future (Giddens 1991; Plummer 1990; Hall 1996a). The problem of narrating origins thus *is* the problem of history, of the haunting of other places and lives and possibilities. So this is not a matter of me as researcher unpacking the political economy of adoption but of analyzing how parents and others unpack it through the problem of narrating the child's origins, which is the problem of the impossible contradictions of her becoming a full member of new family and nation. In other words, the unknowns of abandonment and bio-kinship are compounded by the continuing significance of the multiple dislocations through which children become adopted.

Making sense of abandonment—"getting the story right," for now and in anticipation of children's future queries—is thus experienced as a frustrating and unruly process;[2] there are so many unknowns, multiple ways to make sense of them, and powerful implications for how one does so. And over this unruliness hover birth parents, and more specifically birth mothers; *knowing* a child's past is complicated by the present absence of her other family, the one that abandoned her for reasons only partially known. I consistently encountered contradictions and uncertainties in the narrative framing of abandonment within individual stories, between couples, and across families. Parents waffle between feelings of sadness and anger toward birth mothers who abandon their children and toward a Chinese government that forces children to become "political refugees," as one parent put it. An adoptive mother says how sad her child's birth parents must be; within minutes her husband is berating Chinese people for "throwing their children away." A couple admits how much they resent their child's birth mother for giving up her child; an adoptive father says he will teach his daughter that "people put up kids for adoption not because they don't like 'em, but all the other reasons . . . it's not that they're bad people. It's poverty, and the government, and all of that." One couple insists that it is important to tell their daughter how much her birth mother must have loved her; another single mom protests that her daughter will then wonder, "If she loved me and gave me up, you might, too."

Joyce and her partner, Marion, openly shared the anger and confusion they feel in trying to make sense of abandonment. Their emotional response to the narrative conveys the problem of knowing/not knowing across multiple mothers. Trying to get the story right runs into the "problem" of the birth mother, which circles back around to the meaning of their own motherhood:

> *Marion*: I'm very resentful of her birth mother. I'm like totally protective and I'm not happy about her birth mother [Joyce is giggling a bit ashamedly and Marion starts to snicker, too, at her own level of emotion], and I don't like her birth mother!
>
> *Joyce*: I don't want to convey that.
>
> *Marion*: No, I definitely don't want to convey it, but what I would convey to Corrine is that, for whatever reason, your family had two children and they could only have one, so, so they wanted her to have a better life and so—
>
> *Joyce*: I don't want to call her her family.
>
> *Marion*: [sighing with slight exasperation] Well, her birth parents. Whatever. Her birth parents had more than one child, most likely, and so they gave her to a family that wanted her—us. Not "wanted" her, but . . . Not that they didn't want her.
>
> *Joyce*: We'll probably use different words.
>
> *Marion*: Yes, we'll have to refine it. [We laugh together about them trying to work this out.]

We see here the unruly process of trying to narrate abandonment and the resentment that sometimes surfaces toward Chinese birth parents for leaving to adoptive parents the messy job of explaining it to their children. Because Joyce and Marion are a lesbian couple, this is the problem of accommodating a third mother, who is hard to imagine as the right kind. They and other lesbian adoptive parents I interviewed were relatively comfortable expressing their struggles with this process—perhaps more so than straight couples. Yet even as they had to think about how their adopted daughter would deal with the difference of having two adoptive mothers, Joyce and Marion still wrestled with the desire for an exclusive kinship with her, under the shadow of "traditional ideals of

the nuclear family as the primary contemporary measure of social respectability and value" (Eng 2003: 8). This is a matter of getting the story
right not just for children but also for adoptive parents, in relation to
their children and the Other mother.

Abandonment is powerful because it cuts children off from what we
take to be an essential part of themselves, yet never does so completely—
they carry with them signs of their history that simultaneously provide
clues to their origins and push the boundaries of familial identities.
Writing about her own angst with her "lost and found" daughter's unknowns, adoptive mother Karin Evans (2000) says of a needle she found
in a handmade Chinese quilt: "First, it suggested to me that some things
are impossible to trace; and second, that nothing comes completely
anonymously. The hand of the maker is always there" (212). So when an
adoptive mother remarked to me that "any bit of information makes [my
daughter's] past less a void and more like a pesky shadow," she spoke to
a central tension in origin stories. A narrative that attempts to capture
some kind of authentic past "simultaneously records a certain apparent continuity and emphasizes its loss from memory. . . . Out of this
estrangement comes a conception of personhood, *identity* (yes, you and
that naked baby are identical) which, because it cannot be 'remembered,'
must be narrated" (Anderson 1991: 204). It is no accident, I am sure, that
Anderson uses a baby metaphor to illustrate the historical construction of memory, because there is a certain fetishizing of natural origins
(whether of individuals, objects, ideas, or nations) in identity narratives,
as becomes clear in the treatment of mothers and children in adoption
stories. Trying to get the story of abandonment right exposes a two-sided
obsession with origins; a child's connections to birth family, nation, and
culture are a necessary component of, but also pose a challenge to, the
desire for complete kinship in their new family and nation.

Given the memorialization that "holey" origins seem to call for, American parents of children from China often look not only for clues to their
children's individual stories but also for manageable ways to tell them.
This is illustrated in the phenomenon of life books (albums of textual and
visual materials chronicling the child's early life history). Regional chapters of the support organization Families with Children from China spon-
sor Lifebook Sessions to train parents in this practice; one of the more
popular workshop organizers, Cindy Probst, has a book titled *Adoption*

Lifebook: A Bridge to Your Child's Beginnings. Adoptive mother Jacqueline Farrell describes pulling together clues from disparate sources:

> I found that the bits of information gleaned from various sources could be put together into a more comprehensive story than I expected. Nina's mood, appearance, state of development when we met her, the information we got from the orphanage director, and our personal observations in China all contribute to a history that, if not complete, provides a unique platform for Nina to build her identity on. She didn't drop out of the sky. She has a story that is individual and can be told sensitively.[3]

Life books—which most often exhibit written and photographic evidence of the parents' journey to China to adopt, information on the child gathered before and during the journey, the child's development and transformation after returning home—strive to chronicle and approximate the life of the adopted child, by way of adoptive parents' rendition of historical traces. It is parents who most expressly strive to create that "unique platform" for identity formation. So, while Farrell asserts the importance of dealing with the "truth" of her child's story, or at least a truth that can be approximated from the bits and pieces to which she has access, the fact is that origin stories vary in the truths they convey and the kinds of information they deem important. The narration of Chinese origins can reinscribe desires for exclusive kinship and managed foreignness through what they both include and omit. I have encountered, for example, a number of families who do not remember their child's Chinese name, let alone the town she is from. One life book I saw never mentions birth parents, and O/orients the child's origins to her adoptive home and nation: the opening page of the life book uses a Chinese takeout box to allegorize the story of this girl's migration.

Whether the vehicle for animating narrative identity gaps is a Chinese takeout box, a child's emotional and physical state, or divine intervention, the press of history on these origin stories is thoroughly gendered. Life books are a domesticated "maternal archive" that labors to create a connective, cohesive identity for the child in the tenuous zone between market and care, China and America, biological and adoptive kinship. As such, they mirror the anxieties of white middle-class parenthood under late capitalism, centered on the mother's domestic practice (Anagnost 2000). In China/U.S. adoption, it is almost always adoptive mothers who make life books, plan culture camps, and create and keep stories in conscious response to the unsettled histories of their children—daughters separated from birth mothers. Across racial and national borders, the ghosts of the inequitable gender relations that create "wrong," extra, or excluded bodies (Anagnost 1995; Das 1995) speak all the more loudly. These multiple, transnational dislocations have the effect of undoing the naturalized assumptions of white middle-class motherhood, which is then that much more intensely mobilized toward the cultural construction of domestic kinship. In the sections that follow, I begin to weave together the threads of gender in transnational abandonment stories, focusing centrally on adoptive parents' (especially mothers') narratives. I demonstrate that the narration of girl abandonment is complicated by cultural, class, and national imaginings, as well as by gendered ideals of motherhood.

Engendering Abandonment, Feminizing Culture

All adoptive parents of Chinese children inevitably struggle with some of the same basic facts—nearly every child has been found and brought to an orphanage, most children in orphanages are girls, and the vast majority (95 percent) of the children adopted from China are girls. What's more, the gendered child is a link between disparately situated mothers and motherhoods. A January 2002 Listserv discussion among families with children from China was titled "My Chinese Mom" and was a thread carried solely by half a dozen women wrestling with their daughter's questions about their Chinese birth families, abandonment, and adoption. In the case of both subject and discussants, mothers stood in for families—mothers who want children, mothers who can't take care of children, people who do or don't want girls. Gendered origin stories move back and forth between the "them" of China and birth parents and the "us" of the U.S. and adoptive parents. In the middle stand the daughters whose very presence, practices, and eventual questions link the two, beginning with culture itself.

As anomalies in the case of China/U.S. adoption, the abandonment stories of boys, especially healthy boys, offer some insight into how the bodies of adopted children are continuous with a whole set of gendered cultural explanations. While there is a plethora of specific Internet Listservs for families with children (assumed to be girls) from China—increasingly, for parents of girls from the same orphanage—in 2001 there was just one general Listserv for families with boys, called the China Boys Club. Its director told me he estimated that about 3 percent of the adopted children coming to the United States from China were boys, and that one of the main concerns of their adoptive parents was how to explain abandonment. The adoptive father of a Chinese boy put it this way: "How are we supposed to explain why his parents didn't want a healthy boy? At least with girls you have an explanation." He referred to one of the standard lines of the master narrative of abandonment: gender preferences in Chinese culture discriminate against girls, especially in rural areas. Chinese themselves (especially urbanites) often explain the skewed gender ratio of abandoned children with a somewhat embarrassed reference to the cultural tradition of *zhongnan qingnu*—"boys are more important than girls."

But the "gender explanation" of girl abandonment is not as handy as it might seem; it toggles between negative images of China and the feelings of the child who is Chinese, leaving sadness, bewilderment, and anger in its wake. Adoptive father Aaron Kretz voiced frustration on behalf of himself and his daughter:

> Well you know, the biggest question for me is how does she deal with the fact that her birth mother gave her up—her birth parents. How do you explain that? Now you could say to her well, they did it because they wanted a boy. Well, I don't think that's gonna go over too well. . . . The truth of the matter is, people in China and India give up their kids because they want boys! They give up their girls. That's the reality, and at some point we're gonna have to tell her that.

Joyce Cousins said that her "sense of the culture was 'It's okay, that one's gone now'"—although, she added, she wouldn't present it to her daughter Corrine like that. Gender discrimination is a "cultural" explanation, but an inadequate one that might make a child herself feel inadequate.

Adoptive mom Lila Noonan told me, "I don't want Felicity to feel . . . inadequate in any way? The abandonment, that doesn't reflect on who she is." When I asked Lila what she was afraid might make her daughter feel inadequate, she responded, "Well, just, um, 'Oh well you're a girl, and boys have more value than girls do.' It's gonna take some kind of contemplation on how we're going to approach it. But I want to be really careful, because I don't want her to feel inadequate. I want her to know her story, and I want it to be a wonderful story, because it is!"

One problem lies in the need to construct a unitary Chinese culture, which seems somehow necessary to making the adopted child's identity whole yet is read and imagined off of her body (and reflected back to her)[4] in contradictory ways. The sex of the abandoned child triggers an engendered "cultural" explanation for abandonment that reinscribes a China that is backward, feminized, and patriarchal; yet the construction of a beautiful and strong culture (the one many parents desired to begin with) must equally rely on feminized national figures. Marjorie Sessions, an adoption agency administrator, described adoption as "the pimple" on a culture where women don't count. "All you have to do is watch something as simple as *Mulan,* where you see the problems with basic women's rights. It's retarded," she told me. Yet that same China is seen as a crucial piece in a child's positive identity development. A bit later in our conversation, Marjorie said that when preparing parents for adoption she encourages them to look at the positives of cultural heritage, adding: "You only need to look at *Mulan* to see the rich heritage." How, a number of parents have asked me, do you celebrate the wonder and beauty of Chinese culture when it treats its girls this way? To separate the culture into "good" and "bad" parts is to undermine the cohesion of the child's origin and identity, in part because as a girl, and as an Asian girl, she carries the signs of both cultural beauty and cultural backwardness. And yet cultural heritage must be celebrated, because it is understood as a central conduit between the individual child and a collective, originary human history. As one adoptive parent put it: "I think it's real important to maintain her connection with China itself, with the culture of China, because that is a basic part of her identity. That's where she was born."

Birth parents, birthplaces, and birth cultures can be "blamed" for abandonment, but they cannot be completely written off because they are inextricably linked to each other and to the child. Explanations that begin with gender thus open up the problem of cultural and racial difference, of how to make sense of the Chinese Other that is both over there and right here. An inadequate Chinese culture of inadequate women explains abandonment, but this reality is unpalatable enough that it must be adjusted so that adopted children—*who carry this history with them, on their gendered, raced bodies*—do not feel inadequate. Dislocations of culture, kinship, and birth are made inseparable, bound by the sense that adoption is difficult, unnatural, and risky for a child "severed not only from its 'real' family but also from ethnic roots and cultural heritage: in a word, from its true identity" (Terrell and Modell 1994: 155). The result is a complex interaction among categories of social subjectivity: the gendering of birth origins not only conjures a true cultural identity but also has the strange effect of biologizing the race of the child, through which kinship difference—particularly from the standpoint of whiteness—is read.

The problem of constructing a unitary Chinese cultural identity figures not only through the gendered connection of child to birth mother but through race difference and the making of whiteness. It is important to note that several Chinese American adoptive mothers I talked to were not as worried about gendered abandonment stories. Some said that because they had firsthand experience with how gender inequalities worked in Chinese or Chinese American families and communities, it wouldn't be so hard to explain to their children. For these Chinese American adoptive mothers, using gender inequity as an explanation did not threaten the kind of holistic Chinese culture (that was never there to begin with) that seemed to haunt some white parents' narratives. Furthermore, a condemnation of patriarchal practices seemed to provide the space for the active production of a different Chinese American identity for their daughters and themselves. First-generation immigrant Helen Mah expressed almost a moral righteousness in getting her daughter out of China, proudly telling me about the circle of strong women in which she was now learning Chinese culture. Adoption facilitator Zhuli also made this connection explicit:

> Emotionally as a woman myself, I experienced so much prejudice when I was a child, growing up in China. And I think I definitely

sympathize with these Chinese girls, who are abandoned because of their gender basically. So I feel very good about doing something to help them . . . as an ethnic role model for a lot of children. I think it's important for the girls to know some Chinese, Chinese women particularly.

White parents more gingerly negotiated what seemed liked cultural inadequacies to them, perhaps because whiteness tends to construct recognizable cultural boundaries for racialized others while remaining oblivious to its own secure borders (Frankenberg 1993).

Adoptive mother Karin Evans (2000) writes that she wanted to put together all the pieces—"the baffling causes and conditions"—that might explain her daughter's abandonment, but then gave up on knowing about or making sense of this place called China (248). But such recourse to "inscrutable China" might too easily avoid scrutiny of the Chinese state and its role in reproducing gender hierarchies. Indeed, this thing called Chinese culture blurs with the family-planning policy; *both* become naturalized as that which constitutes children's Chinese origins. As a result, parents feel all the more torn over their children's Chinese identities, stuck between defending and disliking an essential "China." This comes through in Ginger Adley's frustrations:

What am I to say? "This is your country, this is your extraordinary culture, and this is the problem with the culture?" . . . I can say, "Look, this is what happens, this is why, you have to understand, this was a choice, it was good. . . ." I can say all the right things, all the positive things. [But] if I were [a Chinese adoptee like my daughter], and sixteen years old, and I knew my country said, "You have to hide that child, you have to just give it away," I would be very angry, I would be very angry. And no matter how much love and respect I had for my Chinese culture and my Chinese heritage, a part of me would be very angry, and not understand.

Explaining abandonment sets up an impossible contradiction around the child. Her gendered and raced and birthed body demands a normalized continuity of identity; but this relies on gendered cultural explanations that in turn undermine any such coherence. State practices may ab-

sorb some of the blame but become problematically conflated with an essentialized Chinese culture or inadequate to explain the story of an individual child. The more celebratory the universal embrace of such an individual life—the "good" of adoption—the more split the subjectivity
of the girl-child seems to become. This is because explaining her trajectory from abandonment to adoption reveals the particularity of not just
her Chinese origins but of American culture, white middle-class kinship,
and differently located motherhoods. In other words, gendered understandings of origins and motherhood, read off the body of adopted girls,
are a window on how nature and culture, choice and constraint, circulate through national, racial, and class imaginings of adoptive mothers
themselves. These narratives are a reflection of parents' own anxieties
about "right parenting" vis-à-vis other mothers.

Reading Motherhood Across Borders: Blood and Choice, Race and Nation

The narrative link between abandoned girls and Chinese culture is provided by birth families, and more specifically the birth mothers who
serve as feminized representations of Chinese national culture. One the
one hand, birth parents mediate the passing on of a celebrated Chinese
heritage that is at once biological and cultural. As adoptive mother Ginger Adley put it, "We have the man's family that goes back thousands
of years. And we have the woman's family that goes back thousands of
years. And they're *her*." Or as one of the discussants in the "My Chinese
Mom" Internet thread put it, the answer to her anxiety over how to make
her daughter's unknown birth family "come to life" was embodied in her
daughter, since they "look like her, [and] quite possibly have similar
emotional and cognitive tendencies and mannerisms." On the other
hand, birth parents mediate the more suspect engendered and impover-
ished act of abandonment, which in turn is linked to a vilified Chinese
nation and state. But it is crucial that this process of reading *birth* family
and nation is equally a construction of *adoptive* family and nation. One
key place to interrogate this double reading of the child's identity is
in the figure of motherhood, and more particularly differently located

motherhoods. Adoption demands a universalized understanding of the mother-child bond, yet snags on the binary of blood kinship and cultural choice.

Birth mothers loom large in abandonment narratives. For example, as Aaron Kretz talked about the difficulty of abandonment stories, he said, "Her birth mother gave her up—her birth parents," demonstrating a "correction" that occurred several times during my interviews with parents. Indeed, both individual and popular imaginaries of abandonment often envision that it is the birth mother who does the deed, whether willingly or not. As I demonstrate below, the intention and will with which she is imagined to do this can either ennoble her or make her ignoble. Birth fathers, by contrast, become a physically removed afterthought to "tummy mommies." When I asked Lisa Walker and Gerry Lee if they talked about their daughter Pan Pan's birth parents to her, Lisa replied, "We call it her tummy mommy. And actually, we didn't know what to say about her father! (laughs) And we were kind of like, 'Tummy . . . uh. . . .' And Pan Pan goes, 'Father.' Okay, yeah!"

This overrepresentation of birth mothers reflects the continuing power of the notion of a universal maternal bond between biological mother and child—even to the point of "treating mother and child as a single entity with unitary interests" (Glenn 1994: 13)—both of whose identities derive in some basic way from the event of birth. Adoptive parents thus sometimes find the decision to relinquish a child irreconcilable with maternal instincts. As O'Donovan (2002) puts it, underlying discourses of abandonment

> is the assumption that if the woman who gives birth were not a victim, or ill, she would not abandon her child and that giving up one's baby is unnatural for a "real" mother—that is, a woman who has given birth. Her actions therefore have to be constructed in such a way as to assuage people's anxieties about mothers, about what is natural, and about love. (373)

At the same time, idealized bonds between biological mother and child suggest the possible "lesser than" of adoptive motherhood; this hits home in the common reference to birth mothers as "real moms." Cheri Register (1991) captures this notion in the title of her book *Are Those Kids*

Yours? And this is why, at an event for FCC parents that I attended, an adult Korean adoptee told her audience, "I know you're scared of your kids saying to you, 'You're not my mom.'"

These anxieties are all the more intense for adoptive parents who have been through infertility. In this case, both parents and adoption professionals manage the loss of "real" motherhood by narrating the move to adoption as a choice. In fact, adoption is not usually a first choice; most women who seek to adopt are white women who have experienced infertility (Freundlich 2000). But if adoptive kinship is to be valorized, and true parenthood reproduced, adoption must be made of equal weight to bloodlines. Indeed, the adoption profession has increasingly retooled itself around serving the needs of parents and thus embracing adoption as choice ("opt to adopt" is a common phrase). May (1995) dates this to the post–World War II era, when infertility entered the national imaginary as a personal tragedy (especially for barren white women). Many times I heard adoptive parents iterate some version of the mantra that accompanies professional infertility counseling at organizations like RESOLVE: "We decided we were more interested in parenting than in giving birth."

The choice to parent outside of and after the loss of biological reproduction presents a potential identity problem for both adoptive parents and children. A number of parents told me they didn't know how to tell their daughters they had first tried to have children by birth, as this might make adoption "second best." Joyce told me: "I don't want her to maybe know that we tried to have one ourselves. For some reason that's the part I don't want her to know. I'd rather she hears the story from the part where we wanted to [adopt]." Parents feared that a child might feel inadequate for being abandoned as a girl but that she might equally feel inadequate for being adopted as a second choice. *Both* narrations reflect on the nagging problem of adequate motherhood.

Given the discursive power of the "chosen child," especially as a response to the specter of adoption as a second-best form of kinship, it becomes all the more difficult for adoptive mothers' narratives to accommodate what looks like birth mothers' "unchoosing" of motherhood. And what's more, the cultural power of the sacred and sacrificial bonds of biological motherhood—bonds cut short and thus indelibly written on the child herself—raises the question of whether equally strong bonds can be chosen and created in adoptive motherhood. Plagued by the bloodlines of true kinship, explanations of abandonment and adoption labor to restore universalized motherhood. And in doing so, they mine discourses of culture and class difference that show motherhood to be particular and disparate. Just as in the previous section we saw how abandonment stories were filtered through gendered imaginings of cultural difference, so here we see how universal notions of motherhood are filtered through particular imaginings of cultural difference, read in race and nation. Such maternal labor is especially poignant in transracial adoption, where white mother and Asian daughter necessitate an explanation that normalizes motherhood (Eng 2003). The struggle to understand Chinese birth mothers' "choices" becomes a struggle to validate the white middle-class motherhood that best represents and reproduces choice itself (see Solinger 2001).

If right and real mothers do not give up children, how is abandonment to be explained? One explanation is that mothers had no choice and were victims of a system. Adoptive mother Cindy Coombs found herself using such an explanation (if uncertainly):

> I was sitting next to this woman on a trip once, and she started in with the "Oh, aren't you wonderful [for adopting]," and all that stuff, and "Oh, the Chinese must h-a-t-e their children." You know, that whole thing. And I was stuck with her, on this boat! I mean, we're out in the middle of the lake. Like what do I do, just push her over, or what? . . . And you know, I hear comments like that, "How terrible they are" and that sort of thing, and I say hey, anywhere you go, parents do that, and it's not right anywhere. It's not just China. Although, at the same time, I try not to be like, Pollyanna-ish, you know, about China? Because it is harsh, the policy. It's harsh, and detrimental, and for many, many people who have survived so much. So I don't want to paint a happy face on it. But I also feel like it's real easy for people to look at it and ignore the other side of it.

When Cindy responded to the woman who asserted that Chinese must "h-a-t-e" their children, she turned things around to explain that the wrongful act of abandonment is found everywhere but that the Chinese policy left their daughter's birth family with little choice. Similarly,

Christy Kinsler said, "Well, the one thing I can say and feel dead sure of, is that I'm sure that her parents had no choice. I'm sure they felt they had no choice at all. . . . And I think, I just have to believe, *that's the only reason someone could do that,* that they felt there was nothing else to do" (emphasis mine). Christy wanted to demonstrate to her daughter that because of the cultural and political system of which her parents were a part, they had no choice. For her, there was no other way to explain, as some parents put it, "how any mother could do that." Ginger Adley also gave birth families and birth mothers leeway by placing the problem on the shoulders of the Chinese government and an unseemly part of Chinese culture. She and a number of other parents said they could not imagine the heartache of birth mothers who had to give up their daughters—mothers who were victims of a cruel system.

The harshness of China's family-planning policy and the lack of social supports that might make reliance on sons less necessary are explanations that provide some refuge in the narration of adoption origins. As arbiter of both abandonment and adoption, the Chinese state contributes, ironically, to the narrative preservation of ideals of motherhood: adoptive motherhood is legitimated as a sacrificial, responsive choice for children in need of a family, and birth motherhood is saved from the problem of abandonment as unmotherly choice. Through the backward, Third World face of the Chinese state, domestic birth mothers become victims without agency (Mohanty 1988; Briggs 2003); through the forward-looking modern face of the Chinese state (i.e., the CCAA), foreign adoptive mothers exercise choices that restore the child's need for a mother's love. The racialized images, unspoken class privilege, and global hierarchy of nations that help make possible this version of the child's relationship to two mothers are reconstructed in the motherhood ideal (Eng 2003; Riley 1997; Colen 1995, Sollinger 2001).

Yet a second construction of birth mothers—as making a "good choice" in the best interests of their children—further helps shore up mothering ideals. And as I argue below, this narrative also exposes the state, class, and race relations that stratify the reproductive choices of birth and adoptive mothers. Indeed, adoptive parents' personal and published stories of abandonment often conjure a caring, loving mother surreptitiously placing her baby in a train station or near the orphanage gates, then watching to make sure the child is safe until found—this despite the fact that orphanage directors, adoption officials, and birth parents themselves (see Johnson 2004) say that quite often it is a relative or sometimes even a local official who places a child. In this imaginary, birth mothers become both victims and heroes who did the best thing for their child in difficult circumstances. Teresa Huang, adoptive mom to six-year-old Katya, expressed it this way:

> We spend a lot of time explaining how difficult it must have been for her mother not only to have to hide her pregnancy but her birth, and to have her for nine days until it was time to get her someplace where she would be safe. And I think in that respect, we try and portray Katya's mother as more of a hero than this horrible person who abandoned her. I think that's the most important thing, is that the children know they risked a lot, risked jail, risked everything to make sure that Katya got somewhere safe.

Despite, and perhaps because of, the dearth of knowledge about the actual circumstances of a child's abandonment, whatever snatches of information are available are often rendered into signs of care and sacrifice. Motherhood is read off of the physical clues surrounding the child's body. It is not uncommon, as Cindy Coombs alluded to in her response to the woman on the boat, for one small detail to become synecdochically crucial: "I just told her, 'You know, we don't know all the reasons why, but she was left in a safe place, with a note with important information, and that shows that somebody cared.'" Others assert that the circumstances of their daughter's relinquishment don't really count as abandonment because she was wrapped in a warm blanket or left near a police station. Lila Noonan told me, "[Her birth family] did have a plan. Because she was found on a park bench so close to the medical center." Or as Hannah Carter put it,

> Well, the orphanage finally told me that she had been abandoned in a toilet in a public park. I think they thought that didn't sound good, but in reality, the women's bathroom wasn't a bad place—it was sheltered, a woman would find her, and it would be soon. I mean, her natural parents clearly cared, because of the note. It's hard to think that's

what they *had* to do. They knew she would be found, and they wanted her to have a bright future.

Staff members at Chinese orphanages were also impressed by these kinds of details. One read both bravery and desperation in the abandonment of a child in the middle of the day right in front of the orphanage gates. In another instance, the staff told me of a couple of women who had come asking to look around the orphanage for children they said had gotten lost. The women looked around thoroughly and left, leading staff to believe they were checking to make sure babies they had left had been safely found.

I do not want to argue whether or to what extent Chinese birth parents take risks on behalf of their children—obviously many do—but rather that the ways in which narrative gaps about them and their children are filled point to the power of the sacrificial maternal narrative, as it reflects on both birth and adoptive mothers. "A mother's love" is powerful in both Chinese and American adoption discourses. It is quite common to hear people in China speak with a kind of reverence of *mu'ai* (maternal love), especially in reference to *kelian* (pitiful) orphans who have none. The grounds of several orphanages I visited contained statues or other depictions of mothers encircling children in their arms. And in my conversations with orphanage and adoption administrators, anxieties were directed toward making sure children received a mother's love again, and more specifically toward whether foreign adoptive parents could and would supply it. A number of these officials expressed concern that children might go through a second abandonment at the hands of parents who did not have a natural (biological or cultural) connection to a child.

American adoptive parents, in contrast, are anxious to assure their children and observers of their families that there will be no second abandonment because a mother's love is indomitable, despite the lack of a "natural" connection. The symbol of "motherly love" is rife in the popular discourses of both parents and adoption agencies. One adoptive mother has started a business called "A Mother's Love Fundraising"; after referencing her own adoption success upon the heels of infertility struggles, she describes a program of product merchandising whose mission is "to assist people with the hardship of paying for Adoptions

and Infertility costs."[5] A visit to an Internet adoption resource (http://
e-magazine.adoption.com) in August 2004 turned up two articles titled,
respectively, "A Father's Impact" and "A Mother's Love Is for Today and
Always." Fathers come off as socially important, but mothers' love is
natural and permanent (including, as the latter article asserts somewhat
defensively, in adoption).

The million-dollar question for some parents is what to say about a
mother's love. Not knowing exactly why abandonment occurred in the
case of their individual child raises the question of how to imagine what
the birth mother felt. Christy Kinsler and Debra Fine summed up part of
this dilemma in my interview with them:

> *Christy*: And I can imagine saying to Mei, "I wish we had letters from
> your mother. . . . I know that she loves you, that she blesses you,
> that she thinks about you all the time."
> *Debra*: Well, actually I have mixed feelings about saying that much,
> because if she loved her, why would she give her up, kind of thing.
> It's sort of like she cared for her, and wanted the best for her, and
> so therefore—
> *Christy*: No, I didn't . . . I wouldn't say to Mei that her birth mother
> loved her and that's why they took her.
> *Debra*: No, right. 'Cause that, I think, would be really confusing.

What's confusing, as some parents pointed out to me, is that they and
their children will wonder exactly what Debra expressed: "If she loved
her, why would she give her up?" And more poignantly, if she did love
her and give her up, then why wouldn't adoptive parents do the same?
Liz Nickels made clear how real this is in a story about her five-year-old
daughter, Hannah:

> So the other day I was in the car, I wanted to just jump out of the car,
> run into the dry cleaners, run out, right? Just, right there next to the
> car, so she could see me the whole way. I could see she was panicking,
> the terror in her is just rising. And it had been a rough morning with
> her. And I just said, "Hannah, I'm your mother, and I'm not going to
> leave you." And as soon as I said it, I thought, in a few years she is

going to be able to say, "But yeah mom, I had one who did." That does-
n't safeguard anything. You know, it's true. She *was* left by her mother.

Narratives that must make sense of where an adopted child came from
and where she ends up expose the contradictions inherent in the universalizing notion of motherhood and its permanent imprint on identity.
Origin narratives seem to require a particularizing of Other mothers that
must somehow, simultaneously, not particularize motherhood itself.

Most poignantly, then, the labor to reproduce adoptive mothers' love
encounters the problem of reconciling universal ideals of motherhood
with the individual choices of Chinese and American women (see also
Riley 1997). Calling on harshly constrictive social policies or a patriarchal
culture to explain abandonment cannot fully make up for the individual
practices of Chinese mothers, especially in a context where *adoptive*
mothers are perceived to enact their own kind of heroism, carrying out
individual choices that reproduce proper motherhood—against the odds
of infertility or homophobia, for example. "How any mother could do
that" hovers over the narration of a child's kinship, as do queries (including from Chinese adopted children as they get older) about the many
mothers in China, even poor ones, that keep their second or third daughters or disabled children. Reading the Chinese state or Chinese culture as
backward seems to point back to backward mothers. As Joyce put it, "I
have occasionally fantasized about traveling to China and somehow going
door to door if I needed to and saying [laughing a little and lightly
pounding table with fist for emphasis], 'Who left that little . . . who abandoned a baby on . . . ?'"

Urban Chinese observers, like American adoptive parents, sometimes
read abandoning parents with ambivalence (do they care or don't they?
do they have a choice or don't they?). I once asked a taxi driver in China
what she thought birth mothers felt. "*Ayah*," she said, "they have no education or culture, so they just abandon them thinking about the practical stuff." "But surely mothers feel something," I probed. "Well, yes,
they probably care about their children," she replied, "but they think
they have no other *banfa* (way)." A conversation on the same topic over
lunch with several members of the office staff at Hongqi Orphanage in
central China drew similar conclusions:

Sara: American adoptive parents wonder what kind of feelings birth parents have about abandoning their children. I tell them it's probably difficult, but I don't know any birth parents.

Du: We don't know them either.

Li: They have low education, so they probably don't have too much feeling about it.

Sara: So education and feelings are related?

Yuan: No, no, education is related to a sense of responsibility. Of course they have feelings for their children—this is human. They just don't have the sense of responsibility.

Qin: And they don't think about the fact that they are passing on the burden of caring for these children to the nation (*guojia*).

Reading motherhood crucially depends on a particular range of understandings of proper citizenship. It gestures toward producing a modern, educated nation of responsible subjects, with women-as-mothers as the centerpiece. In the case of China, imagining poor rural families as educationally and culturally backward helps explain limitations on mothers' feelings toward the children they abandon, which is in the same moment irresponsible to the collectivity of the nation (which must then take on the burden of caring for the children). Such moralism is linked specifically to the need for China to advance economically— including through population control, for which women are also held most responsible.

Family and motherhood are crucial grounds for the material and ideological molding of class and nation (Balibar 1988a; McClintock 1995; Yuval-Davis and Anthias 1989), not only in China, of course, but also in the United States.[6] In the context of late capitalist America, the mothering tasks of maintaining public virtue are increasingly absorbed into the private, consumerist domain of the individual home (Eng 2003; Solinger 2001), where nurturance is defined through class-abled choice. Marion's and Joyce's rendering of the birth family's choice was read off their daughter's body in ways that hinted at an aversion to the material circumstances of her abandonment. Marion told me, "When Corrine's teeth started coming in, they started coming in a little bit funny and differently than we had expected. So we used to joke, okay, we'll go to the Hongshan mountains and look for the [Joyce chimes in, 'three-toothed'] three-toothed people." Marion and Joyce then went on to say that they thought their daughter was "better off now than if she had stayed in the rice paddies with the three-toothed people," taking us full circle from signs read off of their child's body, to poor birth parents in China, to their own class and national privilege. Indeed, a number of parents referred to a better life for their children in relation to what China could offer. Lila put it innocently enough: "We thought maybe the parents knew the baby would be better off in an adoptive family? Or they wanted to give her a chance of a good life." There were also a number of parents who spoke of "getting girls out" of China in order to give them the education and value they deserved.

This does not mean that parents did not wrestle with the imbalance in fortunes (financial and otherwise) that brought their children to them, especially as it was equally an act of separation from birth mother and culture. Christy felt it "a disturbing thing to take someone away from her country" and that "being poor wasn't an impediment to happiness"— yet she was at the same time comforted that they could at least provide their daughter an education it would be tough to get in China, and as much love as a birth mother could give. Ginger Adley put it this way:

> I want to tell this woman, "I'm sorry. I'm truly deeply sorry that this happened to you. But *look* what has happened for your daughter. Look what I—what we can give to her. Not that you could have given less. But how we maybe have honored your family."

Ginger felt that to honor her daughter's birth mother was to love their mutual daughter and to keep alive the Chinese culture she imagined lived within her daughter. The ability to provide material well-being and an education potentially softened the blow of the biological and cultural dislocation from the original mother. This relationship between class and motherhood gets all the more complicated in the hiring of Chinese nannies for adopted children. On the northern California FCC Listserv, for example, there are regular discussions of how to find a good Chinese nanny who will help a child learn Chinese language and culture. The enactment of good motherhood, of passing on that which would make a child's and mother's identity whole, masks "the need for (and limit[s] the analysis of) the multiple non-kin caretakers—nannies, au pairs, and

domestic laborers—who extend the basis of childcare in capitalist economies" (Ginsburg and Rapp 1991: 329).[7]

For adoptive mothers' choices to "make up for" the choices (or lack
thereof) of birth mothers, they must rely to some extent on the very class,
race, and national privileges that belie claims to universal motherhood.
As Nancy Scheper-Hughes (1992) has argued in her study of a poor
Brazilian shantytown, the political economy of emotions that surround
mothering decisions demonstrates the particularity of the universalized
maternal bond as a social construction of the white Western middle class.
Indeed, as I discussed in chapter 2, we must consider how multiple racial
differences, including the construction of unfit black welfare mothers in
the United States, work together in the white imaginary of Chinese birth
mothers. To understand motherhood in concert with multiple relationships of power is to see the intimacies of biological reproduction and
family in the larger context of the social reproduction of inequalities,
from the ways in which mothers stand as representatives of national culture (Das 1995) to the ways in which transnational reproduction links
quite differently situated mothers (Colen 1995). It is the stark inequity of
choices between two mothers that leads Solinger (2001) to suggest that a
consumerist emphasis on choice undermines all women, pitting them
against each other through the choices afforded by their social location:
"The mutable quality of choice reminds us that sex and reproduction—
motherhood—provide a rich site for controlling women, based on their
race and class 'value'" (223). Writer and adoptive mother Janice Williamson considers the impossible contradictions of choice inherent in her
relationship to her daughter's birth mother in "If This Were an Opera,"
one slide in her visual and textual narrative of adopting from China (see
Figure 9).[8]

Fate and Motherhood

In the context of such contradictory class and race locations of motherhood, the positive hand of fate sometimes appears to explain how the unfortunate structural circumstances of abandonment are converted into
individual good fortunes of adoptive kinship. The language of fortune

Figure 9
If this were an opera—
While this singular *I* writes and grieves my unfortunate infertility,
more than half a billion Chinese women mourn and sing:

> WE LOVE OUR DAUGHTERS
> but must have a son.
> first and second daughters lie
> secreted in our family courtyard
> our third or fourth daughters
> sit close by until a son is born

Shixing jihua shengyu, guanche jiben guoce (Carry out family planning, implement the basic national policy).

Poster is part of the IISH Stefan R. Landsberger Collection (http://www.iisg.nl/~landsberger).

and destiny begins with the heady and reassuring notion that an adoption union was "meant to be" and a particular child was already "chosen" for a particular family. Popular Chinese culture provides convenient tropes. One waiting adoptive parent, for example, sent a posting to an Internet Listserv, excited about a fortune cookie she had received; the fortune read, "A long-awaited package of value will arrive soon." But perhaps the most common of such tropes, borrowed loosely from a Chinese folk practice, is that of a "red thread" connecting an adoptive mother to her adopted child even before they are officially matched. An online catalog of items for adoptive families sells a "red thread bracelet" described in this way:

> This time-honored Chinese legend underscores the belief that when a child is born invisible red threads connect that child's soul to all those people—present and in the future—who will play a part in that child's life. . . . The China Adoption community has taken this legend to heart, and has embraced the tradition of the red thread bracelet as a means of connecting with the children who wait to be united with their new families. Moms-to-be (and Dads!) generally wear their bracelets from the time they begin the paper chase to the day they meet their new daughter or son.[9]

While I return below to the "and Dads!" afterthought to destiny, I first examine how the thread connecting a child to "all those people . . . in that child's life" becomes one fatefully connecting her to adoptive parents in particular. Birth parents, and along with them the realities of whatever led them to abandon a child, are in danger of disappearing. Indeed, by a strange sleight of hand, abandonment might become a blessing. In the "good fortune" account of abandonment and adoption with which I opened this chapter, Teresa and Victor Huang made China a stopping place "on the way down from heaven" for girls like their daughter Katya—girls especially lucky because divinely chosen, as Teresa explained, for abandonment in and adoption out of China. In this rendering of the story, Katya's birth parents become mythologized conduits for a divine plan for Katya: "We have given her birth parents [happy-sounding names] because we want her to have a good association with these people. . . . Well, you know, the whole abandonment thing. We wanted to put a good feeling on that, because it was a good thing. That was the lucky part."

Why this recourse to mythologized birth parents and "destiny"? Part of the answer seems to lie in the irreconcilable positions of birth and adoptive parents vis-à-vis the child. The child is lucky to receive the blessing of parents who want her, and they in turn are lucky to have her; but what of birth parents? As Jennifer Bartz expressed it, "I know that we're all blessed, to have found each other. And you know, in the *best* of all possible worlds, she would still be you know, with a family [in China] that had the luxury and good fortune to keep her. But the blessing got passed on to us." Jennifer insinuates that adoption narratives face the problem of dealing with birth parents' lack of both material and cosmic fortune, especially in such disproportionate relation to adoptive parents' material and cosmic fortune. By taking the ultimate choice out of the hands of *both* families, fate or divinity becomes a narrative device for (at least temporarily) fixing this dilemma—it "avoids recognition of how social structures and international politics of domination enable adoption by these lucky and generous people" (Riley 1997: 97).

But another reason for employing fate, perhaps especially in the case of heterosexual couples that have experienced infertility, lies in the ironic disjuncture of mothering choices discussed above. What else but fate might explain how any mother would give up a child (or allow a child to be taken away), especially when there are other mothers who long to have a child by birth (and work hard to assure their children they will never be given up again)? My research suggests that single and lesbian mothers were less inclined to use fate in this particular way, perhaps because the odds against which they adopted were more often (but not always) about the social choice to adopt as a *first* option. Outside the confines of biological motherhood as fulfillment of heterosexual nuclear family relations, choice and the need to "recruit" progeny were more saliently a part of their narrative to begin with (Hayden 1995). But for a number of straight couples, losing the choice to reproduce naturally became part of a narrative of destiny, especially in relation to people halfway around the world whose choice to give up a child remained to some extent inexplicable. Adoption agencies and popular adoption wisdom

sometimes encourage understanding this as a fateful connection of intertwined "losses"—the birth mother's loss of a child and the adoptive mother's loss of biological birth. My notes on a conversation with
a straight couple that had returned from China just a few months before
illustrate this relationship between destiny and loss:

> Our discussion turns to the issue of fate, and I tell Rhonda and Jake
> how often I run across it in adoptive parents' stories. They both jump
> in to say they think their children were meant to be with them;
> Rhonda suggests that the CCAA and their Minnesota agency did a
> magical thing when matching them with their children, and Jake men-
> tions a Jewish belief ("even if we aren't very religious") that all par-
> ents and children were destined for each other. What about birth par-
> ents? I ask, being provocative; if this child is meant for you, then the
> birth parents are just carriers for your fate? They both look a bit puz-
> zled, and say they had no problem with that. After all, Rhonda says,
> with every fate, every magical gain like this, comes some loss. I ask if
> this is how she views her adoption, as a gain that came with the loss of
> having birth children, and she nods.

Fate, like the state, can take the fall for the unfairness of it all, allowing
birth mothers' losses to be memorialized as tragedy *at a distance* from
adoptive mothers (Anagnost 2000). In fact, as we see in Rhonda's narrative, institutional and supernatural explanations can together balance
out losses and smoothly transfer the blessing of motherhood from birth
to adoptive mother.

In a June 2004 article about her adoption experience, in the progressive Christian magazine *Sojourners,* Indo-American sociologist Ivy
George begins, "I contemplated motherhood well aware that at many
points the line between private matters and public affairs was faint and
broken" (24). While acknowledging that she as an adoptive mother
has "inherited or purchased" certain privileges, that "biological events
should not have to define the entirety of [birth mothers'] lives" (26),
and that "unrelenting social fissures" locate both women in the world,
George finds some solace in the "tragic knowledge" that she and her
"shadow sister . . . have been knit together by a trust without any guarantees. Not faith or hope exactly, because no promise has been given.

Merely the amazement of two distant and unlikely fates inextricably intertwined through one little life" (26). But then, in a celebration of the expansive and revolutionary possibilities of motherhood, George concludes:

> [T]he mother often has the sense of standing in for God or acting as God would unto her . . . adoption has heightened these sensibilities for me. I have a keen sense of what it means to be a recipient of trust. My daughter has been entrusted to me by one woman in particular, and by God at large. (29)

George makes sure that birth mothers are not vilified (she debiologizes motherhood and names the structural factors that constrain their choices), yet even in her careful hands, birth mothers might become vehicles for the divine enactment of sacrificial and exclusive adoptive motherhood.

Indeed, a discourse of fated losses and gains threatens to reduce the birth mother to biological incubator. The notion that "that's the way the system of fate is set up" comes too close to reproducing the mechanistic imagery of women as just happening to be those who carry children—that is, reproducing the idea that "that's the way the system [of biological reproduction] is set up" (Bordo 1993: 91). In this case, such imagery applies to *certain* women, effacing their subjectivity and experience relative to other women. In my conversation with Diane Scott, for example, motherhood was claimed as a destiny radically delinked from physical birth:

> Diane tells me that when their daughter Marianne asks about why she didn't come out of her mommy's tummy, Diane tells her: " 'I couldn't bear you, so another woman had to bear you, and then we had to come and find you.' I tell her about destiny, that *this* is destiny. 'You were always meant to be with Mom and Dad. God wanted for you to be with us.' " Her husband Sean, who has not said much, offers that one difficult thing is the abandonment of females in China, and Diane jumps in, "My feeling is that we can tell her that the reason she was in China was that God had to find a place where they couldn't keep their kids, so we could come find her!" She goes on to say she doesn't know if they'll

have an issue with her birth "mother," adding that she has a hard time
with the term *birth mother*. "I usually say 'the woman who gave you
birth,'" says Diane. "I feel strongly that *I'm* her mother, her soul is
ours, but that other woman gave birth to her."

Diane's narrative is an intense example of the problem of accommodating
two mothers, especially across borders of difference. A divine plan helps
imagine the Chinese birth mother as vehicle for the construction of the
American adoptive mother. Diane strips the "woman who gave you
birth" of her place as mother so that fate can do its job of fulfilling her
own place as rightful mother. The problem of the birth mother's choice
to abandon, which might threaten ideals of motherhood, can be dis-
pensed with. The child is then free to be chosen especially for its adoptive parents. Victor and Teresa Huang, too, emphasized the importance
of telling their daughter "that we wanted to have *her* as a child."

At work here is the ideology of exclusive kinship that marks much of
adoption in Western culture (Gailey 2000; Modell 1994), whereby adoptive families ideally create a new cohesive identity in which children and
parents belong unquestionably to each other. But *belonging* in adoption
sits at the disjointed intersection of two axes of choice. The first axis is
that of biological reproduction: most adoptive parents lack such a
choice, while birth parents seem to "unchoose" it. The second axis is that
of material consumption: most adoptive parents in the China program
can choose a desirable adoption, while many Chinese birth parents lack
the means to choose to keep a child. Both are in their own ways unfair
and perhaps unpalatable, their inequities seemingly irresolvable. Given
this impossible juncture of individual and structural spectra of choice,
fate does the job of managing losses and gains, dislocations and connections, moving the child into the arms of the right mother. To make sense
of abandonment is thus simultaneously a process of producing adoptive
kinship and, more specifically, a normalized version of motherhood.

I have tried to show that, cloaked in fate, these constructions attempt
to resolve both the problems of denaturalized motherhood and privileged class location. But it is also important, as I close this section on fate,
to revisit the place of men and fatherhood in the making of adoptive
motherhood. The cheery afterthought "and Dads!" that appears in the
explanation of red-thread bracelets is a reminder that it falls most heav-

ily on mothers to fulfill the destiny of kinship, but that the absence/presence of men is as important as class location and racial imaginaries to the particularization of motherhood. I have mentioned that single and lesbian adoptive mothers—while no less effusive about the magical fulfillment of mothering desires—seemed less inclined to "make up for" the problems of abandonment and mothering choices with narrative recourse to destiny and red threads. Perhaps this is related to the absence of fathers, or more accurately, the already accomplished absence of normalized heterosexual reproduction. Both single straight and lesbian mothers spoke of dealing with this absence of a father (e.g., deciding to do motherhood without one or explaining to children why they didn't have a father), but they had more often made their peace with the "loss" of biological reproduction prior to and separate from the losses of their children's birth mothers.[10] The absence of sperm-meeting-egg still stigmatizes these women's reproductive choices, but does so one more step removed from the heteronormative script of naturalized reproduction. Because the choice to adopt is already positioned within a nonnormative kinship structure, it is compelled to claim permanent maternal bonds based on love, not blood (Hayden 1995; Weston 2001). Nan Heinman described her trip to China as a single woman claiming and choosing motherhood:

> This is the only irrevocable decision I've made in my entire life. . . . Anything else you do you can turn back from, including marriage, but this is the one thing. I have also thought it was interesting how instantly I, you know, I just bonded with her and that was it. I had wondered, too, how I would feel being all by myself and experiencing this incredible thing of having this child for the first time, and whether I would feel a sadness and a longing, you know, that I was there by myself, or that there were all these other couples. And that didn't happen, that didn't happen.

This does not mean that single and lesbian mothers are any less haunted by the mothers that gave birth to their children. It was Nan Heinman whose heart pounded with anxiety when recalling the woman at her hotel door who might have been her child's birth mother. And many of the parents who most directly expressed frustrations with abandonment and the impossibility of narrating it were lesbian couples. Their adoptions were just as much about fulfilling motherhood as they were for straight couples (see Lewin 1993), and as we have seen, their constructions tapped into domestic imaginaries of whiteness and consumerism. But this is why their narrations, alongside those of straight couples, are important for exploring whether and how transnational, transracial adoption "can be justifiably described as 'poststructuralist' or whether it must be thought about in terms of a constrained (material and psychic) assimilation to dominant social customs and norms" (Eng 2003: 6). This range of voices raises the question of how strongly both blood and choice figure into the continuum of more and less dominant forms of kinship in America (Strathern 1992), and just as important, what particular forms of power those choices enact.

Family Ghosts

The choice to adopt from China challenges heterosexual norms of biological, same-race reproduction, yet the quest to narrate this choice—relative to two (or three) mothers—brings to light the social-historical contingencies of normalized motherhood. Indeed, the presence of two quite differently situated mothers is a reminder that while both abandonment and adoption are outside what is considered normal and natural reproduction, they are necessitated and desired and constructed within those very norms. Abandonment in China may be considered shameful and transnational adoption in the United States may employ the discourse of "an alternative way to build a family," but they both are pursued in the name of reproducing normal families (Modell 1994) and fulfilling proper motherhood. In China, abandonment of girls or special-needs children might make room for the material and symbolic status accorded to women and families by the birth of a healthy boy and/or prevent the burdens on family and nation that come with "wrong" (excess, female, unhealthy, fatherless) children. In the United States, adoption promises to make those children "right" through the fulfillment of the bonds of nuclear kinship, the playing out of social and material status, and the expansive embrace of the nation. As I have argued in earlier chapters, these two sets of circumstances appear as complementary—this is partly why fate works as an explanation. Yet fate, the state, culture, and other forces mobilized to explain adoptive origins can never quite seal the match. The child's history defies narrative closure, haunted by the silences and exclusions that adoptive kinship and motherhood in particular seem to require, both within the United States and in relation to Chinese mother and nation. Adoptive mother Karin Evans (2000) writes of Chinese daughters who are lost and "clearly found," but her fantasies about lost and unknown birth mothers suggest that being found is an ongoing process.

These are the ghosts of unsettled relations of power that haunt adoptive origins—the "ghostly doubles" wrought by abandonment and dislocation (Anagnost 2000). And while those ghostly doubles include children left behind in China, the child that might have been born to parents, unwanted or marginalized immigrants, and (as Eng 2003 insightfully points out) unacknowledged lovers, haunting adheres most centrally to women and mothers. It is women, in my experiences researching adoption, who usually directly or indirectly make reference to or experience what I would call ghostly matters in describing what they know and do and feel. Recent writings by persons in the adoption triad confirm that gendered ghosts of dislocation and loss resonate in adoption, from Ivy George's "shadow sisters," to a short story titled "Ghost Mother" in the anthology *A Ghost at Heart's Edge* (1999), to a poem by a Korean adoptee called "The Living Ghost."[11] A number of adoptive mothers I interviewed indicated they had a "feeling" about their Chinese child's birth mother, a sense of who she was, and some connection with her, especially on their child's birthday.

In Gordon's (1997) exploration of haunting, it is women—and in two of her three cases, mothers who are haunted or recognize ghosts. While she spends little time explicating the gendering of ghosts, Gordon does say that the Mothers of the Plaza de Mayo, whose children disappeared under Argentinian state terror, understood "what it meant to be connected to the disappeared, connected viscerally, connected through kinship, connected through shared social experience" (112). This understanding was not necessarily a product of biological maternal bonds per se but because the mothers "made a special connection with loss and with what was missing but overwhelmingly present" (112). In other words, if haunting attaches more readily to the experience of motherhood, it is because of the ways in which mothers are socially connected to their children, via conflated cultural and biological norms of familial and national citizenship. And in the case of adoption, the child's body and history evoke other motherhood, other times, and other places. Parents must thus create belonging in the midst of difference and construct abandonment in relation to their own adoption story. For American mothers of Chinese children, the haunting they experience is a manifestation of their own structural location outside the norm of reproduction and its inextricable link to the social location of their children's other mothers. It suggests that the "choice" is free for neither mother but rather is embroiled in a set of stories that come to be taken as true.

As we have seen, origin narratives manage the haunting dislocations of abandonment and adoption in a variety of ways: children are materially and emotionally "better off," the onus of blame is placed on an uncaring cultural system or "wrong" mothers, complicated kin relations are put in the hands of fate. The absence of *actual* birth mothers is, for many, a relief; it accommodates exclusive kinship. However, even as distance and difference from birth mothers is a source of comfort, it is also a source of longing—as embodied in the child and her history, it is a reminder that adoptive mothers, too, are distant and different. Parents are haunted by the tangible, physical memories they see or anticipate in their children; such feelings demand something more than explanations employing divine intervention or victimized birth mothers. Especially as children get older, they push the envelope of memory construction, reminding adoptive parents of the dislocations of kinship and motherhood that mark their histories. Some parents told me that while at first they had no interest in birth parents, as their daughters grew older and asked questions, they wished they knew more; one such father was intent on finding a way to start a DNA bank in China to locate birth parents (and there is now a collective effort to start one, through the "a-China DNA Project"). Karin Evans (2000) tells the story of a two-year-old who "was sitting in the bathtub one day, exploring her body":

"What's this?" she asked her mother, and her mother decided it was time for the preliminary facts of life. "That's your vagina," she said.

The little girl looked expectant, so her mother went on. "Someday," she said, "a baby may come from there." The little girl looked down, and then looked up, trying hard to grasp the information. "Va *China?*" she asked.

Explanations of a child's origins have to come again and again, presented each time in a way that's appropriate to her stage of understanding. Along the way, more "whys" may emerge and there will be thorny issues to tackle. (195)

The powerful discourse of exclusive motherhood—especially as it is understood to forge other forms of social and national belonging—can immobilize and fix the birth mother in China, but then there she is, right there in your bathtub, on your child's body, connecting her to a whole set of other people and places, pointing to your "lack" of a biological connection, and pushing the boundaries of your motherhood. This is partly a matter of the physical presence of birth mothers in/on the child's body but also of the physical absence of adoptive mothers in the child's history. Cindy Coombs told me how much she ached to know her daughter's early life. She lacked the kinds of memories mothers are supposed to carry for their children, the legacy of family stories that do not just accompany but predate birth. So, she told me, this incident with her five-year-old daughter Nicola stung:

We had seen a show on TV about C-sections. Nicola came into my bathroom and she had on a hairnet and gloves—from when I dye my hair!—and she said she was going to deliver a baby, and she was going to do the surgery. And I said something like, "You know Nicola, I bet you were born in a different way. I bet you were born vaginally." And I told her what that meant. And she said, "No, I really don't think I was." And I said, "I bet you really were, because you probably weren't born in a hospital." And she said, "Well, you really don't know, do you, you weren't there."

Single mom Betsy Leary told me that although she felt like she had been her daughter Victoria's mother forever, sometimes she caught herself wondering why she couldn't remember Victoria's early months and would have to tell herself, "Oh, that's right, I wasn't there."

This play of remembering and forgetting has a way of dislodging both birth mothers and adoptive mothers from the constructs that constrain and fix women and, in turn, their children: naturalized reproduction, idealized national families, and commodified choice. It is a way, as Eng (2003) reminds us, of bringing the (even unknown) past into the present rather than neurotically fetishizing the lack of a past. Indeed, some mothers' narrations of their children's origins openly willed the birth mother into the room. These parents wanted very much for their children to know something about their families of origin, and since they could not tell them specifics, they wanted at least to try to make those families feel "real." Adoptive mother Joan Spencer told me that she stood over her baby's crib saying, "Birth mother, birth mother, birth mother," forcing herself to conjure her into their family story rather than bury her along with the impossible problem of abandonment. This extended as well to birth siblings, whom many adoptees likely have and probably wonder about as much as they do birth mothers.[12] Jennifer Bartz described playing a kind of game with her daughter Kelly in which they would imagine what Kelly's birth mother might look like, what her siblings might be like if she had any, or what Kelly might be doing if she lived in China: "You know, just so that she feels like she can flesh that life out, and hook it up to whatever she might know or what she might be learning, or what she might be interested in."

Inviting the real subjectivity of birth mothers into the adoption narrative is a way of acknowledging injuries of the past that go beyond the individual child or mother, without necessarily promising resolution. Ghosts are not simply memories, then, of particular people or particular histories (Gordon 1997). Rather, they have a force all their own in the way they constantly remake memories—and this is a social and communal force. Adoptive mother Lindsay Davies (2001) professes her own imbrication in the unequal social relations that brought her daughter to her:

> I don't know what to say to a woman whose greatest tragedy is my good fortune. . . . That you should have your daughter forced from your arms by a government who I then must pay to envelop her in mine is the stuff of which I have fought against my entire career. That I should end up tacitly supporting this policy is my shame, and yet,

my fate. . . . Forgive me, Madam, for my part in ripping off the Women of China and in particular, of course, you. (Quoted in Volkman 2003: 34.)

Making room for two mothers is a way of listening to and talking to ghosts, a key to opening up new possibilities of kinship. Or as Modell (2002) has argued in regard to open adoption, its gift is the necessary forging of relationships among adults, which in turn forces new questions about the exclusions of normalized kinship.

Even to begin to make sense of abandonment and loss is to open the doors to the uneven racial, national, gender, and class relations that condition both abandonment and adoption, and thus at once to bind and separate mothers who have exchanged motherhood. In other words, the open-endedness of the abandonment story coaxes us to keep the story of adoption and its aftermath open-ended as well; because the originary chapters of a child's story do not end, they haunt the uncertainties of her present and future. She is in some measure the living history of the social relations that create the conditions of abandonment and adoption.

One of the most significant of those conditions is race. On the one hand, race becomes a biologized and essentialized link to origins, tying the child to birth mother/China/Asianness; on the other hand, it is an illusory sign mobilized in historically differing ways, tying the child to the desires of adoptive mother/America/whiteness. Anne Anlin Cheng (2001) draws on the work *Dictee,* by Korean American Theresa Hak Kyung Cha, to unpack the relationship between origins and race:

The loss of origin in *Dictee*—simultaneously racial, familial, national, and ontological—speaks of desire and a critique of that desire. The immigrant and the "post"-colonial subject share a similar problem: they are subjects constituted at the site of displacement. And by speaking of the problem of origin, I do not at all mean the difficulty of retrieving a proper origin but rather the impossibility of origin as an empty sign that is always set up as something devoutly to be wished for. Racial "identity," as one of the most powerful forms of collective fantasy, secured at the conjunction of the macro and micro (in Omi and Winant's terms), fails—indeed, cannot afford—to recognize the conditions of its own inception, its own fantasmatic beginnings. (168)

How much more impossible is the unpacking of racial identity when white adoptive parents desire to narrate some kind of origins for their children, but the displacement of those origins leads back to the phantasmatic of race in which their own desires are embedded. As I discuss in the next chapter, whether and how Chinese adoptees and their adoptive parents might be poststructural or even postcolonial subjects has everything to do with their relationship to whiteness, and to the narration and practice of their racial and cultural identities.

CHAPTER 7

American Ghosts

Cultural Identities, Racial Constructions

American children hear no stories about ghosts. They spend a dime at the drugstore to buy a Superman comic book. . . . Superman represents actual capabilities or future potential, while ghosts symbolize belief in and reverence for the accumulated past. . . . In a world without ghosts, life is free and easy. American eyes can gaze straight ahead. But still I think they lack something and I do not envy their life.
—Fei Xiaotong (from a 1944 essay, quoted in Arkush and Leeds 1989: 177)

We want to give her, at the same time, a loving connection and family here, and to help her realize that she also has an identity that's part of her, in China.
—Carl Erdahl, adoptive father

If a central paradox of constructing the adopted child's origins is the double-bind of motherhood (two or more mothers, defined simultaneously as natural and chosen), then a central tension in constructing her postadoption identity is the double-bind of race (as both fluid and fixed). But race often comes in through the back door, through what adoptive parents treat as "the culture question" (Volkman 2003; Yngvesson 2000; Freundlich 2000): how much and what kind of Chinese culture do/should/can we incorporate into the child's and family's life? As I argue in this chapter, claims to a child's cultural identity—in relation to her imagined past and future—are most often the route through which adoptive parents attempt to negotiate racial topographies. But just as important, racial difference is shored up and re-fracted by imaginaries of national belonging, fantasies of gendered de-sire, and enactments of class location. Adoptive parents' conscious tus-sles with cultural identity both illuminate and obscure histories of im-migration (Anagnost 2000), of racial formations (Omi and Winant 1994), and of their own ties to economic opportunity and desire (Alarcón 1996).

In transnational, transracial adoption, it is crucial that the racialized question of culture is also a matter of the nature and choice of kinship. Fei Xiaotong (the "father of sociology" in China) mused six decades ago that Americans are not very good at listening to the ghosts of the accu-mulated past—but what happens when a child, by moving across na-tional and familial spaces, disinters the past from which she came, as well as the one to which she moves? As parent Carl Erdahl suggests, his daughter carries a visceral history of connections and disconnections to people and places that stretch from Minneapolis to China, complicating the future-oriented forgetting of American identity construction. At least two histories converge on the child at once, from behind and in front of her: the history of her birthed past in China and the history of her racialized future in America. And so it turns out that adopted Chi-nese children do not come as baggage-free or as transformable as imag-ined in preadoption narratives of "why China" (as discussed in chapter 2). At one FCC event where I was asked to lead a discussion with adop-tive parents (whose children were busy learning Chinese dances and crafts down the hall), I asked the group what identity issues they felt were the hardest to deal with; the chorus rang out, "Abandonment!" fol-lowed closely by birth parents and race. Whether dislocations of bio-kinship and abandonment are welcomed or mourned, they are made more difficult because they are akin to racial disjunctures, and more specifically, to the dominance of whiteness. Parents usually pose the "culture question" as the main and most friendly passage through this minefield of racial imaginaries and toward domestic belonging.

I use "domestic" quite deliberately here to mean both family and nation—to signal the organizing power of racialization in the history of American national culture. On the one hand, the crossing of racial borders through adoption is celebrated as a sign of the increasingly expansive embrace of nation and family; Adam Pertman, director of the Evan B. Donaldson Adoption Institute, asserts that the growing numbers of families "where the kids aren't going to look anything like their parents [is] starting to make a difference in the way people think of families, of inheritance, of nurture versus nature, you name it."[1] On the other hand, the crossing of racial borders triggers anxieties that "too much difference" will undermine claims to national and familial belonging. Cheng (2001) is eloquent on this point:

> The contemporary American attachment to progress and healing, eagerly anticipating a colorblind society, sidesteps the important examination of racialization: How is a racial identity secured? How does it continue to generate its seduction for both the dominant and the marginalized? And what are the repercussions, both historical and personal, of that ongoing history? (7)

Having been brought into the heart of the "national family," Chinese adoptees disturb the assumptions through which that national family is made. Because they become attached to the nation by way of (usually) white and relatively well-off American families, the social organizing power of racial difference, including as it is articulated with class and gender, is not easily erased or denied. Questions of adoptees' cultural identity prompt us to consider the relationship between hegemonic whiteness and both foreign and domestic minorities (Balibar 1988b), the class expression and consumption of multiculturalism, and the importance the taming of migration has played in constructing the imagined American nation (Lowe 1996; Hondagneu-Sotelo 1994).

Cultural Tools for the Citizenship Blues

Transnational migration has been central to the formation and expression of cultural and national identity in the United States, underwriting both global outreach and national protectionism (Barrett and Roediger 1997; Jacobson 1998; Lowe 1996). For the adoptive families with whom I interacted, interest in immigration was often limited to obtaining legal U.S. citizenship for their children and the paperwork and bureaucracy they often grudgingly waded through to get it. The process was made a bit easier by the Child Citizenship Act, which granted citizenship to children adopted abroad upon return with their citizen-parents to the United States,[2] and was applauded by agencies and adoptive families as long overdue. I flew back to Minnesota from fieldwork in China on February 26, 2001, with the deliberate intention of taking in the following day's celebration of the national launch of the act. From the balcony inside the state capitol, I saw a sea of white adults and mostly nonwhite children gathered around a temporary stage and a large sign announcing "International Child Citizenship Day." The tenor of the day's speeches, delivered by various state officials, was summed up in the words of one state representative: "These children are Americans, they should be treated as such, and now they will be." This pronouncement was greeted with whoops and applause. One official concluded by saying to the adoptive parents gathered there, "You have done a great thing for family, and for our nation."

From the perspective of the state, citizenship for transnationally adopted children is culturally powerful—both in material and symbolic terms—because it feeds the myth that the United States benevolently educates and welcomes the world (as U.S. consular officer Ted Gong suggested), folding diversity into the transcendent national vision of itself. The family, as a crucial site for reproducing ideologies of national order and cohesion (Balibar 1988b), performs the work of carrying out this myth. Yet, as Hall and Held (1989) assert, citizenship raises the question "Who belongs and what does *belonging* mean in practice?" (175); legal citizenship begs the question of the social forms of difference that circumscribe belonging. National membership, for example, conjures a deep comradeship and a sense of continuity only by forgetting the

exclusionary practices through which it has necessarily defined itself
(Lowe 1996; Anderson 1991). What are the unwritten conditions of social citizenship? What is forgotten or warded off, as well as invoked, in
the attempt to achieve it for adopted children?

Perhaps the most obvious condition is the citizenship of adoptive parents themselves, who not only have to be legal citizens of the United
States (or at least one parent, in the case of married couples) but are the
kind of citizens who can be said to have done a great thing for America
by adopting abroad (and whose children therefore *should* be treated as
Americans). They can represent America to the world, and can bring the
world to America, because they carry the social, political, and economic
capital to do so. For example, while the job of the U.S. Citizenship and
Immigration Services (USCIS) is to determine both the eligibility of the
child for adoption and the eligibility of parents to adopt, some of the key
elements for determining eligibility (such as citizenship status and income levels) also confer rights upon parents. As the commissioner of the
agency's predecessor, the Immigration and Naturalization Service (INS),
put it to a House Committee in May 2002, state officials "have a weighty
responsibility to the American citizens—the prospective adoptive parents—who have invested their hearts, and often considerable resources,
in this endeavor."[3]

The child's citizenship is conditional not only on her attachment to
good American citizens but simultaneously on her detachment from her
birth family. This kind of "serial monogamy" of national/familial kinship
is reinforced by USCIS adoption guidelines that exclude adopted children's biological families from immigrating to join their resettled children (Brysk 2004). One Chinese journalist had suggested to me that while
children abandoned in China were *juehu* (orphaned), they could find a
new identity in America because it was a land of immigrants and not
bloodlines. Yet in a letter circulated by an adoptive parent on a number
of Internet Listservs in May 2004, secure national citizenship seemed to
hinge on treating transnationally adopted children *as if* born to American parents. The letter requested support from the adoption community for the pending ICARE legislation, which not only would make
U.S. citizenship automatic upon final adoption in a foreign country but
would issue adopted children a Consular Report of Birth (CRB): "Both the
passport and CRB are recognized under law as proof of citizenship. But

unlike a passport that expires, the CRB never expires. The CRB is the document given to biological children born abroad to U.S. citizens and it functions as a child's birth certificate as well as citizenship certificate forever."

The ICARE legislation goes further than previous legislation in eradicating legal conditions on an adopted child's permanent belonging. But in doing so, it belies its claims to unconditional citizenship by making that very citizenship conditional on the elision of particular histories—not only of birth but also of immigration. The circulated letter further asserted that securing citizenship before migration to the United States would help ensure that the child is not, indeed, an immigrant:

> We must do something about the archaic way our government continues to process international adoptions. We cannot allow the bureaucratic office that is in charge of all immigration into this country, whether it be legal or illegal, to also be in charge of children coming home with their families. Our children are NOT immigrants. They are, once adopted, citizens of the United States.

There is the potential danger here for legal citizenship to be secured at the price of social histories—especially those histories that might be seen to contaminate raced and classed imaginaries of the American family. Why does imagining a better system for processing intercountry adoption entail distancing adoption from other forms of immigration? It is perhaps ironic that in the same contemporary period, activist adult adoptees from other countries, most notably Korea, have been lobbying the governments of their birth countries to give them citizenship rights *as if* they had not been migrated abroad. As Brysk (2004) notes, it is children's combined dependency and mobility to which legal citizenship and rights regimes are so ill equipped to respond.

Citizenship is most readily imagined, even in the best interests of adopted children, as counterposed to "*not* immigrants," which in turn conjures the normalized and invisible power of whiteness, political voice, and consumption. The white adoptive parents I studied—while they would not necessarily have agreed with the rationale for the ICARE legislation—did not usually think of their children from China as immigrants. Perhaps this is all the more salient in adoptions from China because of the particular way in which Asian immigration to the United States has served as a racialized testing ground of national identity, with the historical legacy of fixing Asians as perpetual (if sometimes desirable) immigrants. As I discuss later in this chapter, the experiences of Asian American adoptive parents in both San Francisco and the Twin Cities demonstrate that "race matching" between parents and children, as well as assumptions about Asians as foreigners, can make not just adoption but citizenship status invisible. At a small FCC meeting in Minnesota in which there was discussion of the need to reach out to the Chinese American community, I suggested starting with Chinese American adoptive parents. "There are some?" was the response from the group of white women. One woman offered, "Oh yeah, when we went in for our citizenship, there was this Chinese couple with a child and *we assumed all three of them were there to get their citizenship,* but no, their daughter was adopted and just she was getting citizenship" (emphasis added).

We are reminded that legal citizenship is only the tip of the identity iceberg (see also Ong 1998; Soysal 1994). Further labor is required if social citizenship is to be secured in the face of the haunting of birth families, other kinds of immigrants, and race and class privilege. For most parents, cultural play—whether barely or heavily reliant on things Chinese—is an important component of this labor, even if the child's cultural identity is imagined mostly outside the framework of immigration. Adoptive parent and scholar Mary Watkins (2004) writes of the transnational, transracial adoptee, "She is not exactly a 'migrant,' brought to one culture from another. She moves between multiple cultural locations in the present, not just two. . . . And yet the adoptee is not that different from many others whose identities have had to complexify as a result of migration or exile" (12). For adoptive parents, *culture*—and more specifically, some version of Chinese culture—is often an answer to the unintelligibility of multiple dislocation. This echoes internationally sanctioned agreements on the cultural heritage rights of children[4] but more directly follows from the collective wisdom of adoption experts and professionals: embracing at least portions of a child's birth culture is said to help fill the gaps and heal the "broken" adoptee (see Volkman 2003 and Anagnost 2000 for critiques). This is supposed to correct the problems of earlier professional advice; as the 2004 MSNBC report "All-American, with One Foot in China" described it, there has been "a shift in philosophy in the adoption community—from one that presses for assimilation of their children to one that embraces a different culture."[5]

I argue in this chapter that while such a discursive shift has indisputably occurred, there exists a wide variety of actual practices in adoptive families that in fact do not preclude an assimilationist stance. Across all those practices, parents deal with the aspects of identity that are excess or external to what is promised in exclusive adoptive kinship and citizenship—including the imagined "flexibility" of Chinese children that figures into adoptive choices. How flexible are they, really? When is there "too much" difference?

The cultural identities adoptive parents imagine and seek for their children point to the organizing principles that more generally discipline normalized subjectivity in the United States. As Ong (2004) argues, the American obsession with "culture" as the foundational issue of citizenship misrecognizes a key feature of U.S. history: so-called cultures become equated with race-based traditions because new immigrants are judged and categorized through the racialized lens of an unspoken black-white continuum. Her point is complicated in adoption by the formation of intimate relations of kinship across cultural-national borders. From one side, parents' race and class privilege conditions the flexibility of the child's citizenship; from the other, the child's abandonment and racialized body circumscribe the promise of such flexibility. As Watkins (2004) goes on to say in her essay, adopted children do not choose the alleged mutability and multiplicity of their subjectivity: "They are backed into it. The preclusion of full inclusion in the host country or culture is enforced by the racist surround, where privileges of class that come with many non-family based adoptions in the United States cannot fully offset racial prejudice" (13).

As an effort to integrate a child into a desired family and nation, the construction of an adopted Chinese child's cultural identity has the effect of showing us the social conditions on such integration; she is a symbol of the possibilities and limits of the interplay of dominant and minority categories of citizenship. Adoptive parents' concern about what to say and do about "the culture question" in their and their children's postadoption lives, it turns out, is about the play of race and class in the making of the nation. This plays out with particular poignancy in the adoptive family because of the public/social nature of what might otherwise be private acts of kinship. One couple summed up the consumption of Chinese culture as a useful if tricky tool for responding to the ongoing complexity of their child's sense of belonging:

> *Debra*: We have nooo illusions that this isn't going to be very hard, both within our own country culturally, and with the discovery of the past.
>
> *Christy*: Well, I really think the promise we make to our children is not "You will have no pain." It's "We will give you tools, to deal with this pain" . . . this is not a story about a Chinese girl, this is a story about an *adopted* Chinese girl. And that is a very complicated story that is not cured by watching "Big Bird Goes to China." I mean, both our kids were rejected because of gender alone. I mean, very complicated!

The question is what "tools," as Christy put it, parents employ in response to the relations of difference. Whether adoptive parents err on the side of assimilating their children into mainstream America, immersing them in Chinese schools and activities, or something in between (including, perhaps, watching "Big Bird in China"), unsettled historical relations of power tug at their experiences through the difference represented in their children's and families' identities. Romaine-Ouelette (2001) argues that parents tend to limit the birth origins of children's identity to a contained cultural archive of photographs and souvenirs, while Volkman (2003) responds that "on the contrary, parents seek ways of 'activating' the archive and the connection" (44). I, in turn, contend that it is both—the question is *which* histories are archived and activated, and *how*. Difference and dislocation press upon all adoptive parents, demanding a response, but not all parents respond in the same manner. They vary in how they connect past and present and in how they relate the child's transnational history to the space of American family and nation. One could say, in other words, that adoptive parents vary in how they listen and speak to ghosts.

Children's animated presence—everything from the curl of their hair to the questions they invoke or raise—beckons the ghostly doubles of their lives across borders. The Coombs, for example, ended up adopting a second child they had met in Nicky's orphanage because they were haunted by children "left behind," particularly in relation to their own class privilege. As Fred put it, he didn't want to be sitting on a front-porch swing some day thinking, "I wonder what happened to her." Indeed, many adoptive parents asked me, often anxiously, if I knew what happened to children in Chinese orphanages who were not adopted. But parents also get pulled into the haunting of their child's own imagined past. One adoptive mother repeated for me in whispered fascination how her four-year-old daughter remembered the events of the day she was left alone: "I was sleeping and I was in the bushes. I woke up and said, 'Somebody help me.'" And Debra and Christy, who were frustrated that their facilitator had told them nothing about their daughter Mei's foster-care situation, had only their daughter's unexpected memories to go on—unexpected because she was just over one year old when adopted: "Over the first year, every now and again these things would come out of her mouth. And she talked about China Grandpa. And how he fed her with chopsticks and he called her *wawa,* which is absolutely dead on what somebody would call a baby. And we had never called her that."

Other times the child's actions in the present were connected to her past, and to being Chinese, more because of a feeling than because of the child's own direct narration. At one FCC event, an adoptive mother remarked to me that based on the way they responded to each other, she had the strong feeling that her daughter and another child at the event had been crib mates at their orphanage in China. And Eve Chomsky said of her daughter, "I get the sense that she remembers something, but it must have cast a dark shadow." "She hasn't been verbal about any memories of China," said Lisa Walker, "but you know, oftentimes riding in the car in her car seat, we would look at her, and she was like, zoned out, but sort of actively in another place. *And we would say to each other, 'She's in China'*" (emphasis added).

The unknown people and places of preadoptive life that the child carries into the present continue to be felt in the people and places of her postadoptive life in the United States. Lisa Walker continued, "The first year, we would go to Chinatown sometimes. But actually, going to Chinatown, like in the real stuff, was actually very upsetting to her. With the smells of like, meat hanging out, or the chickens. She'd be very upset and agitated." In a related reading of unknown memories, a number of parents reported their young children's agitation at seeing Asian people, wondering, as Simon Pattuck did, "Is she like reliving this moment, her abandonm—you know, you start projecting all these things." While he and his wife, Ginger, responded by wanting to make Asian people and language a more regular part of her life, others found reason to temper "doing Chinese culture." And a few dismissed the imagined red thread that in popular adoption discourse connects children to their birth families, as Chet Cook did when promising his daughter she would never have to go back to that country that "throws away its children."

We begin to see here how parents, however they respond, are haunted by the history of unsettled difference and dislocation that marks the migration of their Chinese daughters. Adoptees' racialized and gendered American identities, their origins in China, and the conditions of their adoption *recall each other*. In the remainder of this chapter, I demonstrate how the child's past is imagined in relation to her present and future, with particular attention to how narrations and practices of cultural identity in transnational adoption both reproduce and transform meanings of social citizenship. I examine the questions that parents tackle: how much Chinese culture to introduce into their families, why it is or is not important, and where its limitations of efficacy and authenticity lie. These responses to cultural identity, caught as they are between the false dichotomy of "authentic" versus "hybrid" selves, point us to the power of racialization, along with material privilege and gendered imaginings. By showing how questions of cultural identity (understood, in whatever way, as "Chinese culture" and "American culture") reflect, reproduce, and potentially challenge the effects of these intersecting relations of power—especially hierarchies of racial formations—I come back to the larger question of the reproduction and transformation of difference in the political economy of transnational adoption. If, at the same time that Chinese children adopted transnationally are being claimed as insiders, their parents are being pulled to the outside by the history of difference and dislocation brought more intimately to the family by the child, what does this say about the possibilities of poststructural subjectivity?

Constructing Cultural Identity

Even if at a loss for words on other topics, most adoptive parents with whom I spoke had something to say, and sometimes quite passionately, about the limits and possibilities of their children's Chinese and/or American identities. Martha Erdahl told me with great conviction that "the historical and the cultural is a key to understanding self," but this begs the question of *what* histories and cultures. How does one construct an identity that integrates child with self, family, community, and nation, given the histories of difference that her story embodies? And how important is or isn't it to this identity process to make Chinese language, cultural activities, and people part of the family story, and why? The concern with cultural difference hints at a number of issues that haunted all families—the authenticity and exoticism of Chineseness, what it means to be American or Chinese, how parent and family identities (both white and Chinese American) articulate with that of an adopted Chinese child, how to manage multiply intersecting categories of belonging—and invited a range of responses from them. The question of *which* histories is thus not about Chinese versus American cultures but about how American practices and meanings are made through the racialized particularization of Chinese culture. In other words, the construction of children's identities is also a process of delineating and defining family, community, and nation.

In analyzing the ways adoptive parents with Chinese children practice and narrate their children's relationship to Chinese culture, I found four narrative frames that I call *assimilation, celebrating plurality, balancing act,* and *immersion.* Most families I interviewed fell in some way into the middle two of these approaches and understood assimilation and immersion as "extremes." This pseudo-typology grew out of my initial round of interviews in the late 1990s and took on more elaborate nuances in ensuing years; I started to see this range of narrative frames not so much as defining particular adoptive families but as delineating the parameters of a repertoire of cultural identities available to them. Together, these categories help generate the spectral limits and unthought possibilities of forms of belonging in the contemporary United States, especially in the context of intersecting transnational and transtemporal relations of difference. They suggest the configurations of power that structure American culture.

In this section I describe the four approaches to cultural identity in turn, using practices of naming children to illustrate. As a conscious act of narrating and historically locating identity, (re)naming a child adopted internationally encapsulates the contradictory possibilities for responding to difference and constructing cultural meaning. Korean adoptee and author Jane Jeong Trenka (2003), speaking of herself as an immigrant or exile, uses Korean and Anglo names to represent her preadoption and postadoption selves, whom she calls "twins." Mirim Kim, an adult adoptee who has chosen to use her Korean name rather than the name given to her by her adoptive parents, writes about naming as a conscious cultural act:

> Until very recently, my adoptive parents could not accept my name change.
>
> If someone called and asked for Mirim, my mom would hang up the phone.
>
> When we finally could talk about it, she said, "To me, 'Joanna' means 'daughter.' When I say 'Mirim,' it doesn't mean anything."
>
> I've asked her repeatedly why she chose the name Joanna. Did she know anyone with that name? Had she read it in a book or heard it on television? I wanted a special reason, a story for how they re-named me. But she's only said, "We just did. The social worker told us we had to pick a name for the paperwork, and we just liked the name."
>
> I know that a lot of parents don't have a special reason for naming their children, but most kids don't already have a name. The lack of meaning ascribed to "Joanna" is why I have difficulty accepting it as my name. If my parents wanted to erase my Korean name, I wish they had given me a story of why my American name was special. (Kim 2002)

Kim's words suggest that names can take on added significance for the ways they seem to carry and erase the disparate times and places of adoptees' histories; this is why I use them as one kind of proxy for how adoptive parents might think about their children's cultural identity relative to family and nation.

In narratives of *assimilation,* parents emphasized "trying to raise your kids to be happy well-adjusted little *citizens,* not happy well-adjusted little Asian American people," as Chet Cook put it. While most adoptive families were concerned with their children fitting culturally as Americans into family, community, and nation, the Cooks and a few other parents consciously worked against what they saw as practices that particularized their children's identities, unnecessarily connecting them to China or to minority status in the United States. The Leisters, a white couple living in a rural area, explained that they wanted their daughter, as Larry put it, "to know she's American first, and that's her heritage, but she has a background that's Chinese." These parents worried that adoptive families who celebrated all the Chinese holidays or gave their children Chinese names were "cramming it down their throats."

The assimilationist frame eschews setting a child apart or naming difference. Aaron Kretz expressed it this way: "You're basically saying to me that the kid's different, because she's adopted from China. Now I can see saying she's special, but when you start putting them in all these Chinese things, you're saying they're different than other people." (It is important to note that couples did not necessarily agree; Aaron's wife, Eileen, retorted, "Well, they *are* different.") Aaron's concerns about integrating his daughter into family and nation were haunted by the continuity between his daughter's history and the Otherness of China and Chinese culture; he said that he worried, for example, that his daughter Faye would talk as disorientingly fast as some of the local Asian people he knew. He was further haunted by the Otherness of adoption. "I have this ongoing concern that we not do things, and that she doesn't associate the Chinese stuff with being adopted," he said. "I even thought so far as to think, oh my God, we're going to send Faye to this bilingual school, and we're going to wind up with her moving to China and we'll never see her again. She'll take a job over in China because we put her in Chinese kindergarten."

Newfield and Gordon (1996) distinguish the kind of assimilation to the proverbial middle class that immigrants and marginalized citizens might desire from the terms that assimilation*ism* might extract in return: "Assimilationism likes to portray itself as nothing more than the innocent desire for a good life, and indeed this is the foundation of its social influence . . . [it] requires adherence to core principles and behaviors" (80).

I would add that assimilationism neutralizes particular histories, giving the normalcy of "interesting jobs, pleasant neighborhoods, home ownership, financial security, [and] personal leisure time" (80) a kind of timelessness. In the case of the assimilationist bent of some adoptive parents, this takes the form of largely containing Chineseness over there, in the past of China, as "background." As one parent wrote on an Internet Listserv posting in April 1996: "While I do think a sense of heritage is important, our daughters' sense of identity won't come from constantly looking back to China, it will come from making them feel at home in our homes." Making this kind of spatiotemporal distinction between China as "past" and the United States as "present" is what Fabian (1983) calls "the denial of coevalness" or contemporaneity.

Naming practices among some assimilationist parents reflected this interest in adhering to a normalized culture otherwise threatened by attention to difference. The Cooks, a white couple living in a suburb of San Francisco, told me they chose an Anglicized name for their daughter that would look good on a business card someday. Linda Leister said they decided not to keep their daughter's Chinese name because it "was not very easy to spell, or easy to say, and she'd have to pronounce it all the time. So we said no, I'd like to make it easier for her." The name also suggested a distasteful familial connection to the orphanage; Linda added, "We found out that the orphanage named Laney, and everybody has the last name the same because that's the orphanage's name . . . well, does that really mean something to her?" In fact, the Leisters were not sure without looking at the original adoption paperwork what their daughter's Chinese name had been. Cohesion is found in an identity that contains and erases cultural difference, which is also the difference of a child's preadoption life; it nods toward an ideal of American individualism that is tacitly white, middle-class, and exclusive. The concern with assimilation did not mean parents completely shunned things Chinese; rather, they dabbled in Chinese culture, as the Leisters did when they bought a few souvenirs in China.

The second approach, *celebrating plurality,* did not desire so much to erase as to transcend and resolve difference through a celebration of cultural diversity. In this framework, Chineseness is one of many equally interesting ethnic choices, the presence of which enriches and does not undermine national and familial cohesion. This approach has a certain pedigree in the cultural pluralism born in the early-twentieth-century United States that emphasized "multiplicity in unity" as a precursor to multiculturalism (Newfield and Gordon 1996: 83). Victor Huang made a point of saying he enjoyed cooking not just Chinese but German food, and his daughter's Russian name was chosen to reflect his wife's ethnicity. A segment of their daughter's life book read, "While your family is Chinese and German and Russian, you are an American. All these heritages are what makes America." A mosaic of "backgrounds" makes up America, and they are all safely possible in the present. George Lou and his wife, Patty, insisted that their daughter would be exposed to all manner of ethnic celebration, and they had an array of ethnic dolls in her playroom to prove it. George looked out at San Francisco and saw not an abundance of Chinese American resources but a display of diversity: "We've become such a polyglot, just a melting pot. If our daughter wants to go study Zen Buddhism, we'll read up on it. *And* we'll explore things like Octoberfest." While he and Patty had adopted an infant in part "so that she would grow up as an American," being American was equated with the choices multiculturalism seemed to allow. This celebration of pluralism normalized the interracial, intercultural adoptive family by envisioning a glorified global family of "different but the same." Wanda Jones said she had initially wanted to adopt children from all over the world, creating a family that would demonstrate that "we are all human."[6]

Many that emphasized the celebration of diversity were straight couples in which one partner was Chinese American and the other white, and in all six of these cases (four in the Bay Area and two in the Twin Cities), the parents had given their daughters non-Chinese "white" names, with some adding a Chinese middle name. What seemed to be at work here was a desire for a child to fit with family and nation, almost mirroring the ideal of harmonious and apolitical diversity already represented in the marriage. Diane Scott said she was simply being "practical" about the fact of English and Euro-American cultural dominance amid a nevertheless beautiful diversity to which they wanted to expose their daughter. When asked by their agency to "provide the name we were going to give her," Mary Leung and Tom Mining perused a baby-naming book for something that sounded nice with Tom's family name. A child's Chinese heritage was thus something to be celebrated (perhaps as a middle name) but not emphasized; and not unlike assimiliationism, Chinese heritage was woven into the narrative of the present in selective ways. While under the assumptions of assimilationism Chineseness is a potential stumbling block to the ideal of a contemporary "universal" American identity, under the tenets of multicultural celebration Chineseness might preclude an American identity chosen among ethnic options. An individual can choose a cultural identity but does not have to relate to the world *through* it.

For these families, the fluid subordination of Chineseness to American plurality was accomplished in part by downplaying the relevance of a child's birth origins to her identity in the present. Diversity could also be celebrated through an individualist consumptive stance: parents could imagine a smorgasbord of cultural options (Waters 1990), and making those options available to their children enabled a citizenship defined by choice.

In the third narrative frame, that of the *balancing act,* the child's birth history was more closely connected to the here and now, and consuming and choosing things Chinese was a more deliberate endeavor. Whether defining American culture as multicultural or implicitly white, or defining Chinese culture as *Mulan* and fortune cookies or language and history, these parents asserted that their children were Chinese *and* American, and that their children related to the world through both. Eileen Kretz wanted a *"somewhat* greater focus on the Chinese part" because "I think she *is* Chinese—not Chinese like she'd be if she was growing up in China—and she *is* American. But she's *Chinese* American." China and Chineseness were not packaged into the past or into particular days of celebration but were brought into the present through a kind of happy medium that leaned toward a hyphenated identity. As one single white mom put it to me: "There's got to be a happy medium . . . and they're from China, and China is part of their life, after all."

Giving a child a Chinese name, whether as first or middle name, became an attempt to create a live connection between what parents saw as two sides of a child's identity, to activate the archive of a child's life. Cindy and Fred Coombs kept the name given to their daughter by her orphanage director as her middle name—one character for the time of year she was found and the other meaning "good fortune"—because, as Cindy said, "I thought that was nice to have that connection for why she was named that" and "I like that part of her identity." Similarly, Eve

Chomsky told me she and her husband hyphenated the name Chandra, which she thought had a universal and "up" quality to it, with the Chinese name Mei, "like an umbilical cord to China." A Chinese name was understood to ground a child in what little history he or she had; as Terry Schlitz put it, the orphanage name "is as far back as we can go." Lila Noonan agreed:

> *Lila*: I thought it was really important to keep part of her Chinese name. I know a lot of folks just totally Americanize it, and I just couldn't do that to her, because it's who she is. . . .
>
> *Sara*: What would you say to those who say, "Hey come on, they're not Chinese anymore. They're growing up in America," etc. What do you say to that?
>
> *Lila*: I think they're doing the children a disservice, because they're taking away part of them. Because you know what, *they had a life before we came,* and they deserve to keep that. [Emphasis added.]

The haunting of the life before was also evident in cases where, by choosing a new Chinese name, parents tried to redirect the meaning of cultural continuity. For some, this new Chinese name was meant to dispel the impersonality of a name that had been assigned, like a number, by the orphanage. Others, like single mom Jackie Kovich, wanted to circumvent whatever misfortunes might be attached to a name given by and used in the orphanage. Jackie chose for her daughter a name that she recognized from her knowledge of popular Chinese culture and said she was reticent even to use her child's orphanage name in front of her; when I asked why, she teared up and replied, "I guess I don't want her to be confused. And then you have no idea what her memories are."

The attempt to construct a child's identity as a balance of past and future, of Chinese and American, is also experienced as an issue of marginality in relation to dominance and thus is fraught with serious choices about the communities through which a child can identify. One example is the several Jewish families who sought some form of balancing act across multiple hyphens. "We had a baby naming," said Sandra Padding. "And so her name is Sarah Yanfeng Padding Levinson. So she has her Chinese name, she has her English name which is also a Hebrew name!" As has been the case in popular culture, these families drew on comparisons

and resonances between Jewish and Chinese cultures, with the added desire to address the haunted dislocations of adoptive kinship. Sandra's
husband, John, said that he experienced dissonance in "having a Chinese baby without a Chinese past in my life. If she wasn't Chinese, she'd
be a Jewish baby to be raised—and my heritage would be her heritage,
and there wouldn't need to be this other culture added." This couple created a ritual combining the Jewish holiday of Sukkot (the Feast of Taber-
nacles) with the Chinese Mid-Autumn Festival, which fall at the same
time of year; one of their practices on this day was to look at the moon
and remember their daughter's birth family in China. This hybrid cultural practice activated several minority histories at once, even as such
intersections mattered in different ways to people. Aaron Kretz thought
that Chinese and adoption identities together excessively differentiated
his daughter, and therefore he wished to dispel both; his wife, Eileen,
argued instead that (their daughter's) adoption and (their own) Jewish-
ness animated each other: "Being adopted is a minority, just like being
Jewish is a minority. It's all part of our life together." Chinese cultural
and language activities somehow bridged these minority identities, completing the balancing act.[7] In cities like San Francisco and New York,
Jewish families with children adopted from China have formed support
groups around the specific configuration of intersecting differences they
experience.

More generally, many families argue that if there is any one community in and through which their children's identities should be shaped,
it is the community of children adopted from China. Across the country,
the organization Families with Children from China has become the default community for families trying to find some kind of balancing act
among the social categories of "Chinese," "American," and "adopted."
Each chapter of FCC is different, but some have faced painful disagreements over what such a balance looks like. How much of a focus on Chinese culture should there be, and how much on adoption issues? How are
they related? What makes culture, or children for that matter, Chinese?
Martha Erdahl thought that the FCC Dragon Boat Festival was a good
event because "there are some children who want to be involved in the
culture piece and there are some children who want to be involved in the
connections piece [to other kids], and there are some children who just
want to play." For some parents, the (Chinese) cultural content was a side

note to being with other children and families who shared a history of adoption from China. Peggy Peterson organized play dates for groups of Chinese adoptees: "We'll go to the apple orchard or they come to my house and have a tea party. One month we try to do something fun for the kids, and the next month we try to have it be a Chinese theme, like a Chinese tea party, or something like that." But for others, the authenticity of this connection to being adopted from China was inextricable from the authenticity of the cultural content they were handed. Ginger Adley described one of their first experiences at an FCC gathering:

> I thought we'll go, we'll have Chinese food right? I'm sorry, it was Leeann Chin. This is not Chinese food, this is American. So, it's horrible. And this is what we're telling our Chinese daughter is Chinese? Even when we're bringing together all your sisters and your cousins?—and this is how I see these adopted girls.

Disagreements over the relationship between the adoption narrative and the cultural identity narrative raise important questions about the possible ways of belonging in the United States. Does emphasizing the cultural identity of Chinese adoptees as unique by virtue of adoption—not like other immigrants, for example—only convert their difference into a kind of sameness with normative American identity? Or, alternatively, does it free them from some falsely imposed Chinese cultural authenticity imagined and desired by their white parents? Does binding cultural heritage and adoptive identity narratives together only put up obstacles to belonging by overemphasizing difference (as Aaron argued)? Or, alternatively, does it open up belonging by embracing multiple differences (as his wife, Eileen, argued)?

Perhaps it is the impossibility of these questions that spurred a concern among families performing the balancing act that parents might take their desire for balance too far—that there was a line that, if crossed, would signify "too much" Chinese culture. This concern arose from at least two key places: first, an uncertain relationship to authentic representation, and second, a desire not to close the door on choice. In regard to the first, a number of non-Chinese parents said it felt weird or fake to try to pass on or represent Chinese culture, especially "authentic" Chinese culture, to their children. As Jennifer Bartz put it,

We've attended culture camp and attended the Dragon Boat festivities several times. We're kind of enjoying doing Chinese New Year on our own. We've made friends with the folks over at the nearby Chinese restaurant, and so I feel lucky about that. . . . And I think at the same time, we've tried to be cognizant of the fact that what gets passed on to us may not be what people truly do anymore, you know, in cities or towns in China. I don't know, I'm cognizant again of being a story-teller, of transmitting information but not trying to represent the culture.

The question of authentic Chinese culture was inseparable from the question of who could represent it. For example, while it was quite acceptable and even encouraged for adopted daughters to have Chinese names, the few white parents who took on Chinese names were held up as the ultimate eye-rolling example of an unnatural and excessive adoption of Chinese culture. In response, some white families looked to Chinese schools or friends or nannies to fill in where they felt they could not be effective or believable cultural role models. A number of white parents in San Francisco in particular hired Chinese nannies explicitly for this purpose. Nan Heinman, fighting the easy "multicultural chic" by which she thought some people objectified her daughter, hired a nanny as a deliberate act of creating and celebrating an authentic Chineseness she herself could not provide.

In exercising her consumer choice, of course, Nan enacted the choice and individual distinctiveness that American culture is supposed to allow—the second issue that aggravates the concern with doing "too much" Chinese culture. In other words, the balancing act did not want to preclude the same *chosen* and thus fulfilled American identity that cultural pluralism celebrated. The imperative to not fix children to Chineseness was linked to the imperative that parents not become something they are not and cannot be. In an impassioned editorial in the FCC-Minnesota newsletter (*Blessings from China,* December 2000), adoptive mother and writer Lynette Lamb urged parents to stop subsuming their own identities to their daughters', because they "need us to be full human beings and full parents, not full-time Sinophiles. . . . While continuing to expose our daughters to Chinese culture, [we need to recognize that] they are also American girls, after all, and thus heirs to a multicultural richness . . . we owe them the freedom to be the authors of their own lives." Similarly, Sharon Anderson sent her daughter to a bi-cultural Chinese American school and her house was decorated with Chinese art, but she expressed discomfort with immersing her daughter in too much Chinese language and culture, for fear it would be too differentiating and cut off her choices: "How much do you try to expose your child to? I mean, I don't speak Chinese so she wouldn't have a place to practice it really. I mean, they live in this part of the world, and there are a lot of other things going on." Questions of authentic Chinese cultural identity thus bleed into questions of American cultural identity as embodying choice and the authorship of one's own authentic self. Indeed, a Chinese scholar and friend found it curiously American that parents would be so concerned with providing their children with choices—that they would juxtapose "exposing" their children to Chinese culture with "forcing" them to learn it.

For the fourth narrative framework of cultural identity, *immersion*, the chances of "too much" Chinese culture overwhelming "choice" were seen as fairly slim; as one parent put it, "she will get Americanness everywhere anyway." A couple of these families compared their cultural choices to religious ones: you don't ask your children if they want to be Catholic, you take them to church because you want that for them. To do right by a child, then, meant embracing her minority culture, and quite explicitly her place as Chinese American. Parents advocating immersion aimed for some combination of a sustained complement of Chinese activities—language schools, holiday activities, cultural texts, involvement with Chinese American community events and organizations (including churches). Debra Fine and Christy Kinsler spoke of incorporating as many things Chinese as possible, from stacks of Chinese children's books to using a Chinese American mechanic to frequenting a local playground where lots of Chinese nannies hung out (they didn't have one themselves). Joyce Cousins and Marion Frank, a white couple, enrolled their daughter Corrine in a bicultural/bilingual education program. I asked them what they would say to those who said they were forcing the issue, and Marion said, "We didn't force anything on her, this is what her background is . . . and we see it as providing an opportunity." Joyce added that living where they lived, in San Francisco, meant that they could provide a lot of those opportunities. In fact, white adoptive couple

Marie and Fabio Bosco had consciously moved to the Bay Area so their daughter could attend a Chinese language school. Speaking for her seven-year-old daughter, Marie said, "She's investing herself in this second identity, so when this core family isn't so important to her and she's out there in the world, she can say, 'Well yes, I am Chinese, and I've studied Chinese.'"

The immersion approach prompted parents not just to attach things Chinese to their daughters but to narrate their family as transcultural and transracial. As Jason Bradley put it, "We don't want to just sort of sit back and say, 'Okay, we don't have to do anything about her culture, because the Chinese school is doing it all.'" He, the Boscos, Karen Chisholm, and Joyce and Marion said they were committed to learning Chinese language and history along with their children. Karen's daughter was enrolled in a bilingual school, and her house was plastered with Chinese character flashcards. She gave her daughter a gold star "sticker" every time she could teach Karen a new phrase in Chinese—it gave her daughter self-esteem, and it was fun, Karen told me. For David and Joan Spencer, as well as Debra Fine and Christy Kinsler, involving their daughters in the Chinese American community and sending them to a bilingual school were extensions of their own experiences in China. Joan told me, "We chose intentionally to go to China to adopt . . . we thought okay, we're white, but we might be able to do this right for a child; we have a good support network of Chinese friends." David added, "We can make China known and real to her." Some of these parents thus parlayed anxious concern about the right to pass on authentic Chinese culture into constructing themselves as knowledge gatherers who tapped into Chinese and Chinese American resources on behalf of their children.

These parents usually insisted on the importance of language and culture competency for their daughters' multiply positioned identities across borders. Not only would their children be able to function in both Chinese American and white American worlds, but they also would not feel too out-of-place when returning to China. In this way, their daughters' multiple identities—Chinese, Chinese American, American—were not fixed and contained to specific times or places or even bodies. Children's names were selected keeping in mind how they would play with these multiple audiences. Both the Spencers and Christy and Debra consulted with Chinese American friends about what Chinese names to give their daughters, soliciting a list of ten names from which to choose. These names were meaningful because parents thought they could work in white America, Chinese America, and China. The Spencers recalled with some amusement that they had asked their Chinese friend not to suggest names with x's or q's in them, since most Americans would not have a clue how to pronounce them.[8] Christy and Debra chose a new name because the name given to their daughter by the orphanage would be recognized by Chinese people as a "throwaway" name, not to mention that of a cheesy pop music star in China. Lisa Walker and Gerry Tang, in contrast, kept their daughter's name because it did have a concrete and desirable connection to China; their daughter had been named by her Chinese foster family, whom Lisa had met when she was in China.

Parents who erred on the side of immersion thus constructed their families as transnational, transcultural, and transracial, transmitting to their children what they saw as a more authentic choice of moving among China, Chinese America, and white (or multicultural) America— a choice only truly made possible in a white American world, they contended, by embracing and normalizing a Chinese cultural identity.[9] The provision of such choice was, in part, a response to the haunting of involuntary dislocations. The Spencers felt quite strongly that it was their obligation to learn and teach the cultural identities from and to which their daughter had been moved, in part because this occurred through no choice of her own; "You don't get to choose your parents!" Joan said. Joyce Cousins opted for immersing her daughter in the learning of Chinese culture and language; as she put it, "I think part of it is that because she basically can't ever know who her birth parents were, or what the circumstances were, it's like the most we can give her is her birth *country,* kind of?" More pointedly, as Volkman (2003) argues, the fascination with "birth culture" may in part "represent displaced longings for origins and absent birth mothers" (29).

Taken together, the four approaches to Chinese cultural identity—and again, these are not discrete but overlapping categories—demonstrate a range of possibilities for understanding difference in the American context. But that Chinese cultural identity is even an issue, and sometimes a contentious one, means we must ask what is at stake. For *all* parents, responses to Chinese cultural identity were mediated by a range of factors, including their own identities as parents (e.g., white or Asian, married or nonmarried, with or without experience in China); their understanding of what it means to be American (e.g., individualism, choice, multiculturalism); where they lived (e.g., many times parents in San Francisco contrasted the diversity and openness of their city to that of something like "Timbuktu, Iowa"); and the ages of their children (e.g., adopted at an age when they already spoke Chinese or deliberately chosen as an infant to minimize external connections). But most important, cultural practice is illuminated by the multiply intersecting forms of difference brought to the heart of family and nation by transnational adoption. The child's history extends beyond the discrete borders of the family and the nation, stirring simultaneously the ghosts of here and there, now and then. *Belonging* itself is at stake.

This is why the question of culture is not moot for Chinese American couples who adopt from China; rather, their cultural narratives imagined different ways of belonging to family and nation. On the one hand, the child's history and their own Chinese American heritage were sometimes understood as having a "natural" cultural connection. Miriam Lee said of white parents, "I think it's just because their kids are Chinese, they think that they have to have this bond with China, and they have to have knowledge about the culture. And they're not able to give it to them, because they're not Chinese themselves." In the late 1990s, some Chinese American parents in FCC formed their own separate Internet Listserv because, among other things, as one participant told me, "Most of the white parents talk about issues of identity . . . simple things, like 'Should I keep the middle name?' Her Chinese name as the middle name. To us, we don't think that way. . . . Because Chinese naming is a totally different process." On the other hand, shared Chinese cultural identity was fragmented by the differing ways that adoptees and parents related to the nation through birth and immigration. This same parent pointed out that interest in particular Chinese naming practices among Listserv members varied by parents' generation of immigration. And as adoptive father Hugh Chang pointed out, some Chinese American families with children by birth struggled with what it meant suddenly to push attachment to Chinese cultural identity for a child who had immigrated "direct" from China:

One choice they face is, "I have biological kids at home, and they grew up like Americans. Even though they see themselves as Chinese, with yellow skin. But they grew up Americans. Now I have adopted a child, what am I gonna do? Should I treat this one different? Send her to Chinese school, and ignore the other two biological kids? And if I don't ignore it, will they resent it because I forced them to go to Chinese school? Just because the sister is going to Chinese school?" So those are the conflicts.

The Chinese cultural identity Chinese American adoptive couples narrate for themselves and their children is shaped by how race and birth origins are imagined together, although in ways that differ from the concerns of white parents. First, even as Chinese American parents fretted over white parents' lack of authentic representation, they did not worry about their own. The Lees, for example, had a daughter from Vietnam in addition to a daughter from China and were sitting on the fence about whether to do more Vietnamese cultural activities; given that she racially "matched" their family, they could absorb questions of both birth origins and cultural identity into the private space of the family. In addition, there was not as much pressure to find the one right way to do Chinese culture—or perhaps more accurately, whatever way one did it was right in the context of a particular family history and a shared, racialized history of immigration and settlement. Second, Chinese American parents did not as readily hold up a Chinese cultural identity as a panacea for living with the way whiteness and bloodlines dominate normalized belonging.

Adoptive mother Vivia Chen and researcher Andrea Louie, both of whom are Chinese American, profess admiration for white parents' interest in their Chinese daughters' cultural identities. They also provide a pair of related cautionary tales for them. First, the search for an "authentic" Chinese identity is misplaced. As Chen (1999) says, "I fear that some parents might mistake the colorful trappings of Chinese tradition for the experience of being Chinese-American" (cited in Volkman 2003: 41); and furthermore, as Louie told the *St. Louis Chinese American News*,[10] "there is no one way of being Chinese American." Second, the search for cultural identity might make an end run around race. "These snippets of Chinese culture are appealing, fun and just more accessible than grappling with the more difficult issue of identity and the race thing," writes Chen (41). This is why Louie encourages white adoptive families to draw on Chinese American and Asian American resources that "reflect the experiences of living as a racial minority in the U.S."[11] In other words, the culture question is as much about white disconnection from the experience of racism as it is about Asianness.

Many white adoptive parents did indeed recognize this problem, especially as their children got older. In fact, most parents' concerns about adoptive and cultural identity changed over time and with their growing children's changing activities and stories. Some "balancing act" families who had enthusiastically attended FCC cultural events in the first year or two after adoption found their participation tapering off, especially as their children entered school. They cited the time it took from their kids doing "regular" things such as soccer and art and other school-related activities. But even as cultural activities tapered off for some, narrations of birthed and raced identities became more pressing. This was in part because children themselves started asking about "tummy mommies" and adoption but also because they started asking about looking different. One eight-year-old often asked her adoptive mother to act out giving birth to her; she also insisted she wanted blonde hair.

Racing Culture

Latent in all these approaches to cultural identity is the specter of not just biological but racial difference within the family, community, and nation. Race and racial difference haunt China/U.S. adoption at various stages and in various ways, in part because the exclusions of racial formations are built into the national culture itself, or more broadly, into the liberal norms of Western culture (Goldberg 1993). How does "choice" itself, for example, figure as a racialized practice? We know and accept that most parents would have chosen a child born to them, and that many would have preferred a child that looked like them. White adoptive parents get neither of these things. But they choose to adopt from China because it seems to fulfill their needs and desires. As I discussed in chapter 2, already in the choice of where to adopt we see the effects of U.S. racial formations on transnational circulations. Many parents wanted healthy infants, while some wished to avoid the involvement of birth families or to rescue a child from China. For some white parents, the prospect of adopting an Asian child seemed more viable than adopting an African American child, who might also stereotypically be older and/or drug-exposed. And running through many explanations was the imaginary of racially flexible children, shored up by the intrigue of Chinese culture. But then you get a child who wants to look like you, wants blonde hair, and, in wanting to move toward whiteness, belies the flexibility of her difference. Your choice is not her choice.

In this section I examine how the postadoptive racial construction of Chinese adopted children might help us grasp the complexities of the racial landscape of the United States (in the subsequent section, I consider its intersections with class, gender, and family structures). Here I revisit the four approaches to cultural identity to argue that they are all haunted by the way race and adoption speak to and through each other, troubling the notion of flexible citizenship. Race is a pivotal relational category in the narration of biological and cultural difference and belonging, an often unmentioned but always present category. Even as an Asian child is understood as more assimilable in a white family than an African American or Native American child, the unequal meanings of her racialization do not go away. When a white parent at an FCC workshop wondered out loud if perhaps they did not need to worry so much about the things that differentiated them from their children (cultural, adoptive, and racial identities), one of the Korean adoptees on the panel responded, "They're your kids, and they're going to be Asian." He later added that every time he heard a racist comment, it was wrapped up with the difference of adoption: "It reminds me," he said, "that my whole existence is different from theirs."

The salience of racial difference within the family is thus not easily separated from the sometimes painful unequal social formations of which it is a part, stretching from the loss of birth family to the class privilege that enables adoption. Perhaps it is for this reason that in many of my interviews, it was quite common for parents to use the language of culture in response to my questions or comments about race and racism. In the age of multiculturalism, when race is not supposed to matter, the discourse of culture increasingly substitutes for or supersedes that of race (Newfield and Gordon 1996); and how much more is race not supposed to matter in adoptive kinship. While the narration of cultural identity is on the surface relatively safe territory, the ways in which it avoids the language of race points us in the direction of the racial haunting of domestic America. Shiu (2001) puts it this way: "It is the usual non-mention of their children's 'racial' status in America that indicates the parents' recuperation of a generic 'humanity' in which both they and their children live" (10–11).

Interracial kinship incites questions of belonging both within and outside the family, setting adoptive parents up for the awkward embrace and denial of biological, racial, and cultural differences. Indeed, sometimes these blurred together, with race simultaneously translating other categories of identity. Consider the exchange I had with the Lous, who are Chinese American and Irish American, when I asked why they had wanted to adopt an infant:

> *Patty*: There was no issue of culture, different country, different language than she was used to. We just brought her home and she was ours! We want her to know, of course, that she's adopted, and that she's Chinese but also American.
> *Sara*: How do those things fit together for you, that she's both Chinese and American?
> *Patty*: It's not an issue. Because if we had a natural, a biological child, it would be half Chinese, half Caucasian.

Patty mapped national/cultural conceptions of Chinese and American onto racial distinctions that in turn mirrored blood kinship. This tendency to subsume biology and culture under race played itself out most strangely in what I call the "biracial fantasy": in at least three of my interviews, parents wondered if maybe their child wasn't "pure" Chinese. Larry Leister, who had argued that his daughter Laney was "American now," based his suspicion that "she can't be all Chinese" on a combination of cultural behavior (his daughter liked iced instead of hot tea) and physical identifiers (his daughter's hair had red highlights in the sunlight). And the Huangs wondered about the curl in their daughter's hair —maybe her birth father had been a foreign sailor or something, Teresa joked. She and Victor said a couple of times, "Don't you think she could be our daughter?"

Racial passing, or the lack thereof, has a way of managing the remembering and forgetting of other forms of difference. The Huangs admitted that if Victor were not Asian but white, they would probably be pushing harder to integrate Chinese culture into their daughter's life. For some white parents, the lack of racial "matching" underwrote their attention to adoptive and cultural identity, as John Levinson articulated:

> It's just my feeling about it, but if we had adopted a Caucasian child, I wouldn't feel as much a need to find out what their heritage was. . . . It wouldn't be a secret they were adopted, but we wouldn't have to go to Norwegian festivals if the kid happened to be Norwegian. But being Chinese is different, in that she looks so different, and it's clear that she's from China. And just hearing what it's been like for kids who were adopted from Korea, who are teenagers and are older—that having that connection to where they're from is very important, because you can't fit in and get by as a nice Jewish girl when you look like you're from China, and you *are* from China.

Eve Chomsky said she sometimes forgot her daughter was Chinese—"I think of her as looking like me!"—but she was reminded that they did not racially (and biologically) "match" when she saw the social incongruity of her Chinese daughter lighting candles during Sabbath prayers or found people staring at them in public. By contrast, some white parents denied or downplayed the significance of Asian racialization, and along with it other forms of difference. Larry fantasized an "impure" Asianness, miscegenated with whiteness; Aaron fantasized an Asianness "untainted" by blackness, closer to whiteness. Aaron told me, "For me, race just doesn't come up. I've gotta admit that if I had a black child, I'd probably think of us as more biracial."

A strange trio, almost a syllogism, emerges:

If both parents are white, and the child is white, they will probably do less with birth culture. (John)

If both parents are white, and the child is Chinese, they will probably do more with her birth culture. (Victor)

If both parents are white, and the child is black, they will probably see
race more. (Aaron)

At issue here is what I call race-culture matching, whereby racial difference constrains the construction of identity because American society
expects racial difference to mean cultural difference (Omi and Winant
1994; Waters 1990). Or more accurately in this case, whiteness expects it;
race is "seen," let alone seen as racial difference, from a normalized white
gaze. This process is not unique to transracial or transnational adoption
but takes on particular nuances in adoption and in relation to the American constructions of Asian subjects—the foreign and mirror "opposite"
of white and Western and yet sometimes honorary white (Hsu 1996;
Hune 1995; Lowe 1996; Ong 1996), made possible in part through the
black/white binary. This insight alone turns the gaze back on whiteness
as "a set of *cultural* practices that are usually unmarked and unnamed"
(Frankenberg 1993: 1) and as a key component of the quest for cohesion
in adoptive family narratives.

We have seen that the broader social meanings of race-culture matching prompt different responses to "the culture question"; some parents
thought it ridiculous to incorporate things Chinese into a household par-
ented by white Euro-Americans, while others felt it equally strange for a
child racially marked as Asian *not* to know an Asian heritage. Goldberg
(1993) and Stoler (1997), among others, have convincingly argued that
the deep structuring power of race and racism lies precisely in their dy-
namism, as they are reproduced in new and multiple forms across (or
within the same) place and time. As Stoler (1997) puts it, "[T]hat racial
discourses contain and coexist with a range of political agendas is not a
contradiction but a fundamental historical feature of their *non-linear,
spiraling political genealogies*" (191). In other words, the whole range of
approaches to the politics of cultural diversity is haunted by unsettled
histories of racialization. It is thus not surprising that the range of cultural stances I discovered correspond to some extent with the multiple
historical forms that Omi and Winant (1994) argue racial projects have
taken in the United States, for example, assimilation, color blindness,
and multiculturalism.[12]

I have said that race "condensed" the range of cultural identity possibilities parents imagined, and by that I mean that race constrains the

imagined free play of ethnic options. At the same time, as I discuss below, adoptive families' intimate encounters with racism open up possibilities for rethinking inequalities. While conscious attention to race might have been especially prevalent in balancing-act and immersion narratives, crucial to my argument is that racial formations haunted other approaches as well.

The assimilation approach resisted emphasizing Chinese cultural identity for fear it came at the expense of an American identity, but more than this, it "forgot" race and normalized whiteness. When I asked the Leisters about the possibility of racism, Linda Leister smiled at her two-year-old daughter Laney and said, "You're just too cute for teasing." The cover of the children's book the Leisters used to tell the story of adoption to their daughter showed a smiling, blonde, blue-eyed girl. Not only did Larry Leister imagine that perhaps his daughter Laney wasn't "all Chinese," but Laney was also not "all nonwhite" by virtue of her distinction from other immigrants of color. When I asked if there were other racial minorities in their town, the Leisters initially told me there were not. In the context of a later part of our conversation, it turned out that one section of town was occupied by migrant workers from Central America.

Nevertheless, this idealized erasure of racial classification and racism was haunted by the meanings attached to bodies marked as racially and biologically different—the bodies of one's children. Chineseness could not be contained, over there and in the past, but rather demanded some recognition of the white gaze here and in the present, in "our" family. Even the Cooks, conscious about downplaying their daughter's Chinese identity, looked to race to explain disruptions of the assimilationist ideal they espoused:

> *Nancy*: Our daughter is very involved in Scandinavian dancing and really has a talent for it. She's growing so tall and long-legged, and that adds to it. We may or may not encounter prejudice in that.
> *Sara*: Are there other—
> *Nancy*: Not too many. Most are little blonde-haired Scandinavian girls.
> *Sara*: Why do you think it's there that she might encounter prejudice?
> *Nancy*: I don't know that it's there, but it's just that if anywhere in her life where we are right now, that would be the highest possibility? I think just because it's *Scandinavian* dancing. So it kind of makes

one think that Scandinavian people would be doing it. And we just
tell her that judges don't always see every good thing you do. . . .

Sara: So are you saying that you think it's possible the judges aren't
marking her fairly because she doesn't "match" what the part
should look like?

Nancy: Well, I guess Chet and I think there's that potential.

And when I reinterviewed the Leisters four years after our initial interview,[13] I noted changes to their story that reflected the changing racial
formation of their family. Their daughter Laney was older, was noticing
that she looked different from her parents, and now had an adopted sister named Lucia who was not only light-skinned but had a birth mother
with whom they were in contact. Race had implications for other kinds
of belonging.

Larry: You know, out here, Laney will probably be the only person
from—

Linda: —that looks like she does. She knows that already. When she
sees someone Korean or someone Chinese, she says, "Is that person
like me?" And she'll always make a point—someone will ask her if
she's adopted. A lot of people will not realize that Lucia is. And
Laney will always tell them, "Lucia is from Romania, and I'm from
China." [Both parents laugh.] Like hey, we are *all* adopted here.

The Leisters worried about how they would explain to Laney, who already felt different, that they had information about her sister Lucia's
birth mother but not hers. Linda had started to order a few popular children's books about China. And even though she told Laney that a book
with Chinese characters in it "doesn't mean anything to us, honey, because we don't know Chinese," I also heard a subtle unraveling of whiteness: "We're teaching them that everybody's different. Our family isn't
'normal,' you know."

It is worth noting that those who drew on the assimilationist paradigm were usually white heterosexual couples. I do not want to argue
that there is a direct causal relationship between family structure and approach to racial and cultural identity—in fact, many families who best
fit the immersion category were also straight white couples. Rather, I

want to suggest that the locations of families within the racialized structures of the nation might help explain the spectrum of ways in which children's identities could be imagined (see Balibar 1988b; McClintock 1995). Consider, for example, that many of the families that tended toward celebrating plurality were interracial couples. While parents who took this approach embraced what they saw as the beauty and wonder of racial diversity, some did not give much credence to claims of structural racial inequality. Racism was defined as a problem of individual acts of prejudice, left over from a more discriminatory past. When I asked the Huangs and the Lous about racism, they both described their racially mixed home and circle of friends, insisting that racism wasn't much of an issue in their lives, nor did they want it to be for their daughters. Teresa Huang recalled the history of Victor's grandparents, who "had to spend a year on Ellis Island because of discrimination"; but when it came to her and Victor's own encounters with racism, they dismissed an encounter with name-calling as just an isolated incident by ignorant individuals. And George Lou was averse to the idea of his daughter embracing what he called "a racial identity" later in life. In many ways, these parents actively constructed an imagined future of "unmatched" race and culture. Paul Chang, a Chinese American man whose wife is white, asked me rhetorically why people should be expected to be or act a certain way just because they look a particular way. This desire to transcend inequality via the celebration of racial difference is summed up in an Internet Listserv posting from February 1997:

> We have a variety of dolls in our house. Some look Asian, we have African American dolls, brunettes, blondes. I tell my children that the world is like a flower garden and it takes all the flowers to make the garden beautiful. I truly believe that our international families, for that is what we are, will help lead the rest of society to understand and appreciate our global community.

However, at the same time that these parents constructed the private family as a safe locus for transcending difference, they had to confront the miscegenation anxieties and assumptions of racial matching that emanated from the external gaze on their families. Teresa Huang described one such encounter:

There was a Chinese woman with her little boy and her parents, and they came up to me and they asked if Fiona was Chinese, and I said yes. They made some comment about her being adopted, and for some reason I just didn't care for the tone. And um, it just struck me the wrong way, and I said, "Well actually, my husband is Chinese." And the young woman just kind of looked at me and she just didn't know what to say. So finally she turned around and she interpreted to the older couple, and they just gave me this ice-cold glare and turned their backs and walked away. So, yeah, there's some pretty blatant racism from the Chinese in the area. It was okay as long as she was adopted, but for me to marry a Chinese man . . .

And Diane Scott, who is Chinese American, was determined that her daughter Marianne would be proud to be Chinese, especially given the kinds of race-culture (mis)matches she herself had encountered. Diane saw her daughter's name as one way to instill pride and give her the kind of choice that racism might not allow:

Marianne's middle name is Kwan, because I moved my maiden name in the middle. Because a lot of times when I go places, because my name's Diane Scott, now, they think I'm Scottish or Irish or something! They come up to me and say, "May I speak to Diane Scott," and I go, "I'm Diane Scott," and they look at me and go, "Uh, okay." But so I want her to have that Kwan in there to give her that choice; plus Kwan is a very, our family is very proud of their Kwan name. So I wanted her to have that; it's like [I'm telling her], "Marianne, you are a Kwan. You're a Scott, but you're a Kwan."

I sometimes sensed a tug-of-war between pride in cultural distinctiveness and the quest for racial indifference within the family, such as when Mary Leung defended the bits of Chinese culture she wanted to pass on to her daughter against the dismissive chuckles of her white husband, Tom. Their daughter stirred these tensions. Mary professed regrets that, now that she had a daughter from China, she did not know more about her immigrant mother's culture and language; and she found it irritating that her husband didn't seem to care about "adoption stuff."

This tension between celebrating diversity and acknowledging racist formations was alleviated for some Chinese American parents by their historical (and sometimes naturalized) connection to being Chinese American. In contrast, for white families, especially those celebrating plurality, the fun fare of Chinese culture sometimes became a way to deflect the haunting of racial formations. Hugh Chang, a first-generation Chinese American, told me of an FCC meeting where his suggestion to invite a speaker on the history of discrimination against Asians in America was met with discomfort on the part of some white parents; why not just celebrate with Chinese food and dance? they wondered. Hugh said he felt some of the white parents

> were sort of like, "Well, I don't know much about discrimination, so therefore I'm not going to talk about it." As Chinese American families bring up a Chinese kid, she will have no problem identifying with us. But for someone growing up in a Caucasian family, the minute they look in the mirror then they say, "Well, I'm different. How come you never talked to me about discrimination?"

I witnessed a planning meeting for a culture camp in which a similar disagreement arose among a group of white adoptive parents over whether to have a session for kids on racism or, as one mom said, "just the fun [cultural] stuff."

For families trying to do a balancing act or immersion, especially but not only if they were white, Chinese cultural identity was quite explicitly espoused as a tool for responding to race and racism. If there was a difference between the two approaches, it was in the degree to which they lived and embodied difference as a family, which I explain below. What they usually held in common was, first, seeing racialization as more than passing incidents of prejudice; second, perceiving their daughters' cultural identities as inextricably tied to the history of American racial formations; and third, responding to racism by nurturing the cultural identity that tied their daughters to China and/or Chinese America. As Joyce and Marion said, they were doing as much as possible with Chinese culture and language because their daughter would be expected to have that linkage; after all, said Joyce, "[R]ace—people notice that very first thing." Or as Sharon put it, "I mean, it happens in this country in general, that unless you're European, the focus is always on the other ethnic group. Like what does it mean to be Chinese American? Essentially, you're the different one."

These understandings of the racialized white gaze helped shape decisions about cultural practice; Nan Heinman told me that "if in honoring [my daughter's] culture and all the things associated with her race, if I can create a sense of pride and identity, I can only hope that will translate into a strong ego around her race." Liz Nickels anticipated expectations of race-culture matching from not only whites but also first- and second-generation Chinese Americans in the Twin Cities. She introduced Chinese art, food, stories, and holidays into her daughter's life "so that when she meets other Chinese American kids who do grow up in a Chinese American home, she's not completely out of the loop." Chinese cultural activities thus became a tool for somehow giving a child a history— and approximating a normative immigration history—that she and her parents did not have, yet which was marked on her body. Christy and Debra were appalled at a survey that reported a high percentage of Korean adoptees who did not identify as Asian American. You have to have "a sense of belonging, that you're attached to these people," Christy said. White parentage was seen to threaten a detachment from China and Chinese birth parents, as well as from Chinese America, that might become yet another potential "loss" to the child.

It is difficult to say whether and to what extent this fear of the loss of a cultural-racial identity was a kind of "white guilt," or even desire. But a number of white parents narrated their experience of adopting a Chinese child (even one they initially thought might flexibly fit in as an Asian and an infant) as an increasingly wider glimpse into the privileged norm of whiteness in the U.S. national context (Lipsitz 1998; Frankenberg 1993). Ben Houston, an adoptive parent I met at an FCC play group, related a story that illustrates this point. He told me he had initially resisted "doing the Chinese culture thing" not only because it seemed somewhat ridiculous but also because he just didn't find Han Chinese culture very interesting. After all, he said, he had not chosen to call himself "German American," just "American." But Ben was reconsidering, as my notes from the event indicate:

Ben tells me he is beginning to think he and Deena should be doing some things with Chinese culture. He just doesn't want to go over-board (like some parents, is the implication), and calls it a "matter of degree." I ask him why he thinks this is changing for him. One thing he says is that he has realized that while he had the option of not being German American, because of his daughter's race, she will not have that option.

Similarly, Fred and Cindy Coombs said they had at first figured their daughter would just melt into their family, but over time they decided it would be important to address more overtly cultural heritage and national origins, in large part because their daughter had started to no-tice that she looked different from the rest of her family (the Coombses also had birth children). Initially they felt like they were unnecessarily adding another cultural layer, but then their daughter's recognition of race "said something really powerful," according to Fred. Cindy con-tinued:

> She could see that she was Asian, Chinese. She could see it in herself, she could see it in others. And if she could see it in them, then she could probably see that it wasn't in us. And that she noticed those di-fferences means that she may come from some other place. And that meant that because she might look different, it might be okay that some other things are different, too. It's okay to look different, it's also okay to have different heritage. I mean, she recognized that there were differences, and so we shouldn't try to make everything the same.

Realizing that a child would not just "melt into us" sometimes led to a new and playful engagement with the interrelationships and contra-dictions of multiple kinds of difference and the ways in which they defined the family. The Coombses and many other parents would look for ways to demonstrate to their daughters that they had some physical things in common ("Your hair is dark like Mommy's" or "You have dim-ples like Daddy"), even as they wanted their daughters to be proud of the black hair and "Asian eyes" that tied them to another family and nation, as well as to a particular immigrant history. Terry Schlitz, who is white, took it a little further; he told me he now filled out the race or ethnicity slot on official forms "Asian American." "That's who we are now," he said, a bit to his partner Matt's surprise.

The transracial, transnational adoptive family foregrounds, more than anything, the problem of narrative continuity. As Fred Coombs suggested, race difference signals *discontinuities* with the places and families "left behind": China, birth parents, grandparents, siblings, orphans and orphanages. At the same time, it signals an often unanticipated *continuity* with racial formations at home: multiple kinds of racism, immigration histories, the normalized power of whiteness. There was thus growing, nagging recognition of the power race holds as "a concept which signifies and symbolizes social conflicts and interests by referring to different types of human bodies" (Omi and Winant 1994: 55); Frankenberg (1993) calls this "race cognizance." In her move from China to the United States, and as she got older, the attractive, flexible Asian child became suspiciously fixed and foreign. In the words of one parent, "If I have one more family member say how good my daughter is going to be in math, I'm just going to puke." But just as important, race haunted through a continuity from Asianness to blackness—and from the private construction of kinship to the public construction of citizenship—that pushed parents to recognize structural inequality and white privilege. Fred's wife, Cindy, remarked on her new appreciation of the different ways in which race could fix, and be fixed by, whiteness: "It seems almost like well, if your [white] daughter dates or marries out of your race, some people will say 'Well, Asian's okay, that's kind of close.' [She chuckles.] What about somebody who's Nigerian? Or what about somebody who's . . . ? It's one of those things where it really stretches *us*." The significance of race begins with the recognition of its differentiating effect on the child's history within the family but then extends to the recognition of its differentiating effects on the historical formation of American culture. In this context, as I have shown, some parents understood Chinese cultural knowledge as a tool not just for creating racial pride but also for fighting racism—what the Boscos called a "tool of empowerment."

But there was also the sense of being ill equipped as white parents to "authentically" understand racial formations, to help their daughters not feel alone. Karen Chisholm said of her daughter, "She won't be able to look at me and form an identity." This prompted a search for help. Many times I attended events for parents with children from China where white parents were eager to ask adult Asian Americans, "What do we do about racism?" FCC chapters in both California and Minnesota have planned special events on understanding racism and have included reaching out to the local Chinese American community among their organizations' objectives.[14] And individual white parents sometimes sought out Chinese American adult friends as "role models."[15] (One parent also noted wryly that she thought her daughter needed to see that Chinese people really did come in whole families.) When I asked the Erdahls what was important about connecting to Asian people, Martha lamented that she and her husband did not have "the heritage and the stories and the events and things" in their lives, and that "having been a white-blooded American for my whole life, it just sometimes baffles me . . . my Asian American friend helps me understand the underlying system, the structural issues." Martha's words convey the struggle to understand race as a social relation of power.

Tessler and Gamache (2003) found in their survey of adoptive families that few parents (presumably white ones) "appear to have Chinese friends whom they can invite into their home for social occasions" (10). In my own interviews, it was not uncommon for white parents (especially those performing the balancing act) to say that they knew they should seek out Asian American adults in their lives but that they felt awkward or unsure about how to go about it. Some parents looked instead to other families "like ours" (adoptive families consisting of white parents with Chinese kids), or even those particular families with whom they had traveled, for a shared group identity. Increasingly, online information and discussion groups are forming among parents whose children have come from the same orphanage. The desire to build such communities might be seen as haunted by the cultural, racial, kinship, or national communities parents imagine have been disrupted by abandonment and adoption. This is illustrated all the more powerfully by parents who looked to second adoptions to provide narrative continuity for their daughters, as I found with Amy and Ian.

> *Amy*: We would love to have another child from the same orphanage as our daughter. Just so they would have that in common.
> *Sara*: Say more about that. What is it about having that in common that's important to you?

Ian: Well, because she's growing up in a world where she's very different. She's very different from our family, she doesn't look like other people in our family—so wanting her to have a sister who is as similar to her as possible. And common roots, and common backgrounds, a common place to go back to.

Intersections of Race, Class, and Gender

Patricia Williams (1991) has written that the greatest challenge in theorizing intersections of difference "is to allow the full truth of partializing social constructions to be felt for their overwhelming reality" (221)—the reality of racialized political oppression, class formation, and gendered forms of hierarchy. And as Collins (1999) cogently argues in her pivotal work on intersectionality, "partial" means taking each of these social categories of power not as distinct but rather as interrelational, with different kinds of (nonetheless) overwhelming results. I have so far tried to demonstrate how the horizon of possible cultural identities for Chinese adoptees is delimited and challenged by racial imaginaries and formations and that, furthermore, racial haunting connects adopted Chinese children to their dislocations from birth family and nation *and* to the fraught racial territory to which they have been moved. But the salience of racial and cultural identities is fluid, sometimes overshadowed or reconfigured by other social categories of difference. The performance of healthy bodies is one example: one couple reminded me that the growth disorder their child had been diagnosed with a year after they returned from China would probably mark her more than racial difference. To borrow from Williams, the "full truth" of the relationship of the adopted child's biography to racist U.S. culture (Goldberg 1993) must attend to other "partializing social constructions."

In this section I address how heteronormativity, gender, and class intersect with each other, and most especially with racial formations, in the practices and narrations of adopted children's identities. I draw on the popularity of Chinese dolls (especially Mulan and Barbie) and the issue of school choice to illustrate,[16] arguing that the consumer choices of adoptive parents highlight the inextricable linkages of racialization and class identities. Indeed, consumptive practices reframe the questions of cultural authenticity and hybridity as privileges that might accrue to whiteness, class, and heteronormative citizenship (Lipsitz 1998); at the same time, they raise the possibility that cultural play might undo such privileges.

I have already suggested ways in which the racial and ethnic makeup of the adoptive family—for example, whether parents are white or in an interracial partnership or Asian or Jewish—might matter to approaches to cultural identity construction. I want to examine yet another important partializing gaze on the adoptive family, and that is bio-heteronormative reproduction. This starts, quite simply, with the notion that adoption is a family-building strategy outside the norm. Eve and Greg Chomsky felt that this called for unusual measures:

> Eve tells me she has a friend who says that "when you have biological kids, they're yours to do what you want with. But in adoption, you really have to think about the world, your child, racial identity." Eve laments that some adoptive parents of children from China just want to make them Anglo, and Greg agrees: "Kids get teased for all kinds of things, but how often do their mothers get together to plan how to deal with it and prepare their kids for it?"

The felt effects of nonnormative reproduction on approaches to race and culture were in some ways even more salient for families headed by single or queer parents. Single white mothers often said to me that the "absent father" seemed to trump or compound racial difference and again wondered if "too much" culture would unravel the fragility of these family differences. Several told stories of their daughters asking why they didn't have fathers or of people on the street asking them, "Is her father Chinese?" (Sharon Anderson said she would hesitate, smile, and say yes.) Nan Heinman was haunted by the absence of both father and siblings, because while they were missing in the transracial adoption story, her daughter would have had—probably *did* have—them in China:

> For my daughter right now, it's all wound up in "I don't have a daddy and I don't have brothers and sisters and my family's different." I think

those things could come up in a very visceral, deep way, the two things she hasn't had here. . . . And I think that it's possible that that awareness could be the thing, the trigger, that makes her want to really explore her Chineseness.

Vigilance to the historical weight of intersecting social relations of identity thus increases when the transracial adoptive family is further differentiated by heteronormative definitions of the male-female two-parent family. This is true as well for gay and lesbian parents. Most queer parents with whom I spoke fell mostly into the immersion category, erring on the side of putting difference on the table in almost business-like fashion. When I mentioned to Christy Kinsler and Debra Fine that some parents seemed to see Chinese cultural activities as making up for racial and adoptive difference, Christy responded, "I think being lesbian, that's just one of the traps we don't fall into. We know how painful it is to be different. And it doesn't matter in what context you're different, it's painful, and there's no getting around it." Similarly, Terry and Matt sought out Asian adults in their lives because they were pretty sure their son would at some point be "angry that I have two dads, and that they're not Asian."

Gay and lesbian couples' responses to intersecting difference suggest transformative possibilities; they felt prepared in some fundamental way to equip their children for multiple forms of inequality. True, creating a family that crosses racial and heteronormative lines all at once might in some way forge creative new ways of being, but there are certainly no guarantees. Lisa and Gerry, respectively white and Asian American, had a number of stories to tell about their encounters with people for whom an interracial, two-mother family just did not compute. Indeed, one reason they had decided to adopt from China was so that a child would look more like Gerry; Lisa explained that this was to avoid Gerry having to "go through all the questioning of 'Are you the nanny?'" Ironically, this had backfired in painful ways for Lisa: "It's always, I mean, oh god, it's so always out there. Everyone assumes that she's Gerry's birth child, of course, and everyone assumes that I'm the babysitter."

Lisa and Gerry's nanny anxieties bring us to how gender and class intersect with each other and with race across many adoptive parents' constructions of their children's identities. The private, domestic, consumptive space of family labored to absorb the public contradictions of non-normative, transracial kinship (Eng 2003; Anagnost 2000). Nan Heinman hired a Chinese nanny as an identity role model; Eve Chomsky and other mothers, consciously spurred by concerns about racism, "got together to plan how to deal with it." Class privilege thus becomes a means to offer children cultural and racial identity. Indeed, a growing culture industry targets transnational, transracial adoptive parents, from books telling the adoption story and Mandarin language and music tapes to ethnic dolls and engraved pendants celebrating adoptive motherhood.[17]

Adoptive parents looked to the market for representations of Asian girl power and femininity. (Matt and Terry, who have a son, groaned at the difficulty of finding Chinese-looking boy dolls.) Asian girl dolls regularly showed up in discussions on the Internet, on Web sites that market products to white parents with children from China, and in family homes. In the late 1990s, Mulan and Chinese Barbie were especially hot items. As the first cohorts of Chinese children adopted into the United States reached ages four to seven, Hollywood released its movie version of *Mulan*—an ancient story of a gender-bending Chinese girl heroine—along with the action figures and games that touted her. Signs of *Mulan* appeared quite regularly in adoptive households in which I conducted interviews. When I visited Tom Mining and Mary Leung, the contents of a *Mulan* playset were sprinkled around the house—the naked doll on the table, her boyish outfits strewn on the floor, her feminine gowns on a chair. The private consumption of the *Mulan* package mediated the kinds of public representations parents wanted for their children. Several parents expressed what Sharon Anderson said: "*Mulan* came along at just the right time." One single mom at an FCC event told me she was against Barbie dolls but was glad to see her daughter and other adopted Chinese girls identify with Mulan as a strong, independent girl. Not only that, but Mulan provided a narrative connection to their children's Chinese origins. Maria Bosco said that Mulan presented the opportunity, at a perfect age, for her to talk with her daughter about the Chinese "preference for boys." It also seemed to her that the *Mulan* phenomenon had given her daughter a stronger racial identity, as evidenced in how she drew her self-portraits; "the eyes changed" post-*Mulan,* added Maria's husband, Fabio. Sharon Anderson's daughter drew pictures of her birth mother that, as Sharon noted with wry humor, looked an awful lot like "Mulan with earrings."

One reason Mulan hit what Fabio Bosco called "the perfect note" was the blonde beauty standard that plagued many adoptive parents, posing a dilemma at the crossroads of race and gender. Barbie dolls reared their pretty heads in these dilemmas as well, especially for mothers of pre-school-age daughters. Liz related to me a story of her fight with what classic Barbie represented—white as normal, female as blonde and beautiful—after she and Meg took "the Barbie plunge" with Hannah:

> She wanted a blonde Barbie, don't you know. Well, because the others aren't really Barbie. *Barbie* is blonde. But even when she got a number of them—we decided we have to play with them, we might as well get a number of them. And she got them on her birthday . . . and of course, she got an African American, and an Asian, and a blonde. . . . And then she would only play with the blonde one. She refused to play with the dark-haired ones. And finally, I didn't know quite how to handle it, but I said, "It kind of makes me sad. Nobody in our family has blonde hair. We all have brown or black hair, and I love brown and black hair." And we kind of talked it through. . . . But it's insidious. It's very insidious in this culture.

Liz recognized what Clark concluded in his experiments with children's choice of dolls several decades ago: that her daughter's choice was not some simple self-hatred but the result of the social relations that inhabited her psyche (see Cheng 2001: 15).

But relying on consumer power to nurture Asian cultural and racial identity does not and cannot resolve the particularities of raced and gendered intersections. A number of mothers lamented that while they could combat their young daughters' obsessions with blonde hair or longer eyelashes by telling them how beautiful they were, they did not want at the same time to reinforce the idea that beauty was all that mattered, especially given the exoticized Asian female image in popular consumer culture. Sandra Padding was disturbed that people would say her daughter was beautiful and charming, but "they don't take the next step, they just admire her." This problem of the socially celebrated/exploited

Asian girl affected adoptive families' own relationship to the child as object and subject of cultural consumption. I once witnessed a fascinating discussion among adoptive mothers about modeling jobs for their children; an astounding three out of the eight women present had taken their daughters to a photo shoot for potential commercial modeling. "I'm not JonBenet's mother!" one of them insisted, as she passed around copies of her daughter's glossy photos. Advertising agencies were particularly looking for Asian faces, she told us; and wasn't that a good thing, to combat blonde beauty standards with the public display of Asian faces?

Representations of the Asian female body slip uneasily between celebration and commodification, which for parents represented the difference between their children's pride and self-hatred and the haunting of their own relationship to the dominance of whiteness and class privilege. Chinese Barbie is an interesting case; she was of particular interest to a number of families because she represented some kind of alternative to blonde Barbie. (While she has the same anatomically dazzling body and wide-eyed, pixie nose features as Caucasian Barbie, her hair is black and she arrives in her box wearing a traditional Chinese silk dress.) I first encountered Chinese Barbie in conversation on one of the Internet Listservs, where she came to represent the celebration of things Chinese, a reinforcement of racial and gendered pride, and at times Chinese daughters themselves. In this and other conversations, a few parents referred to their adopted daughters as "China dolls." Some parents exchanged information about where to find the elusive Chinese Barbie and how much to spend. But this fetishizing of Chinese dolls—indeed, the conflation of child and Chinese doll—begs attention to cultural and racial representation as part and parcel of the class-enabled desire for the child.

During the Listserv discussion, one parent posted a rebuttal reminding readers that Chinese Barbie is made under exploitative sweatshop conditions in underdeveloped countries, something parents with children from China should be compelled to combat in "this new global community we are joining" (December 1996). This reference to the production side of transnational circulations of capital was a jarring insertion into a conversation otherwise playing out its part on the consumer end of the commodity chain. On top of that, it linked awareness of those transnational circulations to adoption from China itself. Parents looking to the cultural and racial representation of Chinese Barbie were being asked to imagine that desire as part of a broader political economy. The migration of the child into their privileged arms, through the unlikely figure of Barbie, recalls the uneven circulation of capital by which others are *im*mobilized. Did this remark thus come uncomfortably close to recalling the commodification that haunts adoption exchange, and the desire on the part of parents that animates it? In an online resource for China-adoptive families compiled by an adoptive parent,[18] one reader posted an "Actual Items" gag from the television show *Late Night with Conan O'Brien*. It was a cute ad for digital cameras that depicted a grinning Asian child in a straw hat—the kind of advertising often celebrated by parents who were glad to see Asian faces in the media. But then a closer view (the "gag") revealed the fine print in a caption box next to the child: "Record every minute with the kid you just bought in China." The contributor understandably suggested that readers write the show to protest. The advertisement had crassly slipped across the short but crucial distance between desire and consumption, multicultural spectacle and white class privilege.

The advertisement and responses to it reveal what Eng calls "the baby's tenuous transformation from object to subject . . . a tenuous subjectivity continually threatening to undo itself" (8). A child's slippage back into object threatens to reveal the inequality of opportunities through which she has been adopted. Fred Coombs was haunted by the fact that, yes, his daughters were better off, but "I don't want to go there . . . I never cared for people saying how lucky they are." He winced as he recalled his older adopted daughter telling him—as they sat together in their backyard hot tub—how lucky their second Chinese daughter was to be joining them. We come back to how class privilege might shape the imagined possibilities of racial and cultural identity, especially in the service of normalizing kinship.

The issue of school choice further clarifies how the social and material capital families could provide—and reproduce—intersected with the racial, cultural, and national identities they imagined for their children and families. Across the four narrative frames of cultural identity, parents attached different kinds of "trade-offs" to various school choices for their children. There were especially impassioned debates in the Bay Area. The greater availability of public and private Chinese bilingual schools than in the Twin Cities brought to the surface the crosscutting tensions of class, race, and migration through which social citizenship is made. I took part in an FCC discussion group in San Francisco that focused on bilingual and bicultural education, where a number of participants—both white and Chinese American—worried that a Chinese school might take their children away from other normal childhood activities, slow down their English, or, in the words of one parent, "alienate" them from their parents. Concerns about the repercussions of school choice were also common in my interviews, where they reflected the social relations of class and race in which families were embedded.

Chinese American parents discussed a number of issues that shaped their school choices. And while some consciously chose a Chinese-language school or at least a racially and culturally diverse school, others sought the kind of "mainstream" education that promised integration to Asian immigrants otherwise marked as outsiders. Helen Mah, one of the few first-generation Chinese American adoptive parents I interviewed, was blunt about her investment in a well-respected private school: "I want her to get into a top-notch college. We expended all this effort to take her out of China. It doesn't make sense to send her to a crappy school!" For Helen, the social capital of a good education, no matter what the racial and cultural makeup of the school, was what could distinguish her child's new life from her old; it simultaneously reproduced the distinctiveness of Helen's own class location vis-à-vis a backward China. The downside to a Chinese language and cultural education was its downward tug on the material and symbolic demands of normalized citizenship, and its potential reproduction of the struggles of Chinese immigrants. Diane Scott, who is Chinese American, was against the proposal for a Chinese-English bilingual public school in the suburban area where she lived:

> I want my daughter to learn whatever she's supposed to learn in school. That's not what my tax dollars are going for. I don't want math, and science, and English to be pushed aside to learn Mandarin! So that her test scores could be lower? So she could learn less in school? I don't think so. . . . I want her English to be good, I don't want it to be broken. They can talk like my mother if that's what they want! Geez. So I'm totally against it . . . I mean, this is America!

White parents, like Chinese American parents, made school choices that reflected varying intersections of class, race, and culture. Some, like Helen and Diane, resisted Chinese-language school out of concern for how it might further distinguish immigrant and citizen. Aaron Kretz, who told me he worried that his daughter might talk as fast as some of the Chinese people he knew, discussed his uncertainty about sending his daughter to a bilingual school:

> These guys who are Chinese, second-, third-generation Chinese American that I work with don't feel the need to expose their kids to the Chinese culture. If anything, it's like they want to be Americans, and not emphasize the Chinese part. So when a few people who are Chinese American, second or third generation that I've talked to, [even] they don't see the need for Chinese American school . . . we weren't sure of the trade-offs, you know?

But for other white parents, the class location that allowed them to adopt a child from China prompted different schooling decisions. Material resources were mobilized to purchase an education geared toward children's perceived identity needs. Joyce said she recognized that helping their daughter to understand her difference as "normal" by sending her to a private bilingual school with other Chinese adopted children was made possible by their ability and willingness to pay for it. And Joan Spencer passionately told me,

> I think you have to make some concessions. You chose this, your child didn't choose this. And your choice to adopt crammed this down her throat for the rest of her life . . . we all signed on the line, we all pledged to do our best to honor their culture and history. I take that commitment seriously. So you don't have to send your child to a bilingual school, but by golly, it solves a heck of a lot of problems in one place. I mean it does really simplify things.

Jackie Kovich rejected formal Chinese schooling for almost mirror-opposite class reasons. She pointed out that while so many parents with children from China could afford private Chinese schools, she couldn't; besides, she said, private school "just isn't me." Jackie lived in a working-class community of Asian immigrants and thought that her daughter's proximity to other Asians and immigrants was more important than being in a private Chinese-language school that might, ironically, reproduce white class privilege.

The trade-offs inherent in reproducing class location seemed especially to haunt the school choices of those parents, in both San Francisco and the Twin Cities, who were expressly committed to building their children's Chinese racial and cultural identities. The Boscos admitted feeling some guilt over living in a wealthy all-white suburb while sending their daughter into the city for a bilingual education with other Chinese American children; Maria said apologetically, "We're just not city people." Nan Heinman was thrilled that her daughter had gotten into one of the top schools in the Bay Area but was concerned that her daughter seemed obsessed with blonde hair since leaving her less prestigious but more diverse kindergarten. In Minnesota, Terry Schlitz said a bit reluctantly that he thought maybe there was an important trade-off to moving to the white suburb in which they lived, since the school in their old neighborhood included a number of Vietnamese immigrant children. He told me (again, somewhat to the dismay of his partner Matt):

> I was more worried about Sean going to school there and feeling the peer pressure from the kids that have felt pressure to join Asian gangs. I think he's at a higher risk [of acting out] because of having two dads, and being of a different race than his parents. It might be kind of cool to fit in [by joining a gang]—that's my theory, anyway.

Liz Nickels expressed similar anxieties about race-class mismatching:

> Roosevelt School has a magnet program for Hmong kids. And you could argue, send your Chinese American child *there,* because they'll be with all these kids that look like them. *My* feeling, my take on it is, there's probably nothing more different than a first-generation Hmong family and this upper-middle-class family that we are. There's more difference between that and the fact that they just have to look alike. I remember going to Roosevelt, holding Hope, and these little girls, about five of them, came up to me and said [whispering], "Is she your

baby?" They had *no* concept of an interracial adoption. . . . I thought, "No way [is this going to work for my daughter]." And then also there's kind of the clumping. So, they look like each other. Well, Hannah's not struggling with English as a second language. A couple other families I know whose kids are coming up to school, the girls are like three, and they're saying, "Oh wouldn't it be great to send them to Roosevelt." But our take is that it would not be—even though she would be with all these kids that look like her. So, it's so funny, you're just thinking about it on all these different, dumb levels.

All of these "different, dumb levels" at which adoptive parents narrate and act on their children's identities speak to the particular alchemic power of whiteness and class privilege, even when parents espouse transformation. Indeed, as adopted Chinese children get older, some parents have begun to demand changes to school curricula that do not reflect their children's racial and adoptive identities. And so, they put their class privilege to the task of bringing diversity to "good schools"; take, for example, this excerpt from a report by MSNBC:

> The good news, says anthropologist Frechette, is that the families adopting from China are a force for change. "A lot of people adopting from China tend to be wealthier, better-educated and urban," she says, given that this profile is favored by China's adoptions rules. "When they send their kids to homogenous schools, these parents get very frustrated, especially when they start grappling with history, government." History textbooks, for instance, may not even mention Chinese Americans in the battle over civil rights. "They are not prepared for racism in America," Frechette says. But, she notes, these people are pressuring the schools to do things differently. "They are the kind of people who will take this on."[19]

They are in fact the kind of people who can take this on because of the resources at their fingertips. The question remains of what the trade-offs are when diversity is commanded from a position of race and class privilege, or when public problems of difference are absorbed into private acts of choice.[20]

Conclusion: Beginning to Imagine the Future

The cultural, familial, and national identities of adopted Chinese children, as narrated and practiced by their parents, link children's adoption histories to disparate kinds of exclusion and difference. Liz Nickels, for example, combated the blonde beauty standard that pervaded her daughter Hope's life by seeking out Asian images and adults, and she invited her daughter's history into the everyday present by hanging a map of Hope's hometown in China next to a map of the Twin Cities on their dining room wall; at the same time, she actively defended her choice of a school that differentiated Hope from other Asian immigrants. Hope's transnational migration history is indeed different from most by virtue of her proximity to whiteness and wealth. This is why, on the one hand, transnational, transracial adoption practices might be critiqued for reproducing hegemonic white class privilege in the United States, while on the other hand, they might be praised for breaking down those same privileges. But the experiences of adoptive families show neither of these to be a fully realizable possibility. The same factors that make transnational adoption an exceptional form of migration —the legal and symbolic severing of the migrant child from her family and nation of origin (even before migration); her managed reproduction as legal and social citizen; her radical relocation across multiple borders of race, class, nation, and kinship—also challenge the easy citizenship of whiteness, wealth, and multiculturalism. Liz's struggle to do right by Hope's identity shows us with new clarity how cultural practice is the site of both the reproduction and the transformation of difference.

The impossible contradictions of China/U.S. adoption afford a new angle on the race and class imaginaries embedded in American national culture. This is because the process of adoption moves back and forth between a globalized, public complex of exchange and the intimate bonds of kinship. In other words, the individual experience of haunting suggested in this chapter must be understood within the broader political economy of China/U.S. adoption set forth in earlier chapters. The gendered inequalities of abandonment in China and the racial inequalities of American history together haunt in the figure of Mulan and in the process of school choice. The cultural dislocations of absent Chinese birth parents and absent white Jewish birth children are linked in a Sukkot ritual. The hegemony of heteronormative reproduction and racism meet in the biracial fantasy and in the query "So, are you the babysitter?" The quest to instill pride in being an Asian American girl recalls global labor exploitation in the form of Chinese Barbie. These ghosts illuminate not just differences but also local/global inequalities, and thus demand a response. It is in responses to dislocation and difference—responses from not only parents but also agencies, facilitators, and governments in both China and the United States—that relations of power are both reenacted and reimagined.

I conclude this chapter with a sampling of the kinds of responses parents gave to my inquiry into what they imagine and desire for their daughters' futures. If parents cannot count on reflecting the histories of their children's identities back at them, what do they imagine their children will see in the mirror? This is an especially important question in an era when many transracial adoptees have grown to adulthood, telling stories that might foreshadow the experiences of Chinese adoptees. Patton (2000), for example, finds that

> the development of a meaningful sense of racial identity is profoundly complex and problematic for African American and multiracial adoptees raised in White families. While all these adults have managed to work out the racial implications of their lives for themselves, their acquisition of cultural maps to enable such negotiation has typically been a struggle. (170)

In particular, the stories of Korean adoptees—which foreground the "contrasts of normal/abnormal, American/Korean, white/yellow" (Choy and Choy 2003) and the struggle to reckon with the life that might have been and the unknown people with whom it might have been spent—have become a resource from which adoption agencies and parents of Chinese children draw. One of my goals is to suggest where doors are best left open to challenging the inequalities unearthed by adoption's transnational political economy. Of central importance, of course, are the doors left open for, or left to be pushed open by, Chinese adoptee children in years to come.

Not surprisingly, all parents hoped for secure and self-confident children, but the content imagined for accomplishing this goal recalled the four discursive frames of cultural identity I analyzed in this chapter. To imagine transcending racial difference through assimilation or a celebration of diversity was to also imagine transcending the difference of adoption—to be "normal." Nancy Cook had this to say about her daughter's future: "I would hope we would raise a better-rounded person, a child that when she becomes an adult, they wouldn't need an adopted Chinese support group, but would be just, part of life, part of American culture and lifestyle." When I asked Tom Mining how he and his wife might prepare their daughter for questions about her identity as she got older, he briskly deflected the question by retorting, "As somebody who has two loving parents?!" As Cheng (2001) has pointed out, one problematic result of popular psychologies of race identity is "the presumption that having agency or 'a strong ego' makes one impermeable to such [racist] invasions" (Cheng 2001: 15). The universalizing vision of a normalized, loving, two-parent family thus attempts to purge the ghosts of difference—race, class, kinship—conjured at various points in a child's adoption history. Diane Scott put it this way: "I want her to feel secure and confident in who she is. And yes she's adopted, but so what? That's what I kind of want her to have, that 'so what.'" Diane conceded that perhaps her own racial and cultural identification as Chinese American gave her license to be relatively nonchalant about her daughter's ruptured history.

White parents worried by the ghosts of racial difference tended to be worried as well by the ghosts of abandonment and adoption, as John Levinson and Sandra Padding indicated:

> *John*: I think, ten, fifteen years from now, I think she's going to feel she's Chinese. And she's going to look Chinese, and she's going to notice the difference. And that will be a big part of her, I think, that she looks different, and is from China—different from we, her family.
>
> *Sandra*: Yeah, I guess the first thing that leapt into my mind was [the hope that she will identify as] "a Chinese Jewish girl." But what it really is, is that she's managed to feel comfortable with all of her story, all of who she is. Where she came from, what she was raised with.

The inequalities emergent at the conjunction of race with other forms of difference, such as gender and religion and class, made it easier to worry. Eve and Greg Chomsky said they had been at a party where there were several Asian women in their early twenties. "And Eve looked at me," Greg explained, "and said, 'That's Chandra-Mei in twenty years.'" Greg went on to say he found it strange to imagine his daughter as a grown-up Asian woman. He worried that she would "be more exotic, and prettier, and of course maybe more at risk," while Eve wondered if any observant Jewish boy would marry a Chinese Jewish girl.

But it is important that conjunctions of difference within the family were not just a cause of anxiety about the reproduction of inequality and the elusiveness of a whole identity but also a springboard for letting go of the unified self and unified family and unified nation. Some parents took difference and disjunction—that is, a haunted history—as the rule rather than the exception. Lisa Walker expressed listening to the confluence of ghosts in this way:

> I feel an obligation that I'm raising her not just for her and for us, but for the foster family, and for her birth parents. I feel their *presence* in trying to, you know, do the best that we can. . . . I hope that she'll see herself as someone who's a part of many worlds. I mean, that she'll have you know, a strong sense of her birth heritage, and not just in this abstract way. I would want her to have a real relationship with the foster family, and hopefully maybe at some point with her birth parents . . . I want her to have an experience of being Chinese American, and hating going to Chinese school on Saturdays! [Laughs] . . . That she is the child of a gay family, and that she will treasure that diversity. That also, she'll be aware that everyone isn't citizens, and you know. . . . I guess I really want her to see herself as [coming] from a diverse, rich family. And that all of those things are parts of her. And that we fit together, we belong together, because we're different, and because we have all these different parts.

The ability to imagine belonging *through* the differences that bind is not just the province of gay and lesbian families, of course, but I would assert that attending to one set of ghosts allows the possibility of understanding how others are structured into the experience of history. In other words, some families were better than others at listening to "those not present." The Spencers pointed to white people's lack of ability to see with minority eyes *and* worked hard to make Chinese birth parents and orphanage children as real as possible in their child's life. Cindy and Fred Coombs, a straight white couple who already had several birth children, started their daughter's life by bringing "others who are not present" into the narration of her life—they were among very few parents who reported asking the foster family what they would want them to tell their daughter as she grew older. Cindy also reported learning to allow intersecting differences to present possibilities for *making* a difference beyond her individual daughter's life:

> She's going to have a lot of experiences that are different, because she's adopted, because she has a different cultural heritage, because we're older, because we have different financial means. There's a lot of things that are different. . . . And [for my biological children]—I think through their experience with culture, with China, I think it has as a byproduct made them more tolerant, maybe, of a lot of other cultures, a lot of other races.

The accumulation of difference in the history of the adopted child stirs the ghosts that show us where inequalities lie and pushes for something to be done (Gordon 1997). The struggle to construct an identity out of that history corroborates that belonging is made through difference, through the partializing cultural articulations of racial formations, class activations, gendered relations, and national imaginings. In China/U.S. adoption specifically, the struggle shows us how whiteness is made in and through conceptions of the Asian as insider/outsider, how the reproduction of kinship is constructed through globally uneven gender relations, and how ideals of liberal individual citizenship are themselves about the privileges of whiteness and wealth. But difference-as-inequality also presents the possibility of difference-as-change, not just in the individual life of the child but also in the world of difference opened up by her history.

I do not want to suggest that adoption instigates the free and unfettered play of hybrid identity. Watkins (2004) writes that parents can and should be "empathic witnesses" to the multiple, nomadic identities of their adopted children and can best accomplish this by leaving their own comfortable space of whiteness, seriously playing with evacuating the dominant positions of their subjectivity. I find this appealing but wonder if it looks too quickly to the future, prematurely positing a poststructural kinship. Watkins asserts that it is the trauma of exclusion both in the United States and in the birth country that leads to the progressive embrace of a nomadic identity, but then she makes very little mention of the structural privileges that give rise to "identity play" as an option. None of the four narrative approaches to cultural identity with which I began this chapter could be construed as "poststructural" in the sense of producing a free play of identity—not in the context of kin relations made through differences of race and birth.

Perhaps what matters as much or even more than the celebration of heterogeneity is the process of bringing the past into the present (Eng 2003; Cheng 2001), or put another way, listening to the multiple pasts that haunt the Chinese child placed with and desired by white parents. We have seen that racialization plays a key role, on the one hand flexibly enabling exotic appeal and rescuability while on the other hand threatening to spoil the illusion of full kinship and national belonging. A critical analysis tells us it is racist to fix people to a particular place or culture, but given the dislocations of adopted children from China to America, it is perhaps equally racist *not* to affix that history to their stories. When we do so, the privileges of state power, whiteness, and class that migrate the child are provincialized, shown to be particular, unmoored from an easy narrative continuity. The nonnormativity of adoption as kinship formation helps catalyze this recognition. If at the same time that transnationally adopted Chinese children are being claimed as insiders their parents are being pulled to the outside by the history of difference and dislocation brought more intimately to the family, there is perhaps hope for nudging privilege out of its racialized spaces (Haslanger 2004).

Anthony Shiu (2001) is skeptical of the potential challenges to racism I would pin to adoption. In his study of white parents' narratives of their adoption from China, he argues:

Family and whiteness, then, will always embody the form of a decision . . . that which relies upon "difference"—racial, ethnic, linguistic, etc. —will always secure borders, ensure domination, and benefit from the diminution of those who "need" inclusion. . . . And the racial "inclusion" of international adoption only exacerbates the fact that we are replicating the processes that exclude in the first place. (12)

There is no question that adoption can and does replicate processes of exclusion; I have argued as much. But the histories of difference intimately embodied in the adopted child are not always denied in favor of the status quo or blindly held up as exemplars of magnanimous American outreach. Cheng (2001) writes:

> The rhetoric of progress or cure can produce its own blind spots. As Christopher Lasch puts it, "[a] denial of the past, superficially progressive and optimistic, proves on closer analysis to embody the despair of a society that cannot face the future." And when it comes to the future of the race question, to borrow Faulkner's words, the past is not dead; it is not even past. Rather than prescribing how we as a nation might go about "getting over" that history, it is useful to ask what it means, for social, political, and subjective beings to *grieve*. (7)

China/U.S. adoption might be a chance for both white and nonwhite to grieve, if its stories are taken as an invitation to the excluded subjects that haunt it: less mobile migrants both past and present, unknown birth mothers and fathers and siblings, Chinese and black children not adopted, parents and caregivers unable to adopt. The interesting question, the question that remains, is how the stage can be set for both American adoptive parents and their Chinese children to grieve the histories that mold their kinship.

Conclusion

Akin to Difference

> [Consider] the difference between a
> conceptual, declarative mode of speech
> and an experiential, suggestive one.
> While the former, by its very operation,
> tends to be forward-looking—since the
> declarative enunciates by projecting
> ahead—the latter tends instead to
> double back on experiences that are felt
> to be not quite finished, whose effects
> are still with us, haunting us, and
> waiting for some kind of articulation,
> however inchoate such articulation
> might be.
>
> —Rey Chow (2002: 136)

In the late 1990s and early 2000s, a
number of adult Korean adoptees produced stunning autobiographical
work that tried to unpack the blind alleys and broad horizons of their
identities. The titles of their work alone speak to the experience of transitional, multiple, and dislocated selves: *Passing Through, Searching for
Go-hyang* (Hometown), *First Person Plural, The Language of Blood.*[1] In
each of these four works, the adoptee/autobiographer journeys back to
Korea as an adult, searching in different ways for identification. And in
all four, nothing is finally resolved; rather, new and more complex layers
and possibilities for narrating their stories are created. The trajectories
of their identities turn out to be circuitous, referring to geographically
separated mothers and nations, racial and kinship divides, institutional
and state impositions, discursive chasms, historical happenstance. What
connects these facets of their stories, or, more accurately, illuminates the

connections among them, are the authors' own migratory selves. The return journeys turn out to be as much about the adoptees' American families and subjectivities as about their Korean families and selves, and perhaps even more about the stuff "in between" that allows and disallows the simultaneity of the two. All these authors insist, each in his or her own way, on unfixing stable categories of identity, on defying either-or solutions of being Korean or American, birth child or adopted child, abandoned or rescued, universal citizen or unique individual. At the same time, however, they do not settle on "the euphoric valorization of difference" (Chow 2002: 131) or on the emancipatory potential of a Korean cultural identity. Rather, the adoptees' movement between the spatial and temporal locations of their lives asserts that difference matters materially, relationally, and experientially, even as difference is not itself identity (McClintock 1995).

It may seem strange or even essentialist to draw on Korean adoptee narratives in the conclusion to a book on China/U.S. adoption. But the experiences of the former have much to tell us about the geopolitics of identity in the latter—not because Chinese adoptees' experiences do or will exactly mirror those of Korean adoptees but because many of them, too, wrestle with what it means to be akin to difference, and more specifically with the effects of the racialization of Asian females, the "no" of adoption to normalized kinship, and the political economy of abandonment. While completing this book, I launched a new project that is a collaborative exploration of how Chinese adoptees themselves construct and give meaning to their multiply determined lives. In one recent interview, when I asked a lively ten-year-old if she had thought about what it might be like to return to China and meet her birth family, she jumped off the sofa where she was sitting and began an animated dramatization. Vicki acted out the part of an old, bent-over Chinese man who, upon encountering Vicki as she nonchalantly walked down the street, squinted and slowly wagged his finger at her with the words, "You look very familiar. . . ."[2]

Return to China is one way of trying to restore history to the present, "to double back on experiences that are felt to be not quite finished." Indeed, specialized programs of return—sometimes known as "homeland tours"—for Chinese adoptees and their families have sprung up in adoption and travel agencies on both sides of the Pacific. They are a combination of cultural clientelism, packaged identity experiences, professional care, and the labor for kinship reminiscent of the political economy of adoption I have described in this book. They cannot (yet?) officially offer birth-parent meetings. Lotus Travel describes their "Professor Panda Family Tour" as follows (http://www.lotustours.net, accessed October 2004):

> Hold a panda, discover a dinosaur, sail the Yangtze River—all while exploring China with your family . . . each one of our experienced group leaders has a thorough understanding of China adoption, is an expert in cross-cultural opportunities and learning, loves families, and is always available to lend a helping hand.

Another form of "return," one that is ongoing, is the process of building community at home around the shared experience of difference, as specialist Jane Brown does with workshops on racial, cultural, and adoptive identity held across the country for adopted Chinese children. As I read her practices, Brown strives to facilitate adoptees' collective and autobiographical "grope for a 'self-regard' that does not yet exist" (Chow 2002: 142).

In the meantime, however, attempts by adoption practitioners and adoptive families to restore history to children's adoptive journeys will remain sorely inadequate—they do too little, too much, or simply the same old thing—if the gaze of concern rests solely or even mostly on adoptees. Whether we worry a lot, somewhat, or not at all about how "broken" transnationally, transracially adopted children are, we would serve those children well by turning the gaze on our own relational entanglements in the cultural politics of difference. This can be quite uncomfortable (Jane Brown's workshops separate adoptive parents and children into different groups, sometimes to the great nervousness of the former), especially if it means finding ways to mourn the racial grief that transracial adoption reminds us is imprinted on our lives and on the chain of exclusive practices directly and indirectly implicated in the political economy of adoption. But most important, this shift in gaze is not an introspective meditation of self-discovery that neatly resolves itself in globalized multicultural enlightenment; rather, it is a turning outward to the politics of difference that bind people collectively and historically and hierarchically to each other (Chow 2002; Cheng 2001). It envisions transnational, transracial adoption not just as a linear progression from abandonment to intermediate orphanage care to a "new life" but as embedded in the interplay of institutionalized practices and shifting discourses of identity I have attempted to lay out in the chapters of this book.

Mainstream intercountry adoption policies and practices have not always been very adept at making the radical shift to an open-ended, social vision of identity (Melosh 2002)—the kind that can handle more than one mother, multiple origin points, and the haunting of racial hierarchies. Focused on the individual experience of loss and the healing qualities of cultural pride, the adoption world has not fully faced the normalized expectations of market capitalism, the "freedom from the given" that gives whiteness its power, the blindness toward inequalities embedded in progressive narratives of adoption. The same goes for some segments of adoption literature, which can make assertions such as "from a psychological perspective, racial and cultural identity is less critical to self-esteem for Caucasians than for people of color [Phinney 1991; Phinney & Alipuria 1990]" (Freundlich 2000: 114). Such an ahistorical, asocial rendition of identification processes may only reproduce the normalcy of whiteness and the white gaze, rather than provide an opportunity to particularize and problematize them. It is as if race and culture were not crucial to white people's identities, when the point is that they are so crucial as to be normalized. Equally troubling is the corollary tendency to fend off self-esteem problems through the dutiful provision of a cultural identity. What if this well-intentioned focus on the needs of the individual adoptee was repositioned as an interrogation of the cultural politics that make and produce Chinese children as "free" for adoption, as desirable for adoption, and as migrated exclusively for adoption?

The modern or even postmodern promise of freedom from static signifiers (female, of Chinese ancestry, from a poor rural family, abandoned by birth mother, Asian with white parents) might be quite partial and premature; this promise is inadequate to accounting for the minoritization of difference—"the very emotional effects of injustice that persist as the remnants of lived experience" (Chow 2002: 134–35). Melosh (2002) says of author Sherman Alexie's central character in the novel *Indian Killer*—a Native American adopted by well-meaning white parents— "John's problem may not be adoption after all but rather a deluded fixation on stable identity" (190). Alexie poses adoption as a condensed site for interrogating the emotional, psychic effects of social relations that promise choice yet equally insist on identities that conform to universal white color blindness or to predetermined levels of tolerable difference. In similar terms, transnational, transracial adoptees are often assumed to "adjust" to being in domestic white America along some sliding scale ranging from deraced individualism to emblematic multiculturalism. What's more, this imaginary is enabled by contrasting it to those who are "less assimilable" (e.g., black welfare mothers or Vietnamese refugees). These are the impossible conditions of belonging, compounded by the institutionalized desire for exclusive kinship and the marketized routines of care.

The narrative of this book is an attempt to map what injustices might "persist as the remnants of lived experience" in China/U.S. adoption, not just in the lived experiences of the adopted child but in the lived experiences of the people around her. Recall some of the contradictory moments described in the book: the joy of the FCC Chinese New Year celebration next to the neocolonial twinge of the "baby hotel" in China; the orphanage caregiver snapping that the children are "lucky to be in this orphanage" next to the American parent who declared to a room of abandoned babies that "there are families waiting for you in America." These impossible contradictions of class (market and care), gender (biological and social kinship), and race (fixed and flexible citizenship) are an invitation to approach identity as deferred, ambiguous, and above all informed by inequities. The crucial point is not just that these are adoption's contradictions but that adoption disinters these contradictions in American culture in its transnational, historical context. The desire to know the Other through adoption has a way of indicting and implicating "our positions as private, historical, or literary witnesses of submerged histories," as Cheng says of Theresa Hak-Kyung Cha's *Dictee* (Cheng 2001: 150). In trying to read all the fragments of children's stories, to create some wholeness out of them, all those "touched by adoption" bear witness to submerged histories of uneven circuits of globalized and racialized exchange. While often used as a vague (and sentimentalized) reference to the relatives and friends of people who are adopted, "touched by adoption" might lead us to think what it means more generally to mourn the inequalities of social relations of difference.

There are several important dialectics to this process of mourning. And while I refer to adoption to illustrate these points, I mean to refer to any host of processes that promise the transcendence of difference, but perhaps do so too hastily. First, there must be a spatial and temporal refusal of the "post" of adoption, similar to the friendly critiques scholars have made of the unresolved "posts" of structuralism and colonialism. As McClintock writes of the terms of postcolonialism:

> The postcolonial scene occurs in an entranced suspension of history, as if the definitive historical events have preceded our time and are not now in the making. If the theory [of postcolonialism] promises a decentering of history in hybridity, syncreticism, multidimensional time and so forth, the singularity of the term effects a recentering of global history around the single rubric of European time. (11)

The same things might be said about postadoption when it potentially denies or underwrites the inequities that mark the histories of adoption, which are in turn the histories that constitute the stuff of the adopted child's identity. The problem occurs when the "post," by signaling a march of progress into the child's future, produces a fixed and frozen past (of abandonment, Chineseness) that is only selectively revisited in order simultaneously to name the child's origins *and* to normalize her American, adopted self. It might be fruitful for adoptive parents and practitioners to leave themselves "stuck" in this way between pre- and postadoption; it might allow the rift between liberatory and oppressive approaches to difference stand "as a reminder of the ineluctable, overdetermined complexities at hand" (Cheng 2001: 135). This might very well mean abandoning attempts to capture and contain normalized ways of being and representing.

However, we must also reconsider what adoptive parents and adoption agencies and officials might *do*, when the responsibility for the "best interest of the child," for dealing with difference, lies in the first order with them. This is why I so often get asked by adoptive parents what I think, after all this research, is the "best" approach to raising transnationally, transracially adopted children. And here is where I point to the second dialectic of mourning, which is that the histories of adoption also constitute the identities of those "touched" by it, *even before* the adoption happens. It understands that that which constitutes "difference" is historically rendered by what is taken to be normal (whiteness, heterosexuality, liberalized choice), and that, just as important, what is taken to be normal is historically rendered by the differences it names (or refuses to name or rushes to embrace). The seemingly impossible question is how to engage the inequities of difference from a position of privilege, a position that cannot be easily evacuated.

But finally, then, the impossible is not an impasse. A third dialectic of mourning takes—but cautiously—the contradictions of race, class, gender, and nation as a place to reimagine an intimate geography of difference. The movement of adopted children across local and national spaces allows us to understand the political economy of a migration process that is at once caring and consumptive, personal and globe-spanning. We see the intersecting categories of difference that animate the social relations of adoption exchange—not just the child's or her parents' physical migration to meet each other, or the pre- and postadoption construction of her value and identity, but also her birth and abandonment and her imagined future. The symbolic and material linking of these locations through the history of the child *is* the particular political economy of China/U.S. adoption. And it is haunted by raced, gendered, and classed exclusion and denial. But as Derrida (1994) reminds us, these disjunctures represent both injustice and the very possibility of relationship to the Other, that is, justice (22–23). This is where Eng (2003) tentatively asserts the poststructural possibilities of adoptive kinship; the transnational, transracial adoptive family might reproduce white heterosexual middle-class subjectivities, but it does not by any means always do so, or do so in the same way.

It is important here that the focus of transformative possibility is not on what the child represents but on what *relationship with her* represents—especially as a relationship to histories and people otherwise marginalized or made peripheral. Transnational, transracial adoption provides an "internal ethnology of our culture" (Sheridan 1980, quoted in Gordon 1997: 195) because it brings into proximity the reputedly external (marginalized Chinese children) and what is allegedly internal (white middle-class American citizens). This ethnology brings to light the structured hierarchies of gender under which a child is abandoned in China and which in concert with race shape her particular desirability or foreignness in the United States; the material inequalities and privileges of whiteness and heternormativity through which she is culturally transformed for the process of adoption into the United States; and how all these intersecting relations of race, class, and gender shape her possible imagined future. Taken together, the plethora of possible identifications assigned to an adopted Chinese child both reveal and destabilize that which historically overdetermines the social relations around her.

Perhaps, then, we can imagine narrations of self and other that are not so much declarative, as Chow (2002) suggests, but that double back on past events whose effects are still with us—what Cruz (1996) calls the "social hieroglyphics" of identity formation and Gordon (1997) tells us are the unsettled ghosts of historical silences and exclusions. Korean adoptee Ellwyn Kauffman (1997) insists on a doubling back that is tangible in the present when he writes,

> I never want to hear that my past should be left alone
> That what I'm searching for are ghosts.
> Would I be here if my past wasn't real? (159)

Kaufmann points to the historical relations that bring adopted children and adoptive parents together, "enchaining" (Yngvesson 2003) them in a whole set of relations to what Derrida calls "others not present."

But more than that, haunting pushes for something to be done. Writing the child's history, and thus the histories in which she is embedded, is also a process of imagining something else, of "protecting your child from what is waiting for her" (Gordon 1997: 205). Thus, doubling back to an adoptee's past necessarily looks to her future, lest the search for authentic origins becomes a diversion from a politics of possibility. The "history of the present" is about whiteness as much as Asianness, normalized motherhood and heterosexuality as much as abandonment and adoption, the claiming power of care as much as the threat of commodification—and so it is as much about the future of these relationships as it is about their past. Haunting potentially pushes not just adoptive parents, adopted persons, and adoption practitioners but others of us to ask these questions of the racial and sexual and national spaces we occupy.

Something to Be Done

The Power of Fate

Many transnational and transracial forms of migration into the United States carry the burden of representing the transcendence of difference and the flowering of multicultural diversity. But while some migrants, such as temporary or illegal laborers, come to represent the constitutive outside of "good" diversity, other migrants, such as adoptees, are more often hyperemblematic of it. This is enhanced by contemporary adoption myths that play up a special elective affinity ("The right child is out there for you" or "We got the right child") between the members of the adoption triad—birth parents, adoptive parents, and adopted child (Cohen 1994). Such myths of fate present a problem: in whitewashing the uneven terrain of race and class and gender through which choices are made regarding children, they might put an undue and unjust burden on children (and parents) to represent this ideal of belonging (many times parents joked that my interview visit to their home nervously recalled the time when they had had to present their family as "Beaver Cleaver happy" to visiting social workers) and preemptively foreclose the difference and disjuncture through which adoption occurs. The joy most adoptive families experience and the need for children to feel secure are unquestionable; but we need somehow to be able to imagine a narrative of fate that does not erase but rather carries with it the uneven histories of affinity.

H. David Kirk, an early scholar of the psychology of adoption, writes in these terms in his 1964 work *Shared Fate*. Posing an alternative to a language of magic and fate that tries to erase difference and balance out losses (what he calls "rejection-of-difference"), Kirk calls for a "shared fate" based on the recognition that both adoptive parent and adopted child are out of sync with the world (what he calls "acknowledgment-of-difference"). Kirk is referring specifically to the infertility that haunts parent-child relationships (it has a "nagging quality," he says), but his principle is just as easily expanded and applied to other forms of (potentially subversive) difference that mark the adoptive relationship, such as miscegenated class privilege, nonexclusive motherhood, and transnational kinship. In other words, we must look beyond the bounded dyad of parent and child.

The "nagging" of difference-as-inequality pushes for something to be done not only within the family in response to the child's needs but also in response to the others her life recalls. Remember that Linda Leister's acknowledgment that "we're not a normal family" came after adopting a second child from Romania, whose birth mother they had met. And the Petermans, who had asked their daughter's foster mother not to come back to visit them in their hotel in China, told me a year later that they were writing regularly to the foster mother, and it seemed to have "resolved something for us." These simple examples are about acknowledging the multiple narratives in the individual child's and family's disjointed history, and not least of all adoption itself as a form of reproduction outside the norm. The Petermans' sense of resolution came after a painstaking journey; Gretta had said a bit defensively to me in China that, sure, the birth mother lost something, but so did they by not being able to have their own children. Women were more haunted by infertility than men, a gendered form of social haunting that Kirk does not fully address. And this is important because this gendering might further privatize grief, rather than disinterring the politics of reproduction that stratify adoptive and birth mothers and that construct abandonment as an unfortunate and inevitable fate resolved in adoption. I am suggesting instead a politicized fate that is at home with ambiguity.

The Power of Narrative

The power of narrative to mobilize (Hart 1992) is profoundly felt in the adoption process, where biographical pieces are missing but there is almost an excess of histories to tell. Narratives told on behalf of the child start to do justice to forgotten people and places and practices by making them real and present; they look to the future by "doubling back" on the past; they extend acknowledgment-of-difference from the fate of dyadic kinship to that of collective social histories. Lisa Walker indicated a conscious effort to remember otherwise forgotten people along what she called her daughter's "underground railroad":

I imagine that the way this whole thing evolved, that there were many people involved in getting Pan Pan from her birth mother . . . to her foster mother. So she's been on a kind of an underground railroad, with people who've all along the way cared tremendously about her, have made sure that she hasn't had any lapses in any care or any love. I mean, she's been loved and challenged and taught and everything, every step of the way.

There are ways of narrating a child's identity, and narrating identity *to* her, that do not reinscribe or erase difference but rather create a vision grounded in complicated gendered and racial histories. We have seen how some American adoptive parents see the narration of those histories as tools of empowerment, inviting the many possibilities by which the child might tell the story "back to herself," as Jennifer Bartz put it. Or as David Spencer said, "I think we're giving her more tools for both her adoptive self—trying to enable her to form her thoughts and to articulate them—and also her cultural and racial identity." This might mean remembering that there are people in both China and the United States who form the constitutive outside to dominant narratives, whose stories are part of normative adoption through their exclusions from it. The Boscos pointed out that their daughter needed to be able to identify with racially Asian people so that she "will have more to say about her story" and a few minutes later added that they had to be concerned with children still in orphanages, or people with any kind of difference, "all who have stories."

Maintaining ties with China was one way to make the child's story real and present, whether through letters and photos exchanged with orphanage caregivers and foster families or through return trips to China. Increasingly, adoptive families have begun formal programs to collect information about relevant organizations in China, for example, a program whereby parents can order a signed photo from their child's orphanage. Some parents insisted on one or several actual trips to China as the ultimate tool to give their children a sense of China "as a real place," as David and Joan Spencer put it, or "to go and see and feel," as Jennifer Bartz put it. It is also worth noting that return trips to China had the effect of making adopted children real to those in China who "lost" them, such as orphanage caregivers, foster parents, and children in orphanages. At a couple orphanages where I accompanied adopted girls on return visits, caregivers would say, "*Ta shi womende*" (She's one of ours). On one of these visits, a caregiver stroked the head of an eight-year-old adoptee whose hair had blonde highlights. She giggled as she picked up a blonde strand and said that was the girl's "American" part; she then did the same with a black strand and said that was the girl's "Chinese" part. In this moment, she moved toward suspending the dichotomized choice of assimilation or differentiation.

The Power of Difference

But the extent to which stories can dismantle or problematize race, class, and gender privilege remains an open question. A return trip to China, for example, not only depends on the material means to do so but also in some cases reproduces a safe distance from difference. My field notes recorded observations of June, a single white mother, who had brought her seven-year-old Chinese daughter along on her second trip to China to adopt a child:

> Over breakfast at the hotel, June tells me she just doesn't see how her daughter Tara's Chineseness is such a big deal, even as she tells me that Tara doesn't want to leave the hotel. On the tour bus that day, Tara is looking out the window, but then kind of leans and burrows into her mother. June says to her, "What's going on? Is it just really different? Yeah, I know, it's different."

It is not easy for children or parents to return to China because multiple social relations of difference are narrated back to them all over again, in new ways. But it was precisely for that reason that some parents recognized the importance of how China "othered" them. Some parents who made the return trip to China noted that being in China reminded them and their children not of how different Chinese people were from some unspoken norm but of their differential privilege as white Americans. The Spencers' daughter delighted in pointing out to her parents that they were foreigners in China, while she was the one who could blend in.

This triangulated relationship between child-and-parent-in-China had the potential to relativize or reinforce difference but also to bind and separate people in new ways. When the Spencers' daughter was asked by some Chinese schoolchildren why her parents were *waiguoren* (foreigners), she told her mother she didn't know what to say. She had quite readily explained to the school kids that she was adopted, but how do you explain why your parents are foreigners? The impossibility of answering this question is and should be an invitation to adoptive parents and the adoption industry and Chinese and American state officials to tell the story back to themselves in new ways; struggling to help children make sense of being akin to difference opens up the question of what it is about our own social locations and practices that makes it a struggle to begin with.

I have focused on race as a central force in relationships between the us and them, pre and post, here and there of adoption narratives. Race difference signals *discontinuities* with places and families: China, birth parents, grandparents, siblings, orphans and orphanages "left behind." At the same time, it signals an often unanticipated *continuity* with racial formations at home: multiple kinds of racisms, immigration histories, the normalized power of whiteness. And so struggling with race is a key to other kinds of differentiation and forgetting.

For some adoptive parents, concern for the racism their children did or might encounter inspired new forms of activism that might help create a different history for their children's future. Internet Listserv postings by white adoptive parents of Chinese children in both San Francisco and the Twin Cities included the following in the late 1990s and early 2000s: reminders on Martin Luther King Day of the historical indignities suffered by Asian Americans; protests over racist and sexist Abercrombie T-shirts with depictions of subservient Asian women and phrases such as "Two Wongs Can Make It White"; a call for solidarity with Chinese immigrants adversely affected by INS changes in visa regulations; and concern over anti-Asian activities following the April 2001 crash of an American spy plane on Hainan Island in China. Parents who posted on the Listserv usually made connections between their daughters' racial and cultural identities and their responsibilities to respond to injustice. One parent posted a *New York Times* piece about the prosecution of Wen Ho Lee, prefacing it with the words: "For those of you who have been

concerned, as I have been, that the prosecution of Wen Ho Lee was heavily influenced by racial assumptions that will haunt our children in years
to come . . ." (September 15, 2000).

Visions of a different future grow out of the same historically embedded intersections of race, class, gender, and nation that reproduce
inequalities. They take into account narratives of disparate times and
places and stake a struggle (without guarantees) on that shifting ground.
As the political economy of China/U.S. adoption demonstrates to all
transnational migration processes, local-global circulations are haunted
by the intimate relations of difference through which bodies are desired
and excluded. The adoptee's history of dislocation potentially catalyzes
a radical perspective on links between women's reproductive labor and
the privilege of whiteness, between the racialization of Asian females
and the reproduction of class hierarchy, and between citizenship and
heteronormative kinship. In doing so, it rearranges the relationships of
those around her.

The Power of Money

I have argued that identities of adopted Chinese children are haunted by
material and sometimes commodified relations of exchange: the funnel-
ing of adoption fees into particular kinds of children, utterances of
"lucky girl" from Chinese observers, the shops on Shamian selling little
silk dresses, the selection of private schools. This haunting persists in
postadoption transnational activities, as businesses in China scurry to set
up culture camps and "heritage tours" for international adoptive families, and reminders of American wealth make their way back across the
Pacific to China. I remember sitting with Ms. Guo, the head caregiver at
Dayang orphanage, looking at photo albums sent by American parents of
children she had previously cared for. The front pages of some of the albums featured photos of large homes and nicely appointed living rooms
and bedrooms (one of them showed a blonde doll holding a Chinese flag)
before finally showing photos of the child and family. Ms. Guo remarked
that it was good to see that the children were living in such nice conditions, as that helped ease her anxiety (*fangxin*) about them. Whether
those "nice conditions" were about material or psychological security or

both is not clear, but maybe that's the point. Material things convey and create symbolic meaning, just as symbolic processes have weighty material effects.

Money has the power to reinscribe intersecting inequalities but also the power to respond to the haunting of those inequalities. Ms. Guo's orphanage had received much-needed money for school fees, heaters, and washing machines from an organization started by American adoptive parents—parents who told me they were politically committed to demonstrating that it wasn't just about "grabbing kids for adoption." There are many stories of adoptive families and friends of adoptive families who have donated goods and resources to orphanages that badly need them, learning as they go that it is best to ask what orphanages need. This is international charity work that imagines a different future for the orphan children of the child's past and is perhaps akin to the remittances sent home by immigrants through transnational kinship networks. But even as something just can be done in moments "where the sedimented meanings of the socio-economic are contested" (Critchley 1994, quoted in Laclau 1995: 88–89), so are the impossible contradictions of material justice revealed.

Responding financially to the ghosts of a child's history of dislocation can be strewn with difficulties, as comes through with nagging clarity in the following words from Christy Kinsler. She and her partner had adopted a son from Vietnam, whose birth family they had met and whom they were financially supporting:

> Okay [sighs]. We want one single child to be part of our lives and presumably, to do the best we can by that single child. Well, who's to say that our eleven thousand dollars is doing the best for him, bringing him here? And still, I get a catch in my throat thinking about it. Because eleven thousand dollars given to the birth mother . . . ? [I.e., it would have gone a long way for her and her family in Vietnam.] And that's why we have no choice but to be as helpful as we can with his siblings, to send them to school. I want to support them so those children can stay in the family. And if we can help that family, then it's sort of, not that it undoes the loss of this child, the son, but . . .
>
> The agency said, "You better be careful, because they might start saying, 'We want a hundred dollars for a cow.'" And we said, if they

did, we would send them a hundred dollars for a cow. I mean, this is nothing for us. And even if it doesn't buy a cow, who are we to [question it]. What I feel we're doing is hopefully making a difference in her life, but also having the paper trail so our son can find them. If they want money from us, that means we have their address. [Christy laughs lightly.]

As Christy's story suggests, it is impossible to separate the immediate and tangible needs of the adopted child and adoptive relationship from the response to the ghosts of inequality that his presence evokes. Some of the many charitable organizations formed by adoptive families—for example, the Foundation for Chinese Orphanages—make an explicit structural connection between adoptive families and children not adopted. The Orphan Relief Fund, an organization funded and managed jointly by Chinese and Americans, strives to make a difference "to those orphans in China who are 'unseen'" by establishing medical programs, family-like orphanages, and education projects geared specifically for them.[3]

Reframing the Cultural Politics of Adoption

A number of years ago, whenever the local newspaper covered an inter-country adoption story that referred to the agency at which I worked, we would receive a letter from an area resident castigating the agency for its part in adoption. Interestingly, he was upset not only about the "immorality" of interracial kinship but also about the commodification of children; adoption should be free, he would write. His letters spelled the complexity of the politics of adoption, including the question of being "for" or "against" transnational and transracial adoption. He is not alone, of course, in his critique of intercountry adoption. Some adult adoptees have organized against the practice as a whole (e.g., the groups Transracial Abductees and Bastard Nation); some adoptive parents have organized against the power of adoption agencies; and some citizen groups in sending countries have organized against the exploitation of their families and children. In China there have been at least a few reported demonstrations against international adoption; in India there have been some heated struggles between local and foreign adoption interests. And some countries have closed their doors to adoption amid charges of corruption and child exploitation. A couple of state officials in China told me they had consulted with Korean officials in hopes of avoiding the charges of "baby exporting" that contributed to the slowdown in intercountry adoptions of Korean children in the late 1980s.

There is, of course, a politics to being "for" adoption as well. Freundlich (2000) reminds us that those who oppose intercountry adoption usually do so on the grounds of colonialism, cultural genocide, exploitation of women and poor people, and loss of racial and cultural identity. Advocates, by contrast, argue that it meets the needs of children otherwise doomed to institutionalization, bad living conditions, or death. And then there is a compromise position that argues that staying in birth families and birth countries is ideal but that adoption is an "if not in their own country" alternative that works best if cultural and national origins are "honored." Parents and adoption organizations are situated in the midst of all three positions, sometimes caught among the contradictions of their racialized politics. Alice, a single white parent of a Chinese child, told me that one of her relatives had made a reference to "Chinks," while another friend had said, "This is why there shouldn't be any interracial adoption," after Alice shared her daughter's struggles with the loss of birth family.

The problem is partly in the framing. We need to move from asking whether we are "for or against" transnational or transracial adoption to asking what adoption, *as practiced,* is for and against. And this entails understanding how adoption is practiced *in situ.* I was most recently asked about my own stance for or against intercountry adoption at an agency in Seoul, South Korea, that offers classes and support groups to domestic adoptive families—still a rarity in 2004, in a nation where adoption is sometimes disguised as pregnancy and birth, and the social current of bloodlines runs strong. Standing by was a group of adult intercountry Korean adoptees preparing to speak from their own experience to a group of prospective Korean adoptive parents about the problems of international adoption; both they and the agency embraced a certain national and cultural Korean pride that found the contradictions of the global and racialized political economy of intercountry adoption too impossible.

The social hieroglyphics of identity in this location must be considered alongside the situations of already adopted children and their parents, who might try to find ways in their own locations to interrogate the impossible contradictions of belonging. The question is how they might take into account the politics of being for or against adoption, refusing this framing in favor of tackling the conditions of market power, gender inequity, and race privilege under which citizenship and kinship are reproduced. As legal theorist Twila Perry (2004) concludes, "a feminist analysis should support adoption as an institution, but at the same time should be willing to question the justice of a world which often results in the transfer of children of the least advantaged women to the most advantaged" (269). Beyond what adoptive families might do, of course, is the larger question of adoption as an institutionalized set of practices that differentiates among the children and parents it brings together; in the professional practices of adoption agencies and state officials, race, gender, and material privilege mediate kinship at the juncture of domestic and transnational exchanges.

Underlying much of the debate around transnational adoption is the "best interest of children," which we must understand as a political question. For/against approaches often conceptualize "best interests" as measured by the individual self-esteem and adjustment of the child *or* as crushed by hardened global relations of power. The first position neatly sequesters history in the "honoring" of a child's culture (an apoliticized "right to a cultural identity"); the other vilifies adoption with reified historical asymmetries. Both of these too quickly foreclose the more radical transformative possibilities of being akin to difference—the kind of "poststructural kinship" toward which Eng (2003) gestures. Restoring history to the child's story is a process of restoring history to those with whom she has a relationship: caregivers and birth families, other immigrants, hidden gay lovers, children not adopted, and, *just as important,* adoptive parents and adoption professionals. The history of the child and the nation and the family from which she came must be understood as inextricably linked to her adoptive family and nation, *through* forces of market, race, and gender that marginalize and exclude. Under such a framework on the "best interests of children," we can accept that adopted children are not necessarily in crisis, even as we question whether we are doing right by them. This is a tricky pragmatics of being "for" transnational and transracial adoption and "against" the inequities it might practice and conjure. Narratives and practices of identity matter precisely because they both reveal and respond to those social arrangements that dislocate and link actors and institutions across multiple borders.

In transnational, transracial adoption, the proximities of migrant and nonmigrant, Chinese and American, nonwhite and white, poor and wealthy, child and adult, demonstrate that identities are cultural enactments of material and symbolic values and meanings. The question of whether and how China/U.S. adoption accomplishes a "poststructural" global kinship beyond borders of difference does and should remain a question—a question of how social relationships entail an intimate geography against the odds, yet do so through the particular conditions of institutionalized, hierarchical logics. The impossibility of responding to questions of justice within the nuclear family alone suggests a communal responsibility to transracially adopted children that engages in struggle with the restrictions on their imagined belonging, which are also the architectures of race, family, and nation that more broadly haunt the cultural politics of identity in the contemporary United States.

NOTES

NOTES TO THE INTRODUCTION

1. The number of children adopted annually into the United States from Russia and China was about the same in the late 1990s—over four thousand from each—although in FY 2000, China "edged out" Russia at just over five thousand, and by 2004 that number was closer to six thousand.

2. Technically children are "abandoned," but I use this term cautiously because it suggests that children are randomly discarded when, in fact, many of the children are found in public places, including near police stations or orphanage gates. While some children are quite literally left in back alleys or fields, the distinction between abandonment and "leaving a child where he or she will be found" (a phrase preferred by many adoption professionals) is important in a political system that leaves no legal way to place a child for adoption. When I do use the term *abandonment* in the context of China/U.S. adoption, I mean children who have been left and found by others. I persist in using it not only because it is the official term but because it leaves its traces on adopted people and adoptive parents as the feeling of abandonment.

3. This is the first of several slides I use, with her permission, from Janice Williamson's visual essay titled "becoming mah/becoming mommy," found at http://www.arts.ualberta.ca/~jwilliam/baowebsite/story.htm.

4. The U.S. Census Bureau reports that in 2000, 11 percent of adopted boys and 14 percent of adopted girls under age eighteen were foreign-born. ("Adopted Children and Stepchildren: 2000," available online at http://www.census.gov/prod/2003pubs/censr-6.pdf, p. 9). Adoption statistics from the U.S. State Department (number of immigrant visas issued to orphans coming to the United States) are found at http://travel.state.gov/family/adoption/stats/stats_451.html.

5. The actual number of children in China's social welfare institutes is difficult to gauge, and estimates vary widely. Reports in the early 2000s suggested at least 1 million children. The Ministry of Civil Affairs in China, responsible for the social welfare of abandoned children, states that in 1999 there were 1,677 state-run welfare facilities in urban China (Shi 2000: 138). While this number includes institutions other than those that care for orphans, it probably does not include a good number of small, local foundling homes scattered across China, and a growing but still small number of private facilities.

6. These ideas are explicated by Burawoy (2000 and 2001).

7. While the CCAA originally processed only international adoptions, as of September 2005 it also processes domestic adoptions

8. I myself am not a member of the "adoption triad"; I am not birth parent, adoptive parent, or adoptee. But in contradictory ways, my life narrative resonates with the identification processes of transnational, transracial adoptees. I grew up a white missionary kid in South Korea, moving back to the United States at the age of eighteen.

9. The names of people and places I use in the book have been changed to protect anonymity, except where noted. It was very difficult and thus pointless to give aliases to the cities of San Francisco, Minneapolis, and St. Paul, so I have tried instead to take every precaution to disguise people in those cities with whom I interacted.

10. A couple of important changes took place toward the end of the late 1990s that altered the profile of adoptive families. First, China lifted regulations that restricted the adoption of healthy children by childless parents; this meant that a number of families returned to China for second or third adoptions. Second, the waiting time lengthened as the number of international adoption applicants grew, so that children were usually at least ten months of age when placed; in the early years of the program, children as young as four or five months of age were being placed. Third, new restrictions on placements with single and lesbian or gay parents were put into place. But still, in 2003, children adopted from China were 95 percent female, 49 percent under one year of age, and 48 percent from one to four years of age (from *Adoptive Families* magazine, found at http://www.adoptivefamilies.com/china_adoption.php, accessed April 2005).

11. Viviana Zelizer's (1985) book *Pricing the Priceless Child: The Changing Social Value of Children* impressively demonstrates the historical development of a market for adopted children in the United States that was increasingly sentimentalized. Zelizer recognizes the fluidity of multiple forms of value.

12. I am greatly indebted to an anonymous reviewer of the book manuscript for suggesting the framework of "impossible contradictions."

13. From http://www.house.gov/international_relations/cox0522.htm, accessed May 2002.

14. First announced in 1978, the family-planning policy became nationally codified in the Population and Family Planning Law in September 2002. My understanding of changes in abandonment and adoption in the late 1980s and early 1990s is drawn in large part from reading works by and communicating with Dr. Kay Ann Johnson, the leading expert in the United States on abandonment and adoption in China, who has collaborated with Professors Wang Liyao and Huang Banghan in Anhui province.

15. China's "one-child" policy is actually a "one son, two children" policy in most rural areas, meaning that if the first child is a girl, parents may have a second child. For that reason, it is assumed that many of the girls who are left and found are second daughters. (There are also exceptions to the policy for ethnic minority groups, who may sometimes have more than one or two children.)

16. An acquaintance in central China told me an illustrative story of what he called "guerrilla birth." During a family-planning crackdown in the 1980s, his cousin's wife became pregnant when they already had a girl. She went to another city to have the child and then sent a telegram that said, simply, "*Tianli* ["field labor" = boy] *yi anquan daoda*" (The boy has already safely arrived). This was meant as a secret message that she had indeed given birth to a boy. But eventually they were discovered, and as a result her husband was demoted from school principal to teacher. The cousin said he preferred a boy to being a principal. "This is a typical story," my friend concluded.

17. For some of the pivotal work on race and racism in China and the embeddedness of these concepts in notions of nation, family, and blood, see Dikötter 2002.

18. Names of individuals, places, and organizations have been changed, except for government or singular organizations (such as the Immigration and Naturalization Service, the China Center of Adoption Affairs, and the support organization Families with Children from China).

19. See, for example, L. Grow and D. Shapiro (1974) *Black Children, White Parents: A Study of Transracial Adoption,* New York: Child Welfare League of America; L. Lydens (1988) *A Longitudinal Study of Crosscultural Adoption: Identity Development among Asian Adoptees at Adolescence and Early Adulthood,* Ph.D. diss., Northwestern University; R. Simon and H. Altstein (1992) *Adoption, Race, and Identity: From Infancy Through Adolescence,* Westport, CT: Praeger. See Freundlich (2000) for a review of much of this literature.

NOTES TO CHAPTER 1

1. I see this definition of identification as an updated version of C. Wright Mills's (1950) proverbial call to "understand what is happening in selves as minute points in the intersections of biography and history" (7). Nancy Riley (1997) also invokes Mills in her study of the sociopolitical matrices in which individual abandonment and adoption decisions are made in both China and the United States.

2. Portions of this chapter appear also in Sara Dorow, "Racialized Choices: Chinese Adoption and the 'White Noise' of Blackness," in a 2006 issue of *Critical Sociology* (in press).

3. The implications of the differences between the two metropolitan areas are discussed further in chapter 7, as are comparisons of the experiences and practices of Asian American and white adoptive parents. Statistics on the ethnic makeup of cities come from factfinder.census.gov, accessed February 2005.

4. While the kind of research necessary to get an accurate count of the racial and ethnic identities of adoptive parents is beyond the scope of this project, my description of San Francisco is based on informal fact-finding among adoptive parent support groups and my own interactions with a variety of adoptive parents and adoption agencies. It should also be noted that the proportion of Asian American adoptive parents varies quite significantly in different parts of the Bay Area.

5. Paper sons and daughters were Chinese individuals who, after the 1906 fire in San Francisco that destroyed most immigration and citizenship paperwork, immigrated to the United States under manufactured paperwork that claimed they were the children of American citizens of Chinese descent who had returned to China.

6. Dr. Wen Ho Lee was a physicist from Los Alamos National Laboratories, accused by the government in 1999 of violating the Atomic Energy Act. He allegedly mishandled material containing restricted nuclear weapons data, with the intent of unlawfully providing it to China. He was released in 2000 under a plea bargain. The handling of the story in the media and by the government invited accusations of racial profiling and anti-Asian sentiment.

7. In her popular book *The Lost Daughters of China: Abandoned Girls, Their Journey to America, and the Search for a Missing Past,* Karin Evans (2000) remarks on this as well: "In the San Francisco Bay Area or other places with substantial Chinese populations, it's relatively easy to offer children exposure to the Chinese community and the culture into which they were born, even if they have no recollections of it and their parents have to learn from scratch. But introducing children to the dragon dance or Mandarin in a small town in the South or deep in the heart of Amish country, say, may be somewhat challenging" (181).

8. Weak multiculturalism, sometimes associated with the work of Charles Taylor, maintains that differences among people are superceded by certain central values such as tolerance and respect for individual rights. As Steven Yates (1992) puts it, weak multiculturalism asserts that "peoples are different in some respects but alike in others, and can therefore learn by communicating openly with one another" (440); it rejects what it sees as "the naïve view that all cultures are epistemological and moral equals" (451). ("Multiculturalism and Epistemology," *Public Affairs Quarterly* 6: 435–56.)

9. Despite Chinese adoptions being officially closed to gay and lesbian par-

ents, a kind of "don't ask, don't tell" policy characterized much of China/U.S. adoption practice until the CCAA formally instituted guidelines curtailing child placements with gay and lesbian parents in 2000 and 2001.

10. See Linda Gordon's (1999) *The Great Arizona Orphan Abduction* for a fascinating history of a 1905 case in which the courts upheld the "rescue" of white Catholic children from New York originally placed with Mexican families in a town in Arizona. And see Melosh (2002), especially the chapter "Families by Design," on changing and diverse "matching" criteria in the middle decades of the twentieth century.

11. Two things are noteworthy here. First, the largest number of Korean adoptees is found in California and Minnesota, the two states in which I conducted my U.S. fieldwork. Second, parents adopting from China have looked to this large, older cohort of Korean adoptees—online, at adoption seminars, in writings and films—for both affirmation of their own white-Asian adoptive families and advice on how to handle issues of racial and cultural difference.

12. Berebitsky (2000) argues that demand has always exceeded supply. By the 1970s and 1980s, panic over a shortage of infants reflected new kinds of demands from infertile couples and a new focus on meeting their needs. An increased demand for (healthy white) infants also came from newly empowered groups of adopters, namely, gays and lesbians and single straight people. Solinger (2001) has argued that this expansion of the choice to parent must be linked to the choices that contributed to a decreased "supply" of babies: abortion and single parenthood.

13. Only 5 to 10 percent of domestic adoptions in the United States are transracial (Freundlich 2000), but as is the case with China/U.S. adoptions, the cultural impact of the accompanying narratives and imagery are more powerful than the numbers might suggest.

14. Statistics on numbers of international adoption visas issued are from the U.S. State Department: http://travel.state.gov/orphan_numbers.html,

15. This includes a scale of adoptions in the United States ranging from "less adoptable" children that are available not only without fees but also possibly subsidized, to very costly private adoptions of healthy white infants. International adoptions do not vary quite as much but can vary from several thousand dollars to over thirty thousand.

16. See Patton (2000) and Ortiz and Briggs (2003) for more detailed commentary on the Adoption Promotion Act and Personal Responsibility Act of 1996.

17. Rescue serves to resolve distinctions not only between domestic and international adoption but also between adoption and other forms of migration from China. Anagnost (2000) offers a compelling argument regarding rescue

discourse as a way privately to manage the political effects of adoption as an exceptional form of migration; to recognize its distinction among migrating bodies is to bring again to the surface the problem of privilege.

18. While most children in orphanages are girls, there are also a large number of special-needs children of both sexes and some healthy boys. It must be noted that the unbalanced sex ratio cannot be straightforwardly attributed to families not wanting girls. As Greenhalgh and Li (1995) argue, the ideal family in China is "one of each," but under family-planning policies and social expectations of care and labor, girls are more likely to be abandoned than boys.

19. The dismantling of China's state-run work system means a growing demand for social welfare provisions, even as the state tries to put the burden of care back on families. Public institutions of all kinds have been encouraged to start profit-making enterprises or to seek other funding sources.

20. A 1991 report from the U.S. Senate Committee on Intercountry Adoption cited a survey in which parents said they were seeking adoption abroad because they did not meet requirements for domestic adoption (Modell 2002: 193).

21. The importance of a clean break to the attractiveness of adoption reveals the social importance placed on singularity of origin—of the difficulty of belonging to two places and families and mothers at once. See Eng (2003) for a smart discussion of the political and social reasons for a lack of psychic space that can accommodate two mothers.

22. From the Great Wall China Adoption agency (http://www.gwcadopt.org/facts.html), accessed in August 2000. While abandonment is indeed a crime in China, it is difficult to say how often or to what degree the laws against it are enforced.

23. "Hard-to-place" children in the United States, for example, can often be placed for free or with subsidies, while private adoptions of white infants and international adoptions are often U.S. $20,000 or more. It is important to note that from the perspective of adoption professionals, this is understood as a necessary strategy: minimizing costs is a way to attract families for children who might otherwise have little chance of finding homes, perhaps even subsidized by the higher fees paid for "more adoptable" children.

24. Jane Hunter (1984) has documented, for example, that American missionary women to China in this period adopted or fostered local children, even as racial proscriptions from missionary boards warned of such closeness going against "disinterested benevolence." At the same time, Presbyterian organizations in San Francisco established a shelter to "save" orphaned Chinese babies from a Chinatown characterized as unhealthy and uncivilized (even as local protests to the presence of so many Oriental children prompted regulations that would keep them contained) (Shah 2001).

25. For a more detailed explanation of and response to *The Dying Rooms* and the Human Rights Watch report, see Johnson (2004).

26. This was a predictable response, given that the BBC filmmakers, who won a Peabody Award, had apparently received access to Chinese orphanages by posing as social workers and had gathered footage with hidden cameras. In ensuing years, Beijing has opened an increasing number of orphanages to foreigners, starting with "showcase" institutions that have updated facilities, grounds, and equipment. For the most extensive example of Beijing's official (and propagandistic) rebuttal, see The Situation of Children in China (*Zhongguo de Ertong Zhuangkuang*) (April 1996), Beijing: Information Office of the State Council of the People's Republic of China.

27. I am indebted to Dan Kelliher, professor of political science at the University of Minnesota, for his careful, insightful study of the construction of childhood innocence in these events ("The Politics of Childhood Innocence," unpublished manuscript, 2000).

NOTES TO CHAPTER 2

1. U.S. adoption agency workers and parents sometimes speak with both nostalgia and relief (that it's over) of this time when "pioneer" families traveled to China to adopt before clear regulations and procedures emerged in about 1994. There are legendary stories of American parents with Chinese friends who knew someone in China who could find them a child; of a handful of such parents who helped others through the process, sometimes putting together homemade handbooks explaining how others could find their way through murky local adoption processes; and of agency administrators who happened to be in China when the 1991 adoption law was put in place and thus got in on the ground floor of what has now become the largest transnational adoption migration program on the globe. These early families visited orphanages or foster homes in the big cities or small villages where their potential children resided, sometimes getting "stuck" in China for weeks as they dealt with the whims and uncertainties of local bureaucracies. There are even scattered stories of U.S. consular officers in Guangzhou turning a blind eye to irregularities in paperwork in these "frontier-building" times.

2. Some facilitators use their original Chinese names, while others use English given names.

3. The 1993 Hague Convention on Protection of Children and Co-operation in Respect of Intercountry Adoption is a multilateral treaty that creates norms and procedures for the practices in intercountry adoption that are meant to protect the rights of children.

4. For a more thorough discussion of the relationship between family-planning policies and domestic adoption in China, see Johnson (2004).

5. The most difficult part of my research in China was gaining access to officials who oversee adoption at both the provincial and national levels. My conversations with them were usually happenstance, informal, and in one case clandestine.

6. I am indebted to Kay Johnson, Huang Banghan, and Wang Liyao for the important work they have done in tracking the range of practices of domestic adoption in China. I should add that in my own experience at Wangjing and other orphanages, local families sometimes come in to select a child. One staff member told me with a wink that it was too bad I had not been there the day before, when a couple came in and used traditional divining methods to choose the child who was meant for them (it is not just American parents that speak of destiny). Officially, such handpicking is not allowed, since there is a fear that people will "abandon" a child and then pick the same child to "adopt," therefore getting around family-planning policies. As Professor Jiang Zhenghua, vice chairman of the Standing Committee of the National People's Congress, said to me (discussion at University of Minnesota on April 4, 2002), "[P]arents should not get benefit for having more children."

7. Amid these regulations, socioeconomic constraints, and notions of kinship in China, it is not surprising that regulations I saw posted in large lettering in the lobby of one orphanage gave local Chinese families several months to change their minds about a child—perhaps a necessity if adoption is to be encouraged. The farmer I met in Beigang told me he and his family would make their final decision after getting a full medical clearance on the little boy in his arms.

8. As of March 29, 2002, new regulations require that foreign adoption organizations and families must have special qualifications and plans for managing the care of special-needs children. These regulations may indeed improve the quality of care for adopted special-needs children; to what extent they help promote the placement of these children remains to be seen. It should be noted that with the help of donations from adoption agencies in receiving countries, the Ministry of Civil Affairs has launched the "Tomorrow Plan," intended to provide needed surgeries to orphans with physical disabilities.

9. See Guo (2004) for further discussion of cultural nationalism in contemporary China.

10. A summary of Chinese laws and regulations regarding international adoption can be found at http://www.fwcc.org/ccaalaws.htm.

11. Regulations from the CCAA read as follows: "[P]roceeding from the principle that adoption shall be in the interest of the upbringing and growth of the

adopted minors, it would be best for the adopted children to live in a healthy perfect adoptive family with both parents. . . . We shall neither propose nor encourage adoption of children in China by single foreign adoption applicants." The regulations go on to say, "From the Chinese medical point of view, the China Mental Disorder Classification and Diagnosis Standard classifies homosexuality as sexual obstruction, belonging to psychiatric disease of the kind of sexual psychological barrier. In terms of the Chinese traditional ethics and customs and habits, homosexuality is an act violating public morality and therefore not recognized by the society. In accordance with the principle that adoption shall not violate social ethics as set forth in the Adoption Law, foreign homosexuals are not allowed to adopt children in China." (Questions and Answers concerning Policies and Procedures, http://www.china-ccaa.org/ccae-zcwt.htm. China Center of Adoption Affairs, June 18, 2001.)

12. Ibid.

13. A *Business Week* report cited the executive director of the Joint Council on International Children's Services as saying that "the ad might prompt China to end all single-parent adoptions" and that it was disingenuous of John Hancock to issue the following statement defending the ad: "There was nothing in this commercial that defines the nationality of the child or the relationship of the women. Anyone drawing such a conclusion is demonstrating their own prejudice." (Robert McNatt and Catherine Arnst, "Did Hancock Go a Mom Too Far?" *Business Week,* September 25, 2000, p. 12.)

14. The level of emphasis on race and culture awareness varies by adoption program and, it seems, in a "direct correlation" between them (the darker the child, the more cultural awareness may be emphasized). When culture- and race-awareness training does take place, it often takes the form of referring parents to cultural resource groups such as FCC and reminders that knowledge of birth culture is important for adopted children's self-esteem. Much attention to being transracial and transcultural families happens postadoption, through elective programs offered by agencies and parent-led support groups, as well as through informal Internet communications.

15. It is instructive that when Chinese American parents came through agencies, adoption practitioners often felt that children would more naturally "feel connected to the family." Rita Jasper admitted that the agency would just assume that Chinese American applicants "know something about Chinese culture," but that even if they were wrong, it was ultimately a matter of a child fitting because of race matching. In these cases, the professional concern focused instead on the risk that Chinese American parents might not adequately deal with abandonment and adoption questions.

16. At the same time, the social and cultural capital of trans-Pacific "flexible citizens" poses its own kind of unease. Rita Jasper, who works at an agency without a Chinese facilitator, asked: "If you've got a Chinese American facilitator, does that make your program better? Because that person really has an in? Does China feel that that's a more worthwhile agency to go to?" In reality, the answer to that question is yes, and Rita and other non-Chinese administrators know it. Some of the newer agencies started and run by Chinese nationals, as well as those with especially well connected Chinese facilitators, were placing a large percentage of children from China into U.S. families in the late 1990s. Administrators from some of the older agencies suggested that some of the new (Chinese-run) agencies and facilitators sacrifice standards of adoption practice that then hurt their own more established businesses. I interviewed Carrie during a period when the CCAA was slowing and limiting the number of adoption files it handled, and her resentment toward these agencies showed: "These other agencies are taking clients from MIA, providing home studies that obviously we feel are inferior to ours, and their preparation process is not as good, they're charging far less, and they're doing it much more quickly. And our China program is in trouble. We are losing families."

17. In the United States, for example, the Families with Children from China organization regularly raises money for Chinese orphanage children, including through linkages to China-based organizations such as the Amity Foundation. The organization Half the Sky has donated resources for schooling and staff support for the care of children, among other things. Some authors of books and films about Chinese adoption, as well as merchants of Chinese goods, donate profits to supporting abandoned children in China.

18. For example, the head of an orphanage in Nanping City, Fujian Province, was convicted of embezzling more than U.S. $12,000 of orphanage donations in 2001. ("Abandoned Chinese Babies Find Love from Foreign Parents," *People's Daily*, December 18, 2003; at http://english.peopledaily.com.cn.)

19. Some Western charitable organizations have made a concerted effort to reach special-needs children who are outside of the loop of resources; in other cases they have been "given" these children to take care of because the orphanage cannot (or will not) put in the extra effort to meet their needs.

NOTE TO CHAPTER 3

1. Excerpted from "Wild Cards," by adoptive mother Mary Cummings (first published in *Touched by Adoption: Stories, Letters and Poems*, compiled and edited by Nancy A. Robinson, 1999).

NOTES TO CHAPTER 4

1. Bourdieu (1987) writes that "fundamental social powers are, according to my empirical investigations, firstly *economic* capital, in its various kinds; secondly *cultural* capital or better, informational capital, again in its different kinds; and thirdly two forms of capital that are very strongly correlated, social capital, which consists of resources based on connections and group membership and *symbolic* capital, which is the form the different types of capital take once they are perceived and recognized as legitimate" (3–4).

2. These are managed by a host of offices, including the Ministry of Civil Affairs and its local branch offices (managing orphanages and adoption paperwork), the Ministry of Justice (issuing final legal approval of parents' and children's documents), and the U.S. consulate and Citizenship and Immigration Services (issuing the visa for a child's immigration into the United States).

3. The numbers in parentheses indicate the tone of the word. In Mandarin, *xiang* with a third tone means "to miss or think about," while with a fourth tone it means "to be or look like."

4. In *Specters of Marx*, Derrida (1994) employs the phrase "the time is out of joint" from Shakespeare's *Hamlet* to point to moments of disjuncture both spatial and temporal.

5. From the China Center of Adoption Affairs (http://www.china-ccca.org, accessed September 2001).

6. From http://www.usembassy-china.org.cn/consulates/guangzhou, accessed December 2000.

7. A kind of hierarchy of facilitators emerges in China/U.S. adoptions. There is a handful of well-seasoned facilitators who are mostly based in the United States, although some are independent businesspeople based in China who travel back and forth between China and the United States on a regular basis. They come closest to what Ong (1998) calls "flexible citizens," transnational elites who can bank on their personal networks and social capital to move between nations and cultures. In the next tier down is a range of young men and women in China who might work for a Chinese travel agency that has entered the adoption business or who "moonlight" as assistants to the seasoned facilitators.

8. See, for example, Zhu (1996). Friends in China also reported seeing feature news items about American adoptive families' celebrations of Chinese culture and holidays.

9. For insightful discussions of evolving discourses of the gift, especially around children and more specifically in adoption exchange, see Yngvesson

(2002) and contributions to the anthology *Transformative Motherhood: On Giving and Getting in a Consumer Culture,* edited by Layne (1999).

10. From "It's Different for Girls," a September 19, 2003 article in *The Guardian.*

11. Yngvesson (2002: 229) points out that gift discourse is sometimes disliked (see Rapp 1999, for example) for suggesting that debtor developing countries have only their children to give, but in the case of China, it rather suggests that the giving nation is doing the right thing "in the best interest of the child."

12. Adult Korean adoptee Mirim Kim (2002) uses the work of Chandra Mohanty (1988), "Under Western Eyes: Feminist Scholarship and Colonial Discourses," to argue that Asian orphan girl-children are made rescuable by the uniform oppression Third World women are imagined to experience.

13. Colen (1995) draws on her study of West Indian child-care workers and their New York employers to explain: "By *stratified reproduction* I mean that physical and social reproductive tasks are accomplished differentially according to inequalities that are based on hierarchies of class, race, ethnicity, gender, place in a global economy, and migration status . . . reproductive labor—physical, mental, emotional— . . . is differentially experienced, valued, and rewarded according to inequalities of access to material and social resources in particular historical and cultural contexts" (78).

14. Stryker (2001) effectively draws on Scheper-Hughes's (1992) *Death without Weeping* to make this point.

NOTES TO CHAPTER 5

1. My description of Shamian Island includes the actual names of most locations and organizations (but not most individuals), since there is no point in trying to disguise these one-of-a-kind places. These "present-tense" descriptions apply to 2000–2001.

2. Portions of this chapter first appeared in Sara Dorow (2002), "Adopted Children's Identities at the China/US Border," in *Immigrant Life in the US: Multidisciplinary Perspectives,* edited by D. R. Gabaccia and C. W. Leach. London: Routledge.

3. This innocuous sign does not convey the full symbolic weight of that history of boundary violation and resolution. It does not, for example, tell visitors that in 1925, British troops on Shamian Island fired on Chinese demonstrators who passed too close to the concession, killing fifty-two and wounding over one hundred. The crowd of students, soldiers, workers, and Boy Scouts were protesting foreign imperialism. This history of Shamian Island is adapted from

Jonathan Spence's 1990 *The Search for Modern China,* New York: W. W. Norton and Company, p. 340.

4. The U.S. consulate in Guangzhou is one of very few in the world with a special adoption visa unit. It issues more adoption visas than any other post worldwide ("The Triennial Comprehensive Report on Immigration," U.S. Immigration and Naturalization Service, http://www.ins.usdoj.gov/graphics/aboutins/repsstudies/addition.html, p. 242).

5. Reported in David Barboza (2003) "A Chinese Hotel, Full of Proud American Parents," *New York Times,* March 31, p. A4.

6. Items include brocade-covered photo albums, children's clothing with brocade borders, copper rubbings of zodiac animals, porcelain dolls, handmade teabags, panda backpacks, panda quilts, fuzzy panda costumes.

7. There is certainly child trafficking in China, although there is only limited evidence to date of connections to international adoption. In late 2005, the international media reported allegations of baby trafficking in Hunan Province with potential links to intercountry adoption.

8. I use Ted Gong's real name with his permission.

NOTES TO CHAPTER 6

1. Lack of information on adopted children would usually apply to formal domestic Chinese adoptions as well.

2. An adopted friend of mine suggested that "unruly" sounded too much like a naughty child, "as if this process *should* be disciplined and linear and predictable." But that is part of the point—the great desire to bring coherence to and to discipline the story, even as it refuses to be tamed and contained. I borrow from what Nancy Fraser (1989) suggests in the title of her book *Unruly Practices: Power, Discourse and Gender in Contemporary Social Theory.*

3. From "Talking to Nina," at http://www.fccne.org/lb (2000, 2001), accessed January 2002.

4. In a study of Chinese adoptees in middle childhood, Tessler and Gamache (2003) find that "the more children were exposed to Chinese language and culture, the more distress they showed in response to having the circumstances in China that led to their being adopted explained." They then go on to surmise that "the distress they exhibited might be due to the dissonance between the positive connotation associated with China . . . and the negative connotation implied by the circumstances that led to their adoptions" (8–9). Yet such an explanation only further begs the question of the essentialist conception of culture that underlies the impetus to give China such positive connotations.

5. From http://www.amotherslovefundraising.com, accessed August 2004.

6. See also Kaplan's (2002) exploration of "manifest domesticity"—the double-edged woman-centered labor of, on the one hand, fulfilling the national destiny of expanding into the world and, on the other hand, keeping the home safe from the disorderly threats of doing so.

7. This "shadowing" of motherhood in other caregivers was poignantly represented in a family drawing done by the daughter of a single mother I interviewed. She and her adoptive mother appear in the center of the page, dressed identically but distinguished by their black and blonde hair; off to the side is an all-gray female figure that the adopted child told her mother was her Chinese nanny.

8. Williamson, at http://www.arts.ualberta.ca/~jwilliam/baowebsite/story .htm.

9. From http://www.adoptshoppe.com/red_thread_bracelets.htm, accessed May 2000. I say that the phrase is quite loosely borrowed because, as adoptive parent Amy Klatzkin points out, the red thread traditionally attached a girl at birth to her future spouse and was not necessarily celebratory (cited in Volkman 2003: 41).

10. Many if not most of the women who tell their adoption stories in the collection *New American Families: Chinese Daughters and Their Single Mothers* (Liedtke and Brasseur 1997) begin by telling their readers they had thought about adoption for many years before finally acting on it.

11. Marly Swick (1999), "Ghost Mother," in *A Ghost at Heart's Edge: Stories and Poems of Adoption,* edited by S. Ito and T. Cervin. Berkeley: North Atlantic Books, pp. 40–49. Eun Jung Che (1997), "The Living Ghost," in T. Bishoff and J. Rankin (1997).

12. The preliminary stages of my project examining how Chinese adoptees narrate their own identities suggests that Chinese girls think just as much about possible siblings (especially older sisters) as they do about their birth mothers or birth fathers. I should also note that in 2004 and 2005 there was increasing interest among adoptive families in using DNA testing and historical records to try to match siblings who might have been separately abandoned and then adopted internationally.

NOTES TO CHAPTER 7

1. From Mary Witenburg and Amanda Paulson, "All in the (Mixed-Race) Family: A US Trend," *Christian Science Monitor,* August 28, 2003 (http://www .csmonitor.com).

2. There are exceptions to this rule. For example, the child must be already legally adopted in the home country to be eligible for automatic U.S. citizenship (e.g., Korean children are not legally adopted until they return to the United States).

3. From a speech on international adoption delivered to the House Committee on International Relations on May 22, 2002 (www.house.gov/international _relations/ziglo522.htm). Brysk (2004) notes that while the USCIS is mandated to ensure a child's immigration eligibility as well as adoptive parents' qualifications to adopt, receiving states in transnational adoption tend to be especially responsive to private and transnational concerns.

4. See the UN Convention on the Rights of the Child and the Hague Convention on Intercountry Adoption, for example. Such conventions call for due regard "to the desirability of continuity in a child's upbringing and to the child's ethnic, religious, cultural and linguistic background" (Stephens 1995: 38).

5. James Cheng, "All-American, with One Foot in China: Adoptive Parents Grapple with Race, Culture, and Growing Up," March 25, 2004 (http://www .msnbc.com).

6. Wanda Jones and Paul Chan, an interracial couple, cannot quite as easily be put in the category of celebrating plurality, since they sent their children to Chinese-language school. But it is also worth noting that unlike the other Chinese American parents with white partners, Paul is first-generation Chinese American and had business and family connections with China that took him there on a regular basis.

7. Ginger Adley told with some pride a story about the humorous and subversive social effects these resonant layers of identity can have. Once, while riding in an elevator, her three-year-old daughter Francie was singing a Hebrew children's song to herself, and from the back of the elevator a wry voice said, "And there go three thousand years of Chinese history." It is worth noting that, as a number of Jewish parents of Chinese children will point out, Chinese history contains plenty of Jewish stories, including the now-famous Jews of Kaifeng and the large number of Jewish refugees that settled in China (especially in Shanghai) before and during the Holocaust.

8. In the *pinyin* romanization system of Chinese, "x" and "q" are not pronounced in ways intuitive to English speakers; the former is pronounced as a thin "sh" and the latter as a thin "ch."

9. I must note that at least two families protested mildly that I characterized them as immersionists in earlier published pieces. I take their protests to mean two things: (1) no one likes to be categorized (this is why I insist that these are ideal types that in reality overlap), and (2) "going too far" or being seen as

"extreme" in approaches to Chinese cultural identity holds great power. One parent pointed out to me that she sees immersionists as those adoptive families who pack up and go live in China, and that was not what she had done.

10. From an interview by Donna Coble published as "Research Shows FCC and Chinese American Families Share Similar Issues" at http://www.scanews .com, August 2004.

11. Ibid.

12. The equivalent of "immersion" does not appear in Omi and Winant (1994), perhaps because there is very little in the broader structural politics of the United States to promote such a position.

13. The Leisters were one of two families I officially reinterviewed, although I kept up with a number of other families informally in the months and years after my interviews with them.

14. This outreach to Chinese American communities is not without its problems. Some FCC chapters have experienced tension, as I have indicated, over what is being sought: "authentic" cultural role models, or people who can help understand the history and experience of Asian racialization? Apparently one Chinese American club in the Bay Area expressed concern at the influx of adoptive families.

15. Tessler and Gamache's (2003) survey of adoptive families—to the authors' surprise—found that when children looked at photos of adults, they "more often picked the Chinese males and females as the adults who would understand them the best" (9).

16. Mulan/Barbie and school choice were not subjects I deliberately pursued in my interviews. Rather, they just kept coming up, depending in part on the timing of interviews (i.e., age of child at the time, popular cultural phenomenon in that year, how much parents were plugged into Internet discussions).

17. Of course, adoption itself becomes marketized as well. One especially unnerving example is the "NewBorn Nursery Adoption Center" offered by Lee Middleton Original Dolls, Inc. Young "shoppers" can "feast their eyes" on a nursery viewing area, choose a doll to adopt, simulate adoption paperwork, and then shop for all the wonderful accessories their new babies deserve. "When you peek through the glass, you'll see a variety of babies with all different complexions and hair and eye colors. It's almost too difficult to choose just one bundle of joy to take home!" (At http://www.newbornnursery.com/about.php, accessed September 2004.)

18. From the January 20, 2004 edition of *China Adoption News* (http://caswell .blogspot.com/china).

19. See Cheng, "All-American," in note 5, above.

20. One trade-off might be the occlusion of nonwhite people of privilege. In the summary of their research findings, Tessler and Gamache (2003) express surprise that adopted Chinese children "enrolled in more racially diverse public schools were more likely than children enrolled in less racially diverse public schools to choose the photo of the white girl and less likely to choose the photo of the Chinese girl" as someone with positive character traits. They conclude that this may be because of economic disadvantage among their minority classmates; "children adopted from China are much more similar to their white classmates than they are to their non-white classmates" (9). While I do not entirely disagree, I think it important that children in more racially diverse schools might also be more attuned to the classlike privileges of racial hierarchy. Might Chinese adopted children be picking up on their own tenuous position as racial minorities with attachments to privilege through an inextricable link between whiteness *and* class?

NOTES TO THE CONCLUSION

1. The first three are films: *Passing Through,* by Nathan Adolfson (1998); *Searching for Go-hyang,* by Tammy Tolle (1998); and *First Person Plural,* by Deann Borshay Liem (2000). *The Language of Blood* is the title of the book by Trenka (2003).

2. Such chance meetings are not completely unheard of. In an article titled "Walking Down the Village Path," adoptive mother and organizer of "return" tours to China, Jane Lietdke, shares several anecdotes of adoptive families who through "twists of fate" end up encountering birth families when visiting their daughters' hometowns in China (fccm@yahoogroups.com, January 2005).

3. From the *FCC–Northern California Orphanage Assistance Digest,* no. 1, September 2003.

BIBLIOGRAPHY

Ahn, Me-K. 1994. *Living in Half Tones*. Third World Newsreel.

Alarcón, Norma. 1996. "Conjugating Subjects in the Age of Multiculturalism." In *Mapping Multiculturalism*, edited by A. F. Gordon and C. Newfield. Minneapolis: University of Minnesota Press.

Allport, Gordon W. 1979 [1954]. *The Nature of Prejudice*. Reading, MA: Addison-Wesley Publishing Company.

Althusser, Louis. 1979. "Contradiction and Overdetermination." In *For Marx*. London: Verso.

Anagnost, Ann. 2000. "Scenes of Misrecognition: Maternal Citizenship in the Age of Transnational Adoption." *positions: east asia cultures critique* 8 (2): 390–421.

———. 1997. *National Past-Times: Narrative, Representation, and Power in Modern China*. Durham, NC: Duke University Press.

———. 1995. "A Surfeit of Bodies: Population and the Rationality of the State in Post-Mao China." In *Conceiving the New World Order: The Global Politics of Reproduction*, edited by F. D. Ginsburg and R. Rapp. Berkeley: University of California Press.

Ancheta, Angelo N. 1998. *Race, Rights, and the Asian American Experience*. New Brunswick, NJ: Rutgers University Press.

Anderson, Benedict. 1991. *Imagined Communities: Reflections on the Origin and Spread of Nationalism*. New York: Verso.

Anderson, Perry. 1980. *Arguments within English Marxism*. London: Verso.

Anthias, Floya. 1998. "Rethinking Social Divisions: Some Notes towards a Theoretical Framework." *Sociological Review* 46 (3): 503–35.

Appadurai, Arjun. 1996. *Modernity at Large: Cultural Dimensions of Globalization*. Minneapolis: University of Minnesota Press.

———. 1986. "Introduction: Commodities and the Politics of Value." In *The Social Life of Things: Commodities in Cultural Perspective*, edited by A. Appadurai. New York: Cambridge University Press.

Arkush, R. David, and Leo O. Leeds. 1989. *Land without Ghosts: Chinese Impressions of America from the Mid-Nineteenth Century to the Present*. Berkeley: University of California Press.

Balibar, Etienne. 1988a. "The Nation Form: History and Ideology." In *Race, Nation, Class: Ambiguous Identities,* edited by E. Balibar and I. Wallerstein. London: Verso.

Balibar, Etienne. 1988b. "Racism and Nationalism." In *Race, Nation, and Class: Ambiguous Identities,* edited by E. Balibar and I. Wallerstein. London: Verso.

Barrett, James R., and David Roediger. 1997. "Inbetween Peoples: Race, Nationality and the 'New Immigrant' Working Class." *Journal of American Ethnic History* 16 (Spring): 3–44.

Bauman, Zygmunt. 1999 [1973]. *Culture as Praxis.* London: Sage Publications.

———. 1990. "Modernity and Ambivalence." *Theory, Culture and Society* 7 (2–3): 143–69.

Becker, Howard. 1998. *Tricks of the Trade: How to Think about Your Research While You're Doing It.* Chicago: University of Chicago Press.

Becker, Uwe. 1989. "Class Theory: Still the Axis of Critical Social Scientific Analysis?" In *The Debate on Classes,* edited by E.O. Wright et al. London: Verso.

Berebitsky, Julie. 2000. *Like Our Very Own: Adoption and the Changing Culture of Motherhood, 1851–1950.* Lawrence: University Press of Kansas.

Berger, Bennett M. 1995. "Sociology and Culture." In *An Essay on Culture: Symbolic Structure and Social Structure.* Berkeley: University of California Press.

Bhabha, Homi. 1994. *The Location of Culture.* London: Routledge.

Biernacki, Richard. 1997. "Work and Culture in the Reception of Class Ideologies." In *Reworking Class,* edited by J. R. Hall. Ithaca, NY: Cornell University Press.

Bishoff, Tanya. 1997. "Unnamed Blood." In *Seeds from a Silent Tree,* edited by T. Bishoff and J. Rankin. San Diego: Pandal Press.

Bishoff, Tanya, and Jo Rankin, eds. 1997. *Seeds from a Silent Tree.* San Diego: Pandal Press.

Blalock, Hubert M. 1967. *Toward a Theory of Minority-Group Relations.* New York: Wiley.

Blauner, Robert. 1969. "Internal Colonialism and Ghetto Revolt." *Social Problems* 16 (4): 393–408.

Bonilla-Silva, Eduardo. 1996. "Rethinking Racism: Toward a Structural Interpretation." *American Sociological Review* 62 (June): 465–80.

Bordo, Susan. 1993. *Unbearable Weight: Feminism, Western Culture, and the Body.* Berkeley: University of California Press.

Bourdieu, Pierre. 1991. "Social Space and the Genesis of 'Classes.'" In *Language and Symbolic Power,* edited by J. B. Thompson. Cambridge, MA: Harvard University Press.

———. 1990 [1980]. *The Logic of Practice.* Palo Alto, CA: Stanford University Press.

———. 1987. "What Makes a Social Class? On the Theoretical and Practical Existence of Groups." *Berkeley Journal of Sociology* 32: 1–18.

Bourdieu, Pierre, and Loïc J. D. Wacquant. 1992. *An Invitation to Reflexive Sociology*. Chicago: University of Chicago Press.

Briggs, Laura. 2003. "Mother, Child, Race, Nation: The Visual Iconography of Rescue and the Politics of Transnational and Transracial Adoption." *Gender & History* 15 (2): 179–200.

Brysk, Alison. 2004. "Children Across Borders: Patrimony, Property, or Persons?" In *People Out of Place: Globalization, Human Rights, and the Citizenship Gap*, edited by A. Brsyk and G. Shafir. New York: Routledge.

Buell, Frederick. 1994. *National Culture and the New Global System*. Baltimore: Johns Hopkins University Press.

Burawoy, Michael. 2001. "Manufacturing the Global." *Ethnography* 2 (2): 147–59.

———. 2000. "Reaching for the Global." In M. Burawoy et al., *Global Ethnography: Forces, Connections and Imaginations in a Postmodern World*. Berkeley: University of California Press.

———. 1998. "The Extended Case Method." *Sociological Theory* 16 (1): 4–33.

Burke, Timothy. 1996. *Lifebuoy Men, Lux Women: Commodification, Consumption, and Cleanliness in Modern Zimbabwe*. Durham, NC: Duke University Press.

Butler, Judith. 1997. "Merely Cultural." *Social Text* 52/53: 265–78.

———. 1993. "Introduction." *Bodies That Matter: On the Discursive Limits of "Sex."* New York: Routledge.

Calhoun, Craig. 1997. *Nationalism*. Minneapolis: University of Minnesota Press.

———. 1995. *Critical Social Theory: Culture, History, and the Challenge of Difference*. Cambridge: Blackwell Publishers.

Cartwright, Lisa. 2003. "Photographs of 'Waiting Children': The Transnational Adoption Market." *Social Text* 21 (1): 83–109.

Cha, Theresa Hak Kyung. 1995 [1982]. *Dictee*. Berkeley: Third Woman Press.

Chakrabarty, Dipesh. 1997. "The Time of History and the Time of Gods. In *The Politics of Culture in the Shadow of Capital*, edited by L. Lowe and D. Lloyd. Durham, NC: Duke University Press.

Chan, Suchong. 1990. "European and Asian Immigration into the United States in Comparative Perspective, 1820s to 1920s." In *Immigration Reconsidered: History, Sociology, and Politics*, edited by V. Yans-McLaughlin. New York: Oxford University Press.

Chang, Robert S. 2000. "Why We Need a Critical Asian American Legal Studies." In *Asian American Studies: A Reader*, edited by J. Yu-wen Shen Wu and M. Song. New Brunswick, NJ: Rutgers University Press.

———. 1995. "Toward an Asian American Legal Scholarship: Critical Race Theory, Post-Structuralism, and Narrative Space." In *Critical Race Theory: The Cutting Edge*, edited by R. Delgado. Philadelphia: Temple University Press.

Charles, Carolle. 1992. "Transnationalism in the Construct of Haitian Migrants'
    Racial Categories of Identity in New York City." In *Towards a Transnational
    Perspective on Migration: Race, Class, Ethnicity, and Nationalism Reconsid-
    ered,* edited by N. Glick-Schiller et al. Annals of the New York Academy of
    Sciences 645. New York: The New York Academy of Sciences.

Cheng, Anne Anlin. 2001. *The Melancholy of Race: Psychoanalysis, Assimilation,
    and Hidden Grief.* New York: Oxford University Press.

Cheung, King-Kok. 2000. "The Woman Warrior versus the Chinaman Pacific:
    Must a Chinese American Critic Choose between Feminism and Heroism?" In
    Asian American Studies: A Reader, edited by J. Yu-wen Shen Wu and M.
    Song. New Brunswick, NJ: Rutgers University Press.

Chow, Esther Ngan-Ling. 1998. "Family, Economy, and the State: A Legacy of
    Struggle for Chinese American Women." In *Shifting the Center: Understand-
    ing Contemporary Families,* edited by S. J. Ferguson. Mountain View, CA:
    Mayfield Publishing Company.

Choy, Catherine Ceniza, and Gregory Paul Choy. 2003. "Transformative Terrains:
    Korean American Adoptees and the Social Constructions of an American
    Childhood." In *The American Child,* edited by C. Levander and C. Singley.
    New Brunswick, NJ: Rutgers University Press.

Cohen, Phil. 1994. "Yesterday's Words, Tomorrow's World: From the Racialisa-
    tion of Adoption to the Politics of Difference." In *In the Best Interest of the
    Child: Culture, Identity and Transracial Adoption,* edited by I. Gaber and J.
    Aldridge. London: Free Association Books.

Colen, Shellee. 1995. " 'Like a Mother to Them': Stratified Reproduction and
    West Indian Childcare Workers and Employers in New York." In *Conceiving
    the New World Order: The Global Politics of Reproduction,* edited by F. D.
    Ginsburg and R. Rapp. Berkeley: University of California Press.

Collins, Patricia Hill. 1991. *Black Feminist Thought: Knowledge, Consciousness,
    and the Politics of Empowerment.* New York: Routledge.

Cornell, Stephen, and Douglas Hartmann. 1998. *Ethnicity and Race: Making
    Identities in a Changing World.* Thousand Oaks, CA: Pine Forge Press.

Coronil, Fernando. 1998. *The Magical State: Nature, Money, and Modernity in
    Venezuela.* Chicago: University of Chicago Press.

Crenshaw, Kimberle W., et al. 1995. "Introduction." In *Critical Race Theory: The
    Key Writings That Formed the Movement,* edited by K. Crenshaw et al. New
    York: New Press.

Cruz, Jon. 1996. "From Farce to Tragedy: Reflections on the Reification of Race
    at Century's End." In *Mapping Multiculturalism,* edited by A. F. Gordon and
    C. Newfield. Minneapolis: University of Minnesota Press.

Das, Veena. 1995. "National Honor and Practical Kinship: Unwanted Women and

Children." In *Conceiving the New World Order: The Global Politics of Repro-duction,* edited by F. D. Ginsburg and R. Rapp. Berkeley: University of California Press.

Davis, Angela. 1998. "Reflections on Race, Class, and Gender in the USA." In *The Angela Davis Reader,* edited by J. James. Malden, MA: Blackwell Publishers.

Denzin, Norman K. 1990. "The Sociological Imagination Revisited." *Sociological Quarterly* 31 (1): 1–21.

Derrida, Jacques. 1994. *Specters of Marx: The State of the Debt, the Work of Mourning, and the New International.* Translated by P. Kamuf. New York and London: Routledge.

Dikötter, Frank. 2002. "Race in China." In *A Companion to Racial and Ethnic Studies,* edited by D. T. Goldberg and J. Solomos. Malden, MA: Blackwell.

di Leonardo, Micaela. 1993. "What a Difference Political Economy Makes: Feminist Anthropology in the Postmodern Era." *Anthropological Quarterly* 66 (2): 76–80.

Dill, Bonnie Thornton. 1979. "The Dialectics of Black Womanhood." *Signs* 4 (3): 543–55.

Dorow, Sara. 2006 (in press). "Racialized Choices: Chinese Adoption and the 'White Noise' of Blackness." *Critical Sociology.*

———. 2004. "Adopted Children's Identities at the China/US Border." In *Immigrant Life in the US: Multi-disciplinary Perspectives,* edited by D. R. Gabaccia and C. W. Leach. London: Routledge.

———. 2002. " 'China 'R' Us'? Care, Consumption, and Transnationally Adopted Children." In *Symbolic Childhood,* edited by D. Cook. New York: Peter Lang Publishers.

Dorow, Sara, and Doug Hartman. 2000. "Ghosts and Haunting as Sociological Evidence: Building on Avery Gordon." Conference paper presented at the Annual Meeting of the American Sociological Association, Washington, D.C.

Duncan, William. 1993. "Regulating Intercountry Adoption: An International Perspective." In *Frontiers of Family Law,* edited by A. Bainham and D. S. Pearl. London: John Wiley & Sons.

Eng, David L. 2003. "Transnational Adoption and Queer Diasporas." *Social Text* 21 (3): 1–37.

———. 2001. *Racial Castration: Managing Masculinity in Asian America.* Durham: Duke University Press.

Evans, Karin. 2000. *The Lost Daughters of China.* New York: Tarcher/Putnam.

Fabian, Johannes. 1983. *Time and the Other.* New York: Columbia University Press.

Feagin, Joe R., and C. B. Feagin. 1993. *Racial and Ethnic Relations.* Englewood Cliffs, NJ: Prentice-Hall.

Ferguson, James. 1992. "The Cultural Topography of Wealth: Commodity Paths and the Structure of Property in Rural Lesotho." *American Anthropologist* 94 (1): 55–73.

Ferree, Myra Marx, and Elaine J. Hall. 1996. "Rethinking Stratification from a Feminist Perspective: Gender, Race, and Class in Mainstream Textbooks." *American Sociological Review* 61: 929–50.

Firestone, Shulamit. 1997 [1970]. "The Dialectic of Sex." In *The Second Wave: A Reader in Feminist Theory,* edited by L. Nicholson. New York: Routledge.

Fong, Timothy P. 1998. *The Contemporary Asian American Experience: Beyond the Model Minority.* Upper Saddle River, NJ: Prentice-Hall.

Fonseca, Claudia. 2002. "Inequality Near and Far: Adoption as Seen from the Brazilian Favelas." *Law & Society Review* 36 (2): 397–431.

Foucault, Michel. 1991a. "Governmentality." In *The Foucault Effect: Studies in Governmentality,* edited by G. Burchill et al. Chicago: University of Chicago Press.

———. 1991b. *Remarks on Marx: Conversations with Duccio Trombadori.* Translated by R. J. Goldstein and J. Cascaito. New York: Semiotext(e).

———. 1980. "Omnes et Singulatim." *The Tanner Lectures on Human Values.* Salt Lake City: University of Utah Press.

Frankenberg, Ruth. 1993. *White Women, Race Matters: The Social Construction of Whiteness.* Minneapolis: University of Minnesota Press.

Fraser, Nancy. 1997 [1992]. "Structuralism or Pragmatics? On Discourse Theory and Feminist Politics." In *The Second Wave: A Reader in Feminist Theory,* edited by L. Nicholson. New York: Routledge.

———. 1989. *Unruly Practices: Power, Discourse, and Gender in Contemporary Social Theory.* Minneapolis: University of Minnesota Press.

Freundlich, Madelyn. 2000. *Adoption and Ethics.* The Role of Race, Culture, and National Origin in Adoption 10. Washington, D.C.: Child Welfare League of America, The Evan B. Donaldson Institute.

Fuss, Diana. 1995. *Identification Papers.* New York: Routledge.

Gailey, Christine Ward. 2000. "Ideologies of Motherhood and Kinship in US Adoption." In *Ideologies and Technologies of Motherhood,* edited by H. Ragoné and F. Winddance Twine. New York: Routledge.

———. 1999. "Seeking 'Baby Right': Race, Class, and Gender in US International Adoption." In *Mine, Yours, Ours . . . and Theirs: Adoption, Changing Kinship and Family Patterns,* edited by A. Rygvold, M. Dale, and B. Saetersdal. Oslo: University of Oslo.

Galang, M. Evelina. 2003. *Screaming Monkeys: Critiques of Asian American Images.* Minneapolis: Coffee House Press.

Gans, Herbert. 1999. *Making Sense of America: Sociological Analyses and Essays.* Lanham, MD: Rowman & Littlefield.

George, Ivy. 2004. "The Past, Interrupted." *Sojourners* 33 (6): 24–29.

Gibson-Graham, J. K. 1996. *The End of Capitalism (as We Knew It): A Feminist Critique of Political Economy.* Cambridge: Blackwell Publishers.

Giddens, Anthony. 1991. *Modernity and Self-Identity: Self and Society in the Late Modern Age.* Stanford, CA: Stanford University Press.

Gilroy, Paul. 1993a. *The Black Atlantic: Modernity and Double Consciousness.* London: Verso.

———. 1993b. "Nationalism, History and Ethnic Absolutism." *Small Acts: Thoughts on the Politics of Black Cultures.* New York: New York University (Serpent's Tail).

Ginsburg, Faye D. 1989. *Contested Lives: The Abortion Debate in an American Community.* Berkeley: University of California Press.

Ginsburg, Faye D., and Rayna Rapp. 1995. "Introduction: Conceiving the New World Order." In *Conceiving the New World Order: The Global Politics of Reproduction,* edited by F. D. Ginsburg and R. Rapp. Berkeley: University of California Press.

Glenn, Evelyn Nakano. 1998. "Gender, Race, and Class: Bridging the Language-Structure Divide." *Social Science History* 22 (1): 29–39.

———. 1994. "Social Constructions of Mothering: A Thematic Overview." In *Mothering: Ideology, Experience, and Agency,* edited by E. Nakano Glenn et al. New York: Routledge.

Glick-Schiller, Nina, Linda Basch, and Cristina Blanc-Szanton. 1992. "Transnationalism: A New Analytic Framework for Understanding Migration." In *Towards a Transnational Perspective on Migration: Race, Class, Ethnicity, and Nationalism Reconsidered,* edited by N. Glick-Schiller et al. Annals of the New York Academy of Sciences 645. New York: The New York Academy of Sciences.

Goldberg, David Theo. 1997. *Racial Subjects: Writing on Race in America.* New York: Routledge.

———. 1993. *Racist Culture: Philosophy and the Politics of Meaning.* Cambridge: Blackwell.

Gordon, Avery F. 1999. *Ghostly Matters: Haunting and the Sociological Imagination.* Minneapolis: University of Minnesota Press.

Gordon, Linda. 1999. *The Great Arizona Orphan Abduction.* Cambridge, MA: Harvard University Press.

Gordon, Milton. 1964. *Assimilation in American Life: The Role of Race, Religion, and National Origins.* New York: Oxford University Press.

Gotanda, Neil. 2000. "Multiculturalism and Racial Stratification." In *Asian*

American Studies: A Reader, edited by J. Yu-wen Shen Wu and M. Song. New Brunswick, NJ: Rutgers University Press.

Gramsci, Antonio. 1971. "State and Civil Society." In *Selections from the Prison Notebooks,* edited and translated by Q. Hoare and G. Nowell-Smith. New York: International Publishers.

Greenhalgh, Susan, and Jiali Li. 1995. "Engendering Reproductive Policy and Practice in Peasant China: For a Feminist Demography of Reproduction." *Signs: Journal of Women in Culture and Society* 20 (31): 601–41.

Gregory, Steven. 1998. *Black Corona: Race and the Politics of Place in an Urban Community.* Berkeley: University of California Press.

Grewal, Inderpal. 1996. *Home and Harem: Nation, Gender, Empire, and the Culture of Travel.* Durham, NC: Duke University Press.

Gruskey, David B. 1994. "Introduction." In *Social Stratification: Class, Race, and Gender in Sociological Perspective,* edited by D. B. Gruskey. Boulder, CO: Westview Press.

Guarnizo, Luis, and M. P. Smith. 1998. "The Locations of Transnationalism." In *Transnationalism from Below,* edited by M. P. Smith and L. E. Guarnizo. Comparative Urban and Community Research 6. New Brunswick, NJ: Transaction Publishers.

Guo, Yingjie. 2004. *Cultural Nationalism in Contemporary China: The Search for National Identity under Reform.* London and New York: RoutledgeCurzon.

Gupta, Akhil, and J. Ferguson. 1992. "Beyond 'Culture': Space, Identity, and the Politics of Difference." *Cultural Anthropology* 7 (1): 6–23.

Hall, John R. 1997. "Introduction: The Reworking of Class Analysis." In *Reworking Class,* edited by J. R. Hall. Ithaca, NY: Cornell University Press.

———. 1992. "The Capital(s) of Cultures: A Nonholistic Approach to Status Situations, Class, Gender, and Ethnicity." In *Cultivating Differences: Symbolic Boundaries and the Making of Inequality,* edited by M. Lamont and M. Tournier. Chicago: University of Chicago Press.

Hall, Stuart. 1996a. "Cultural Identity and Diaspora." In *Questions of Cultural Identity,* edited by S. Hall and P. duGay. London: Sage Publications.

———. 1996b. "Gramsci's Relevance for the Study of Race and Ethnicity." In *Stuart Hall: Critical Dialogues in Cultural Studies,* edited by D. Morley and K. H. Chen. New York: Routledge.

———. 1986. "The Problem of Ideology—Marxism without Guarantees." *Journal of Communication Inquiry* 10 (2): 28–44.

Hall, Stuart, and D. Held. 1989. "Citizens and Citizenship." In *New Times: The*

Changing Face of Politics in the 1990s, edited by S. Hall and M. Jacques. London: Lawrence and Wishart.

Haraway, Donna. 1991. "Gender for a Marxist Dictionary." In *Simians, Cyborgs, and Women.* New York: Routledge.

Hart, Janet. 1992. "Cracking the Code: Narrative and Political Mobilization in the Greek Resistance." *Social Science History* 16 (4): 631–68.

Hartmann, Douglas. 1999. "Toward a Race-Critical Sociology." *Critica: A Journal of Critical Essays* (Spring): 21–32.

Hartmann, Heidi. 1997 [1981]. "The Unhappy Marriage of Marxism and Feminism: Towards a More Progressive Union." In *The Second Wave: A Reader in Feminist Theory,* edited by L. Nicholson. New York: Routledge.

Harvey, David. 1995. "Globalization in Question." *Rethinking Marxism* 8 (4): 1–17.

———. 1989. *The Condition of Postmodernity.* Oxford: Basil Blackwell.

Haskell, Thomas. 1985a. "Capitalism and the Origins of the Humanitarian Sensibility (part 2)." *American Historical Review* 90 (3): 547–66.

———. 1985b. "Capitalism and the Origins of the Humanitarian Sensibility (part 1)." *American Historical Review* 90 (2): 339–61.

Haslanger, Sally. 2004. "Racial Geographies." In *Families by Law: An Adoption Reader,* edited by N. R. Cahn and J. H. Hollinger. New York: New York University Press.

Hayden, Corrine P. 1995. "Gender, Genetics, and Generation: Reformulating Biology in Lesbian Kinship." *Cultural Anthropology* 10 (1): 41–63.

Hays, Sharon. 1996. *The Cultural Contradictions of Motherhood.* New Haven, CT: Yale University Press.

———. 1994. "Structure and Agency and the Sticky Problem of Culture." *Sociological Theory* 12 (1): 57–72.

Higham, John. 1999. "Instead of a Sequel, or, How I Lost My Subject." In *The Handbook of International Migration: The American Experience,* edited by C. Hirschman et al. New York: Russell Sage.

Hing, Bill Ong. 1993. *Making and Remaking Asian America through Immigration Policy, 1850–1990.* Palo Alto, CA: Stanford University Press.

Hirschman, Charles. 1999. "Theories of International Migration and Immigration: A Preliminary Reconnaissance of Ideal Types." In *The Handbook of International Migration: The American Experience,* edited by C. Hirschman et al. New York: Russell Sage.

Hobsbawm, Eric. 1983. "Introduction: Inventing Traditions." In *The Invention of Tradition,* edited by E. Hobsbawm and T. Ranger. Cambridge: Cambridge University Press.

Hochschild, Arlie. 1983. *The Managed Heart: Commercialization of Human Feeling*. Berkeley: University of California Press.

Hoffman-Riem, Christa. 1990. *The Adopted Child: Family Life with Double Parenthood*. New Brunswick, NJ: Transaction Publishers.

Hollingsworth, Leslie D. 1997. "Effect of Transracial/Transethnic Adoption on Children's Racial and Ethnic Identity and Self-Esteem: A Meta-Analytic Review." *Marriage and Family Review* 25 (1–2): 99–130.

Hondagneu-Sotelo, Pierrette. 1995. "Women and Children First: New Directions in Anti-Immigrant Politics." *Socialist Review* 25 (1): 169–90.

———. 1994. *Gendered Transitions: Mexican Experiences of Immigration*. Berkeley: University of California Press.

Horkheimer, Max. 1986 [1972]. "Traditional and Critical Theory." In *Critical Theory: Selected Essays*. Translated by M. J. O'Connell et al. New York: Continuum.

Hsu, Ruth Y. 1996. "'Will the Model Minority Please Identify Itself?' American Ethnic Identity and Its Discontents." *Diaspora* 5 (1): 37–63.

Hune, Shirley. 1995. "Rethinking Race: Paradigms and Policy Formation." *Amerasia Journal* 21 (1 & 2): 29–40.

Hunter, Jane. 1984. *The Gospel of Gentility: American Women Missionaries in Turn-of-the-Century China*. New Haven, CT: Yale University Press.

Ito, Susan, and Tina Cervin, eds. 1999. *A Ghost at Heart's Edge: Stories and Poems of Adoption*. Berkeley, CA: North Atlantic Books.

Jacobson, Matthew Frye. 1998. *Whiteness of a Different Color: European Immigrants and the Alchemy of Race*. Cambridge, MA: Harvard University Press.

Johnson, Kay Ana. 2004. *Wanting a Daughter, Needing a Son: Abandonment, Adoption, and Orphanage Care in China*. St. Paul, MN: Yeong & Yeong Book Company.

———. 1996. "The Politics of the Revival of Infant Abandonment in China." *Population and Development Review* 22 (1): 77–98.

———. 1993. "Chinese Orphanages: Saving China's Abandoned Girls." *Australian Journal of Chinese Affairs* (30): 61–87.

Johnson, Kay, Huang Banghan, and Wang Liyao. 1998. "Infant Abandonment and Adoption in China." *Population and Development Review* 24 (3): 469–510.

Kang, Laura Hyun Yi. 2003. "Conjuring 'Comfort Women': Mediated Affiliations and Disciplined Subjects in Korean/American Transnationality." *Contents: Journal of Asian American Studies* 6 (1): 25–55.

Kaplan, Amy. 2002. *The Anarchy of Empire in the Making of U.S. Culture*. Cambridge, MA: Harvard University Press.

Katz, Cindi. 1996. "The Expeditions of Conjurers: Ethnography, Power, and Pretense." In *Feminist Dilemmas in Fieldwork,* edited by D. L. Wolf. Boulder, CO: Westview Press.

Kauffman, Ellwyn. 1997. "Never." In *Seeds from a Silent Tree: An Anthology by Korean Adoptees,* edited by T. Bishoff and J. Rankin. San Diego: Pandal Press.

Kearney, Michael. 1995. "The Local and the Global: The Anthropology of Globalization and Transnationalism." *Annual Review of Anthropology* 24: 547–65.

Kelley, Robin D. G. 1997a. "Identity Politics and Class Struggle." *New Politics* (Winter): 84–96.

———. 1997b. *Yo' Mama's Disfunktional! Fighting the Culture Wars in Urban America.* Boston: Beacon Press.

Kim, Eleana. 2000. "Korean Adoptee Autoethnography: Refashioning Self, Family and Finding Community." *Visual Anthropology Review* 16 (1): 43–70.

Kim, Mirim. 2002. *Reconstructing Narratives of International Adoption: A Korean Adoptee Talks Back.* Unpublished M.A. thesis, North Dakota State University.

King, Thomas. 2003. *The Truth about Stories: A Native Narrative.* Toronto: House of Anansi Press.

Kirk, David. 1964. *Shared Fate: A Theory of Adoption and Mental Health.* New York: Free Press.

Kirton, Derek. 2000. *'Race', Ethnicity and Adoption.* Buckingham: Open University Press.

Laclau, Ernesto. 1995. "The Time Is Out of Joint." *Diacritics* 25 (2): 86–96.

Lal, Shafali. 2002. "Orphaned, Adopted, and Abducted: Parents and Children in Twentieth-Century America." *Radical History Review* 84 (Fall): 174–84.

Lamont, Michele. 1991. "Introduction: Beyond Taking Culture Seriously." In *The Cultural Territories of Race: Black and White Boundaries,* edited by M. Lamont. Chicago: University of Chicago Press.

Lauria-Perricelli, Antonio. 1992. "Towards a Transnational Perspective on Migration: Closing Remarks." In *Towards a Transnational Perspective on Migration: Race, Class, Ethnicity, and Nationalism Reconsidered,* edited by N. Glick-Schiller et al. Annals of the New York Academy of Sciences 645. New York: The New York Academy of Sciences.

Layne, Linda. 1999. "The Child as Gift: New Directions in the Study of Euro-American Gift Exchange." In *Transformative Motherhood: On Giving and Getting in a Consumer Culture,* edited by L. Layne. New York: New York University Press.

Lee, Erika. 2003. *At America's Gates: Chinese Immigration during the Exclusion Era, 1882–1943.* Chapel Hill: University of North Carolina Press.

Lee, Jayne Chong-Soon. 1995. "Navigating the Topology of Race." In *Critical Race Theory: The Key Writings That Formed the Movement,* edited by K. Crenshaw et al. New York: New Press.

Lee, Robert G. 1999. *Orientals: Asian Americans in Popular Culture*. Philadelphia: Temple University Press.

Lewin, Ellen. 1993. *Lesbian Mothers: Accounts of Gender in American Culture*. Ithaca, NY: Cornell University Press.

Li, Yamin. 2000. "Zhongguo Gu'Er Zai Meiguo." *Xin Guangjiao* (December): 4–12.

Liedtke, Jane, and Lee Brasseur. 1997. *New American Families: Chinese Daughters and Their Single Mothers*. Bloomington, IL: Our Chinese Daughter's Foundation.

Lipsitz, George. 1998. *The Possessive Investment in Whiteness: How White People Profit from Identity Politics*. Philadelphia: Temple University Press.

Liu, Lydia H. 1999. "The Question of Meaning—Value in the Political Economy of the Sign." In *Tokens of Exchange: The Problem of Translation in Global Circulations*, edited by L. H. Liu. Durham, NC: Duke University Press.

Lofland, John, and Lyn H. Lofland. 1995. *Analyzing Social Settings: A Guide to Qualitative Observation and Analysis*. Belmont, CA: Wadsworth.

Lopez, Ian F. Haney. 1998. "Race, Ethnicity, Erasure: The Salience of Race to Latcrit Theory." *La Raza Law Journal* 10 (1): 57–125.

Lovelock, Kirsten. 2000. "Intercountry Adoption as a Migratory Practice: A Comparative Analysis of Intercountry Adoption and Immigration Policy and Practice in the United States, Canada and New Zealand in the Post W.W. II Period." *International Migration Review* 34 (3): 907–49.

Lowe, Lisa. 1996. *Immigrant Acts: On Asian American Cultural Politics*. Durham, NC: Duke University Press.

Lowe, Lisa, and David Lloyd. 1997. "Introduction." In *The Politics of Culture in the Shadow of Capital,* edited by L. Lowe and D. Lloyd. Durham, NC: Duke University Press.

Luke, Carmen, and Allan Luke. 1998. "Interracial Families: Difference within Difference." *Ethnic and Racial Studies* 21 (4): 728–53.

McClintock, Anne. 1995. *Imperial Leather: Race, Gender and Sexuality in the Colonial Contest*. New York: Routledge.

McKeown, Adam M. 1999. "Conceptualizing Chinese Diasporas, 1842 to 1949." *Journal of Asian Studies* 58 (2): 306–37.

Mackerras, Colin. 1989. *Western Images of China*. New York: Oxford University Press.

Ma, Sheng-mei. 2000. *The Deathly Embrace: Orientalism and Asian American Identity*. Minneapolis: University of Minnesota Press.

Madsen, Richard. 1995. *China and the American Dream: A Moral Inquiry*. Berkeley: University of California Press.

Mahler, Sarah J. 1998. "Theoretical and Empirical Contributions toward a Research Agenda for Transnationalism." In *Transnationalism from Below,* edited by M. P. Smith and L. E. Guarnizo. Comparative Urban and Community Research 6. New Brunswick, NJ: Transaction Publishers.

Mansnerus, Laura. 1998. "Market Puts Price Tags on the Priceless." *New York Times,* October 26, p. A1.

Manzo, Kathryn A. 1996. "Nationalism and Global Politics." In *Creating Boundaries: The Politics of Race and Nation.* Boulder, CO: Lynne Rienner Publishers.

Marcus, George E. 1995. "Ethnography in/of the World System: The Emergence of Multi-Sited Ethnography." *Annual Review of Anthropology* 24: 95–117.

Marx, Karl. 1976. *Capital: A Critique of Political Economy.* Volume 1. Translated by Ben Fowkes. New York: Penguin Books.

Matsuda, Mari. 1995. "Looking to the Bottom: Critical Legal Studies and Reparations." In *Critical Race Theory: The Key Writings That Formed the Movement,* edited by K. Crenshaw et al. New York: New Press.

Matsuda, Mari J. et al. 1993. "Introduction." In *Words That Wound: Critical Race Theory, Assaultive Speech, and the First Amendment,* edited by M. Matsuda et al. Boulder, CO: Westview Press.

May, Elaine Tyler. 1995. *Barren in the Promised Land: Childless Americans and the Pursuit of Happiness.* Cambridge, MA: Harvard University Press.

Maynes, Mary Jo. 1992. "Autobiography and Class Formation in Nineteenth-Century Europe: Methodological Considerations." *Social Science History* 16 (3): 517–37.

Melosh, Barbara. 2002. *Strangers and Kin: The American Way of Adoption.* Cambridge, MA: Harvard University Press.

Mills, C. Wright. 1999 [1959]. *The Sociological Imagination.* New York: Oxford University Press.

Mirza, Heidi. 1997. "Mapping a Genealogy of Black British Feminism." In *Black British Feminism: A Reader,* edited by H. Mirza. London: Routledge.

Mitchell, Tim. 1998. "Fixing the Economy." *Cultural Studies* 12 (1): 82–101.

Modell, Judith S. 2002. *A Sealed and Secret Kinship: The Culture of Policies and Practices in American Adoption.* New York: Berghahn Books.

———. 1994. *Kinship with Strangers: Adoption and Interpretations of Kinship in American Culture.* Berkeley: University of California Press.

Modood, Tariq. 1997. "'Difference', Cultural Racism and Anti-Racism." In *Debating Cultural Hybridity: Multi-Cultural Identities and the Politics of Anti-Racism,* edited by P. Werbner and T. Modood. London: Zed Books.

Mohanty, Chandra. 1988. "Under Western Eyes: Feminist Scholarship and Colonial Discourses." *Feminist Review* 30: 61–88.

Morawska, Ewa. 1990. "The Sociology and Historiography of Immigration." In

Immigration Reconsidered: History, Sociology, and Politics, edited by V. Yans-McLaughlin. New York: Oxford University Press.

Nagel, Joane. 1998. "Constructing Ethnicity: Creating and Recreating Ethnic Identity and Culture." In *New Tribalisms: The Resurgence of Race and Ethnicity,* edited by M. Hughey. New York: New York University Press.

Newfield, Christopher, and Avery F. Gordon. 1996. "Multiculturalism's Unfinished Business." In *Mapping Multiculturalism,* edited by A. F. Gordon and C. Newfield. Minneapolis: University of Minnesota Press.

Niemonen, Jack. 1997. "The Race Relations Problematic in American Sociology: A Case Study and Critique." *American Sociologist* (Spring): 15–41.

O'Donovan, Katherine. 2002. "'Real Mothers' for Abandoned Children." *Law & Society Review* 36 (2): 347–78.

Okihiro, Gary Y. 2001. *Common Ground: Reimagining American History.* Princeton, NJ: Princeton University Press.

Omi, Michael. 1996. "Racialization in the Post–Civil Rights Era." In *Mapping Multiculturalism,* edited by A. F. Gordon and C. Newfield. Minneapolis: University of Minnesota Press.

Omi, Michael, and Howard Winant. 1994. *Racial Formation in the United States: From the 1960s to the 1990s.* New York: Routledge.

Ong, Aihwa. 2004. "Latitudes of Citizenship: Membership, Meaning, and Multiculturalism." In *People Out of Place: Globalization, Human Rights, and the Citizenship Gap,* edited by A. Brysk and G. Shafir. New York: Routledge.

———. 1998. *Flexible Citizenship: The Cultural Logics of Transnationality.* Durham, NC: Duke University Press.

———. 1996. "Cultural Citizenship as Subject-Making." *Current Anthropology* 37 (5): 737–51.

———. 1992. "Limits to Cultural Accumulation: Chinese Capitalists on the American Pacific Rim." *Towards a Transnational Perspective on Migration: Race, Class, Ethnicity, and Nationalism Reconsidered,* edited by N. Glick-Schiller et al. Annals of the New York Academy of Sciences 645. New York: The New York Academy of Sciences.

Ortiz, Ana Teresa, and Laura Briggs. 2003. "The Culture of Poverty, Crack Babies, and Welfare Cheats: The Making of the 'Healthy White Baby Crisis.'" *Social Text* 21 (3): 39–57.

Ortner, Sherry B. 1984. "Theory in Anthropology since the Sixties." *Comparative Studies* 26 (1): 126–66.

Ouellette, Françoise-Romaine, and Hélène Belleau, with the collaboration of Caroline Patenaude. 2001. *Family and Social Integration of Children Adopted Internationally: A Review of the Literature.* Montreal: INRS-Urbanisation, Culture et Société.

Palumbo-Liu, David. 1999. *Asian/American: Historical Crossings of a Racial Frontier.* Stanford: Stanford University Press.

Park, Robert E. 1950. *Race and Culture.* Glencoe, IL: Free Press.

Patton, Sandra L. 2000. *BirthMarks: Transracial Adoption in Contemporary America.* New York: New York University Press.

Perrons, Diane. 1999. "Reintegrating Production and Consumption, or Why Political Economy Still Matters." In *Critical Development Theory: Contributions to a New Paradigm,* edited by R. Munck and D. O'Hearn. New York: Zed Books.

Perry, Twila. 2004. "Transracial and International Adoption: Mothers, Hierarchy, Race, and Feminist Legal Theory." In *Families by Law: An Adoption Reader,* edited by N. R. Cahn and J. H. Hollinger. New York: New York University Press.

Pessar, Patricia R. 1999. "Engendering Migration Studies: The Case of New Immigrants in the United States." *American Behavioral Scientist* 42 (4): 577–600.

Plummer, Kenneth. 1990. "Herbert Blumer and the Life History Tradition." *Symbolic Interaction* 13 (2): 125–44.

Poulantzas, Nicos. 1973. *Political Power and Social Classes.* London: Sheed and Ward.

Polanyi, Karl. 1944. *The Great Transformation: The Political and Economic Origins of Our Time.* Boston: Beacon Press.

Prashad, Vijay. 2003. "Bruce Lee and the Anti-Imperialism of Kung Fu: A Polycultural Adventure." *positions: east asia cultures critique* 11 (1): 51–82.

Ragoné, Heléna. 1999. "The Gift of Life: Surrogate Motherhood, Gamete Donation, and Constructions of Altruism." In *Transformative Motherhood: On Giving and Getting in a Consumer Culture,* edited by L. Layne. New York: New York University Press.

Rapp, Rayna. 1999. "Foreword." In *Transformative Motherhood: On Giving and Getting in a Consumer Culture,* edited by L. Layne. New York: New York University Press.

Register, Cheri. 1991. *"Are Those Kids Yours?" American Families with Children Adopted from Other Countries.* New York: Free Press.

Reimers, David M. 1992. *Still the Golden Door: The Third World Comes to America.* New York: Columbia University Press.

Rice, J. S. 1992. "Discursive Formation, Life Stories, and the Emergence of Co-Dependency: 'Power/Knowledge' and the Search for Identity." *Sociological Quarterly* 33 (3): 337–64.

Richmond, Anthony H. 1994. *Global Apartheid: Refugees, Racism, and the New World Order.* Ontario: Oxford University Press.

Riley, Nancy E. 1997. "American Adoptions of Chinese Girls: The Socio-Political

Matrices of Individual Decisions." *Women's Studies International Forum* 20 (1): 87–102.

Roediger, David. 1994. "Whiteness and Ethnicity in the History of 'White Ethnics' in the United States." *Towards the Abolition of Whiteness: Essays on Race, Politics, and Working Class History.* New York: Verso.

Rofel, Lisa. 1999. *Other Modernities: Gendered Yearnings in China after Socialism.* Berkeley: University of California Press.

Rosaldo, Renato. 1988. "Ideology, Place, and People without Culture." *Cultural Anthropology* 3 (1): 77–87.

Rose, Sonya O. 1997. "Class Formation and the Quintessential Worker." In *Reworking Class,* edited by J. R. Hall. Ithaca, NY: Cornell University Press.

Rubin, Gayle. 1997 [1975]. "The Traffic in Women: Notes on the 'Political Economy' of Sex." In *The Second Wave: A Reader in Feminist Theory,* edited by L. Nicholson. New York: Routledge.

Rumbaut, Ruben G. 1999. "Assimilation and Its Discontents: Ironies and Paradoxes." In *The Handbook of International Migration: The American Experience,* edited by C. Hirschman et al. New York: Russell Sage.

Sacks, Karen Brodkin. 1989. "Toward a Unified Theory of Class, Race, and Gender." *American Ethnologist* 16: 534–50.

Said, Edward. 1994 [1978]. *Orientalism.* New York: Vintage Books.

Sayer, Andrew. 1994. "Cultural Studies and the Economy, Stupid." *Environment and Planning D: Society and Space* 12 (6): 635–38.

Scheper-Hughes, Nancy. 1992. *Death without Weeping: The Violence of Everyday Life in Brazil.* Berkeley: University of California Press.

Scott, Joan W. 1988. "Women in *The Making of the English Working Class.*" In *Gender and the Politics of History.* Princeton, NJ: Princeton University Press.

Sevenhuisen, Selma. 1998. "Has Head, Hands, Feet and Heart." In *Citizenship and the Ethics of Care.* New York: Routledge.

Shah, Nayan. 2001. *Contagious Divides: Epidemics and Race in San Francisco's Chinatown.* Berkeley: University of California Press.

Shanley, Mary L. 2001. *Making Babies, Making Families: What Matters Most in an Age of Reproductive Technologies, Surrogacy, Adoption, and Same-Sex and Unwed Parents.* Boston: Beacon Press.

Shi, Zhengxin, ed. 2000. *Zhongguo shehui fuli yu shehui jinbu baogao.* Beijing: Social Science and Literature Publishing Company.

Shiu, Anthony. 2001. "Flexible Production: International Adoption, Race, Whiteness." *Jouvert: A Journal of Postcolonial Studies* 6 (1–2). At http://social .chass.ncsu.edu/jouvert/v6i1-2/shiu.htm.

Smelser, Neil. 1998. "The Rational and the Ambivalent in the Social Sciences." *American Sociological Review* 63 (1): 1–16.

Solinger, Rickie. 2001. *Beggars and Choosers: How the Politics of Choice Shapes Adoption, Abortion, and Welfare in the United States.* New York: Hill and Wang.

———. 1994. "Race and 'Value': Black and White Illegitimate Babies, 1945–1965." In *Mothering: Ideology, Experience, and Agency,* edited by E. Nakano Glenn et al. New York: Routledge.

Somers, Margaret R. 1997. "Narrativity, Narrative Identity, and Social Action: Rethinking English Working-Class Formation." *Social Science History* 16 (4): 591–630.

Soysal, Yasemin Nuhoglu. 1994. *Limits of Citizenship: Migrants and Postnational Membership in Europe.* Chicago: University of Chicago Press.

Spivak, Gayatri. 1995. "Ghostwriting." *Diacritics* 25 (2): 65–84.

———. 1988. "Subaltern Studies: Deconstructing Historiography." In *In Other Worlds: Essays in Cultural Politics.* New York: Routledge.

Steinmetz, George. 1992. "Reflections on the Role of Social Narratives in Working-Class Formation: Narrative Theory in the Social Sciences." *Social Science History* 16 (3): 489–516.

Stephens, Sharon. 1995. "Introduction: Children and the Politics of Culture in 'Late Capitalism'." In *Children and the Politics of Culture,* edited by S. Stephens. Princeton, NJ: Princeton University Press.

Stoler, Ann Laura. 1997. "Racial Histories and Their Regimes of Truth." In *Political Power and Social Theory,* edited by D. Davis. Volume 11. Greenwich, CT: JAI Press.

———. 1995. *Race and the Education of Desire.* Durham, NC: Duke University Press.

Strathern, Marilyn. 1992. *Reproducing the Future: Essays on Anthropology, Kinship and the New Reproductive Technologies.* New York: Routledge.

———. 1988. *The Gender of the Gift: Problems with Women and Problems with Society in Melanesia.* Berkeley: University of California Press.

Stryker, Rachael. 2001. " 'Trading Children for Childhood': Deciphering Modes of Exchange in Russia's State-Run Orphanages." *CSEES Newsletter* 18 (1): 4–5 and 23–25. Berkeley: Institute of Slavic, East European, and Eurasian Studies, University of California–Berkeley.

Sturken, Marita. 1997. *Tangled Memories: The Vietnam War, the AIDS Epidemic, and the Politics of Remembering.* Berkeley: University of California Press.

Suransky, Valeri Polakow. 1982. *The Erosion of Childhood.* Chicago: University of Chicago Press.

Takaki, Ronald T. 1989. *Strangers from a Different Shore: A History of Asian Americans.* Boston: Little, Brown.

Tanaka, Stefan. 1993. *Japan's Orient: Rendering Pasts into History*. Berkeley: University of California Press.

Telfer, Jon. 2000. "Partial to Completeness: Gender, Peril and Agency in Australian Adoption." Conference paper presented at the Annual Conference of the European Association of Social Anthropologists, Krakow, Poland.

———. 1999. "Relationships with No Body?—'Adoption' Photographs, Intuition and Emotion." *Social Analysis* 43 (3): 144–58.

Terrell, John, and Judith Modell. 1994. "Anthropology and Adoption." *American Anthropologist* 96 (March): 155–61.

Tessler, Richard, and Gaile Gamache. 2003. "Learning about Chinese Adoptees in Middle Childhood." *China Connection: A Newsletter for New England Families Who Have Adopted Children from China* 9 (3): 8–11.

Thompson, E. P. 1978. "Eighteenth Century English Society: Class Struggle without Class?" *Social History* 3 (2): 133–66.

Thorne, Barrie et al. 2001. "Transnational Childhoods: The Participation of Children in Processes of Family Migration." *Social Problems* 48 (4): 572–91.

Trenka, Jane Jeong. 2003. *The Language of Blood*. St. Paul, MN: Borealis Books.

Tsing, Anna Lowenhaupt. 1993. *In the Realm of the Diamond Queen: Marginality in an Out-of-the-Way Place*. Princeton, NJ: Princeton University Press.

Tuan, Mia, and J. Shiao. 2001. "Racial and Ethnic Identity Salience: The Case of Asian Adoptees." Unpublished manuscript.

U.S. Census Bureau. 2003. "Adopted Children and Stepchildren: 2000." U.S. Department of Commerce Economics and Statistics Administration.

Volkman, Toby Alice. 2003. "Embodying Chinese Culture: Transnational Adoption in North America." *Social Text* 21 (1): 29–55.

Waltner, Ann B. 1990. *Getting an Heir: Adoption and the Construction of Kinship in Late Imperial China*. Honolulu: University of Hawaii Press.

Wang, Gungwu. 2001. *Don't Leave Home: Migration and the Chinese*. Singapore: Times Academic Press.

Waters, Mary C. 1998. "The Costs of a Costless Community." In *New Tribalisms: The Resurgence of Race and Ethnicity,* edited by M. Hughey. New York: New York University Press.

———. 1990. *Ethnic Options: Choosing Identities in America*. Berkeley: University of California Press.

Watkins, Mary. 2004. "Adoption and Identity: Nomadic Possibilities for Re-conceiving the Self." At http://uploads.pacifica.edu/gems/watkins/Adoption-Identity.pdf.

Wee, Vivienne. 1995. "Children, Population Policy, and the State in Singapore." In *Children and the Politics of Culture,* edited by S. Stephens. Princeton, NJ: Princeton University Press.

Weston, Kath. 2001. "Kinship, Controversy, and the Sharing of Substance: The Race/Class Politics of Blood Transfusion." In *Relative Values: Reconfiguring Kinship Studies,* edited by S. Franklin and S. McKinnon. Durham, NC: Duke University Press.

Wheeler, Wendy. 1999. *A New Modernity? Change in Science, Literature and Politics.* London: Lawrence & Wishart.

Widdershoven, Guy A. M. 1993. "The Story of Life: Hermeneutic Perspectives on the Relationship between Narrative and Life History." In *The Narrative Study of Lives,* edited by R. Josselson and A. Lieblich. Newbury Park: Sage Publications.

Williams, Brackette F. 1996. "Introduction: Mannish Women and Gender after the Act." In *Women Out of Place: The Gender of Agency and the Race of Nationality,* edited by B. Williams. New York: Routledge.

Williams, Patricia. 1991. *Alchemy of Race and Rights.* Cambridge, MA: Harvard University Press.

Williams, Raymond. 1983. *Culture and Society: 1780–1950.* New York: Columbia University Press.

———. 1980. "Base and Superstructure in Marxist Cultural Theory." *Problems in Materialism and Culture.* London: Verso.

Williams, Rhonda M. 1997. "Living at the Crossroads: Explorations in Race, Nationality, Sexuality, and Gender." In *The House That Race Built,* edited by W. Lubiano. New York: Vintage Books.

Willis, Paul. 1977. "Notes toward a Theory of Cultural Forms and Social Reproduction." In *Learning to Labor.* New York: Columbia University Press.

Wilmsen, Edwin. 1989. *Land Filled with Flies: A Political Economy of the Kalahari.* Chicago: University of Chicago Press.

Wilson, Rob, and Wimal Dissanayake. 1996. "Introduction: Tracking the Global/ Local." In *Global/Local: Cultural Production and the Transnational Imaginary,* edited by R. Wilson and W. Dissanayake. Durham, NC: Duke University Press.

Wolf, Diane L. 1996. "Situating Feminist Dilemmas in Fieldwork." In *Feminist Dilemmas in Fieldwork,* edited by D. Wolf. Boulder, CO: Westview Press.

Yanagisako, Sylvia J. 1985. "Transforming Orientalism: Gender, Nationality, and Class in Asian American Studies." In *Transforming the Past: Tradition and Kinship among Japanese Americans.* Stanford, CA: Stanford University Press.

Yans-McLaughlin, Virginia. 1990. "Metaphors of Self in History: Subjectivity, Oral Narrative, and Immigration Studies." In *Immigration Reconsidered: History, Sociology, and Politics,* edited by V. Yans-McLaughlin. New York: Oxford University Press.

Yngvesson, Barbara. 2003. "Going 'Home': Adoption, Loss of Bearings, and the Mythology of Roots." *Social Text* 74 21 (1): 7–27.

———. 2002. "Placing the 'Gift Child' in Transnational Adoption." *Law & Society Review* 36 (2): 227–55.

———. 2000. "'Un Niño de Cualquier Color': Race and Nation in Intercountry Adoption." In *Globalizing Institutions: Case Studies in Regulation and Innovation,* edited by J. Jenson and Boaventura De Sousa Santos. Burlington, VT: Ashgate.

Yngvesson, Barbara, and Maureen A. Mahoney. 2000. "'As One Should, Ought and Wants to Be': Belonging and Authenticity in Identity Narratives." *Theory, Culture & Society* 17 (6): 77–110.

Young, Iris Marion. 1994. "Gender as Seriality: Thinking about Women as a Social Collective." *Signs: Journal of Women in Culture and Society* 19 (3): 713–38.

Yuval-Davis, Nira, and Floya Anthias. 1989. *Woman-Nation-State*. New York: Palgrave Macmillan.

Zelizer, Viviana A. 1985. *Pricing the Priceless Child: The Changing Social Value of Children*. New York: Basic Books.

Zhu, Xiaohui. 1996. "Haizi, Gei Ni Yige Jia, Gei Ni Yige Shijie." *Zhongguo Minzheng* 12: 4–5.

Adoption, China/U.S. *(continued)*
actors in, 11, 72, 114; by black families, 10; Chinese view of, 18–19,
78–79, 101, 128, 131–134, 139, 156,
209, 274; Chinese American response
to, 239, 298n14; and citizenship,
208–215; and commodification/con-
sumption (*See* Commodification of
adoption); in contrast to other adoption programs, 68; cost of, 12, 61, 81;
as cultural economy, 11–12, 16–17, 57,
93–103; as East Asian migration, 2, 8,
38–49; forced v. voluntary migration,
7; by gay/lesbian couples, 10, 49,
286n9, 290n11; and gender choice, 48,
59–61; history of, 49–63, 68, 72,
289n1; as humanitarian act, 55, 78–79;
injustices of, 261–262, 265–266,
267–268; and orphanages (*See also* Orphanages, Chinese); political economy
of, 28, 64, 104, 114, 124, 148, 256–257,
269, 276; popularity of, 2, 58, 68,
283n1; process of, 10–12, 13, 14f, 15,
113–114, 116–119; and provincial Civil
Affairs Offices, 117–118, 121–122, 151;
statistics, 10; and "the culture question," 206, 235; standardization of,
68–70; and tourism, 152–162
Adoption, China/U.S. in media, 9–10, 60,
62, 63–64, 83, 128, 134, 211–212, 251,
255, 291n13, 293n8, 295n7
Adoption, transnational. *See also* Adoption, China/U.S.; Postadoption; Preadoption; and abandonment, 167; advocacy of, 279; "clean break" of, 60–61,
67, 138, 166–167, 288n21; and com-
modification/consumption (*See* Commodification of adoption); as cultural
economy, 23–24, 25; cultural politics
of, 278–281; dichotomies of, 22; and
domestic U.S. adoption, 52–55; history
of, 50–52 (*See also* Adoption, China/
U.S., history of); as humanitarian act,
25, 36–38, 50–53, 61–62, 66–67; and
identity, 266–267; and imperialism,
118–119; and kinship, 5–6; from Korea,
52, 58, 279; as market/business, 62,

66–67, 104–105, 138, 155–156 (*See also*
Commodification of adoption); as migration, 24–25, 38–49, 161–162,
210–211, 256, 264, 271; opposition to,
96, 278–281; political economy of, 13,
104, 170, 251, 269; risks of, 88; from
Russia, 58, 61, 80, 145, 283n1; by
single parents, 290n11; statistics, 53,
283n1, 283n4, 287n14; transformative
possibilities of, 5, 26, 32, 105–106,
133, 203, 237, 256–262, 263–281;
transnational influences on process
of, 71–73; transnations, perspective
of, 6
Adoption, U.S. domestic, 287n13,
287n15; adoptive parent's attitudes
toward, 55; cost of, 288n23; history
of, 50–56; as market/business, 53;
and race, 52–56; of special-needs
children, 55
Adoption agencies, 55, 83. *See also* Great
Wall China Adoptions (agency); adoptive parents response to, 85–86; advertising of/recruiting practices, 48, 60,
86–87, 89; charitable programs of,
100–101; competition between, 69–70,
84, 83–87, 292n16; preadoption
process, 85–86
Adoption Consumer Assistance and Protection Service, 18
Adoption exchange: actors in, 31, 117;
and birth parents, 113–151, 142, 269;
and business card, 120–121; and caregivers, 144–145; and China/West relations, 124; Chinese onlookers of,
18–19, 118, 127–128, 130–132, 136,
139–140, 141, 144, 159f; and choice,
125; demands of adoptive parents in,
122–23, 125–126, 135, 146; and exclusions, 114–116, 138; and gender,
141–142; gifts and favors given in,
120–123, 135, 140, 293n9; and hotels
in China, 148–149; and international
onlookers of, 154–155; and narratives,
121; political economy of, 66, 114–115,
150–151; process of, 113–119; representations of, 115; and social ex-

ABOUT THE AUTHOR

Sara K. Dorow is Assistant Professor of Sociology at the University of Alberta. She is the author of *When You Were a Child in China: A Memory Book for Children Adopted from China* and editor of *I Wish for You a Beautiful Life: Letters from the Korean Birth Mothers of Ae Ran Won to Their Children.*